Quick Reference to
Neurological CRITICAL CARE NURSING

Quick Reference to *Neurological* CRITICAL CARE NURSING

Noreen M. Leahy, MS, RN, CNRN
The University Hospital at Boston University Medical Center
Boston, Massachusetts

Aspen Series
Quick Reference to Critical Care Nursing
Joan Vitello-Cicciu, Series Editor

AN ASPEN PUBLICATION®
Aspen Publishers, Inc.
Rockville, Maryland
1990

Library of Congress Cataloging-in-Publication Data

Leahy, Noreen M.
Quick reference to neurological critical care nursing/ Noreen M. Leahy.
  p. cm.--(Aspen series. Quick reference to critical care nursing)
  "An Aspen publication."
  Includes bibliographical references.
  ISBN: 0-8342-0127-5
  1. Neurological nursing--Handbooks, manuals, etc.
  2. Intensive care nursing--Handbooks, manuals, etc. I. Title. II. Series.
  [DNLM: 1. Critical Care--nursing--handbooks. 2. Nervous System
    Diseases--nursing--handbooks. WY 39 L434q]
  RC350.5.L43   1990   610.73'68--dc20   DNLM/DLC
                                            for Library of Congress
                                                    89-18022
                                                        CIP

Copyright © 1990 by Aspen Publishers, Inc.
All rights reserved.

Aspen Publishers, Inc., grants permission for photocopying for limited personal or internal use. This consent does not extend to other kinds of copying, such as copying for general distribution, for advertising or promotional purposes, for creating new collective works, or for resale. For information, address Aspen Publishers, Inc., Permissions Department, 1600 Research Boulevard, Rockville, Maryland 20850.

> The authors have made every effort to ensure the accuracy of the information herein, particularly with regard to drug selection and dose. However, appropriate information sources should be consulted, especially for new or unfamiliar drugs or procedures. It is the responsibility of every practitioner to evaluate the appropriateness of a particular opinion in the context of actual clinical situations and with due consideration to new developments. Authors, editors, and the publisher cannot be held responsible for any typographical or other errors found in this book.

Editorial Services: Marsha Davies

Library of Congress Catalog Card Number: 89-18022
ISBN: 0-8342-0127-5

Printed in the United States of America

1 2 3 4 5

*To Tom, Sean, Colleen, and Michael, for their love and understanding;
to Mom and Dad, for their faith and constant support;
and to my sisters, for all the hours of child care.*

Table of Contents

Preface ix

Acknowledgments xi

Chapter 1— Review of Neuroanatomy and Neurophysiology 1
    Bones of the Cranial Vault 1
    Bones of the Spinal Column 4
    Meningeal System 8
    Cellular Composition 9
    Neurotransmitters 10
    CNS Structures 11
    Spinal Cord 19
    Cerebral Vasculature 26
    Peripheral Nervous System 30

Chapter 2— Neurological Assessment 37
    Overview of the Neurological Examination 37
    General Cerebral Function 37
    Motor Function 41
    Sensation 45
    Cerebellar Function 46
    Cranial Nerves 46
    Neurological Assessment 48

Chapter 3—Neurodiagnostic Procedures 61

Computed Tomography 61
Magnetic Resonance Imaging 62
Single-Photon Emission-Computed Tomography 63
Skull Radiographs 65
Spine Radiography 66
Lumbar Puncture 67
Cisternogram 68
Myelogram 69
Cerebral Arteriography 70
Digital Subtraction Angiography 71
Cerebral Blood-Flow Studies 72
Noninvasive Carotid Artery Studies .. 73
Transcranial Doppler Sonography ... 75
Electroencephalogram (EEG) 75
Electromyography 77
Nerve-Conduction Velocity Studies .. 77
Evoked Responses (Evoked Potentials) 78

Chapter 4—Increased Intracranial Pressure 80

Munro-Kellie Hypothesis 80
Blood-Brain Barrier 80
Volume-Pressure Relationships 81
Cerebral Blood Flow and Perfusion .. 82
Cerebral Edema 83
Brain Swelling 84
Entities Associated with Increased ICP 85
Herniation Syndromes 85
Signs and Symptoms of Increased ICP 89
Management of the Patient with Increased ICP 92
Intracranial Pressure Monitoring ... 98

Chapter 5—Brain Death 103
Definition 103
Application of the Criteria 104
Declaration of Brain Death 106
Organ Donation 107

Chapter 6—Head Trauma 111
Types of Head Injuries 111
Skull Fractures 114
Management of Skull Fractures 116
Scalp Lacerations 117
Injuries to the Brain 117
Secondary Problems 125
Management 131

Chapter 7—Spinal Cord Injuries 137
Mechanisms of Injury 137
Vertebral Fractures 138
Types of Spinal Cord Injury 141
Management of Spinal Cord Injuries 146
Secondary Problems 150

Chapter 8—Central Nervous System Neoplasms 157
Classification of CNS Tumors 157
Clinical Presentation 158
Identified Risk Factors 160
Intracranial Tumors 161
Spinal Canal Tumors 166
Management Concerns 167

Chapter 9—Cerebrovascular Events 172
Risk Factors 172
Classification 173
Diagnosis of Cerebrovascular Events 174

Ischemic Stroke Syndromes 175
Management of Ischemic Events 179
Hemorrhagic Stroke Syndromes 181
Nursing Management Concerns 188

Chapter 10— Seizures and Status Epilepticus **194**
Definition of Seizure Activity 194
Classification of Seizure Activity 196
Diagnosis of Seizure Activity 198
Treatment of Seizure Activity 199
Status Epilepticus 202

Chapter 11— Infectious Processes **205**
Access Routes 205
Meningitis 206
Encephalitis 209
Brain Abscess 211
Neurological Complications of AIDS 212

Chapter 12— Acute Neurological Conditions **215**
Myasthenia Gravis 215
Amyotrophic Lateral Sclerosis 220
Guillain-Barré Syndrome 222

Index **227**

Preface

This text is written for critical care nurses caring for adult patients with neurological dysfunction. Its purpose is to provide readily accessible and clinically applicable information on neurological diagnoses commonly seen in the intensive care setting. In-depth discussion of the material presented is beyond the scope of this text, and the reader is referred to the Notes and Suggested Readings for more detailed medical and nursing information. The author hopes that the text will validate the clinical decisions of some nurses and demystify the nervous system for others.

Acknowledgments

I express my deepest appreciation to my colleagues in the Nursing Department of The University Hospital at Boston University Medical Center, whose encouragement and support have been paramount in the completion of this text; and to Jim Harrington, for his expertise in preparing some of the artwork.

1

Review of Neuroanatomy and Neurophysiology

The nervous system has two primary functions. The first is to control and to coordinate all body parts. The second function entails processing of internal and external data through the sensory system, with subsequent determination of appropriate responses to the particular stimuli. Concomitant with these functions, the nervous system is continuously processing and storing information.

There are two main divisions within the nervous system:

1. Central nervous system (CNS)—containing the brain and spinal cord
2. Peripheral nervous system (PNS)—comprised of the cranial and spinal nerves and the autonomic nervous system (ANS), which has two components:
   (a) Sympathetic nervous system
   (b) Parasympathetic nervous system

BONES OF THE CRANIAL VAULT

There are a number of protective, physical structures enveloping the nervous system. The cranial vault itself is covered by a thick layer of skin, under which lies subcutaneous tissue, galea, and the blood supply to the scalp. The bones that comprise the cranial vault are the frontal, occipital, sphenoid, ethmoid, and the paired parietal and temporal plates (Figure 1-1).

Cranial Sutures

At the time of birth these bones are normally not well fused but are held together by cartilage. As the human body ages, ossification occurs at bone junctions. The fusion of these bones is referred to as sutures, and the sutures are used as anatomical landmarks (see Figure 1-1), which include the following:

2   QUICK REFERENCE TO NEUROLOGICAL CRITICAL CARE NURSING

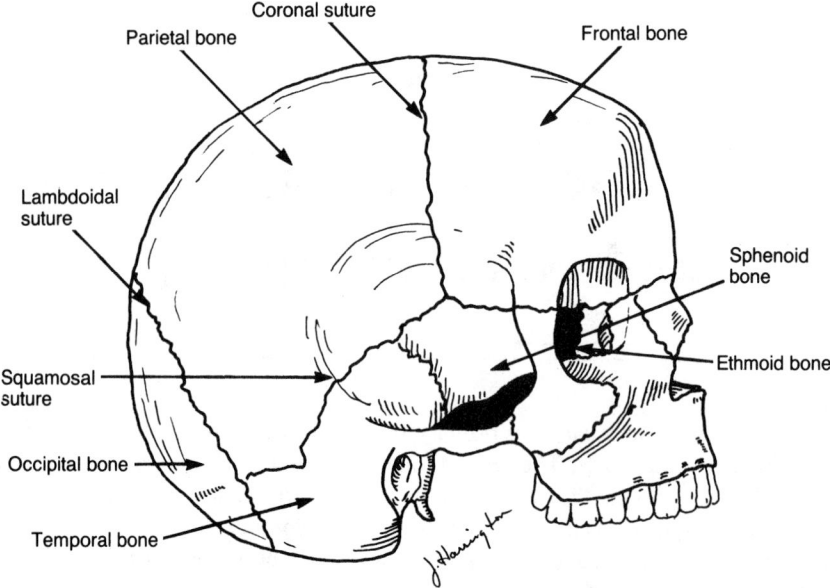

Figure 1-1 Lateral View of the Skull.

- Sagittal suture—located between the parietal bones
- Coronal suture—located between the parietal and frontal bones
- Squamosal suture—located between the parietal and temporal and temporal and occipital bones
- Lambdoidal suture—located between the parietal and occipital bones

Fontanels

In the neonate there are several fontanels, or soft spots, normally present at birth. Along with the bone plates that have not yet fused, they allow molding of the infant's skull as it passes through the birth canal and permit expansion of the cranium in the event of increases in intracranial pressure. Normally these fontanels, described below, fuse as the infant grows.

- Anterior fontanel—located at the junction of the sagittal and coronal sutures. It normally closes around the age of eighteen months. Once complete ossification occurs, it is referred to as the bregma.
- Posterior fontanel—located at the junction of the sagittal and lambdoidal sutures. It normally closes around the age of two months. Upon complete ossification it is called the lambda.

- Anterolateral fontanel—located at the junction of the frontal, parietal, temporal, and sphenoid bones. It also closes approximately two months after birth and is referred to as the pterion with complete ossification.
- Posterolateral fontanel—located at the junction of the parietal, temporal, and occipital bones. It closes around the age of two years and is referred to as the asterion with complete ossification.

These fontanels, and later in life their ossification sites, serve as anatomical landmarks for skull radiography and during cranial surgery.

Cranial Floor and Fossae

The base of the skull is comprised of a jagged and irregular surface resulting from bone formation (Figure 1-2). The irregularity of the inner skull table is a

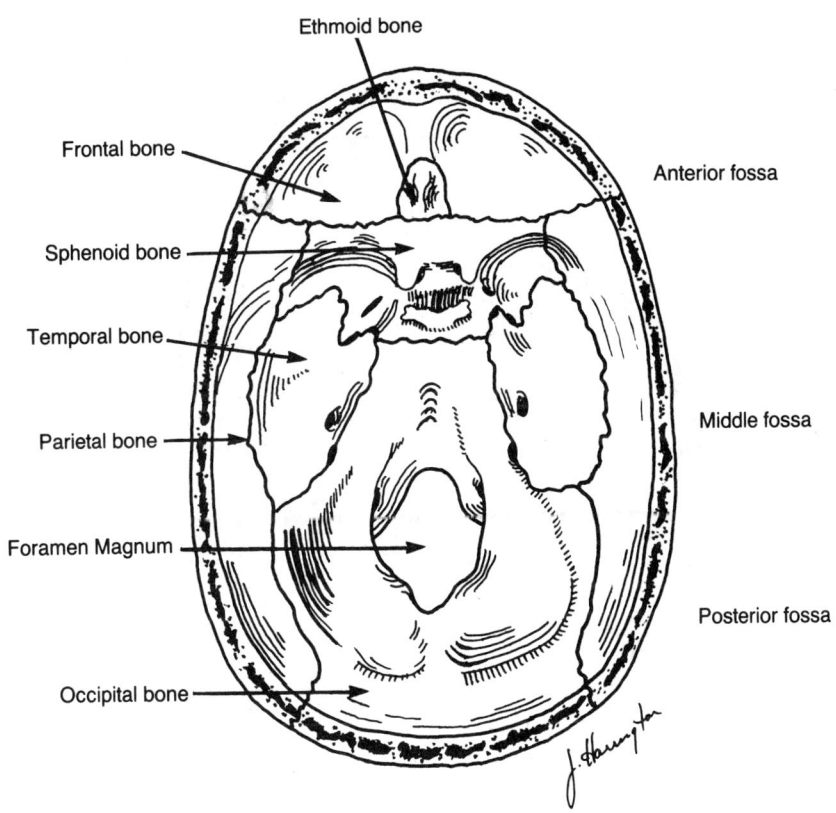

Figure 1-2 View of the Skull Floor.

contributing factor in the brain injuries incurred with head trauma. The skull is often divided into divisions, or fossae, to describe particular neuroanatomical areas (Figure 1-3). The anterior fossa holds the frontal lobes, while the middle fossa houses the temporal, parietal, and occipital lobes. The cerebellum and brain stem are contained within the posterior fossa.

BONES OF THE SPINAL COLUMN

The vertebral column is the bony enclosure for the spinal cord. It is divided into five major parts, with the total number of vertebrae equaling thirty-three. There are seven cervical vertebrae, twelve thoracic, five lumbar, five sacral, and four to five coccygeal. The vertebral bodies within the sacral and coccygeal regions are normally fused together (Figure 1-4).

Vertebral Components

There are specific anatomical components to each vertebra to facilitate its proper alignment with the cranial vault and each subsequent vertebra. With the

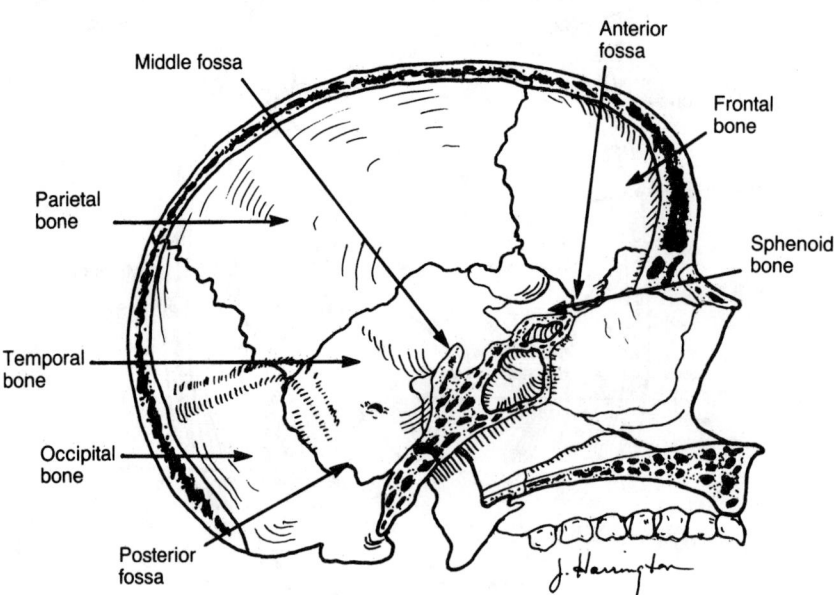

Figure 1-3 Sagittal View of the Skull.

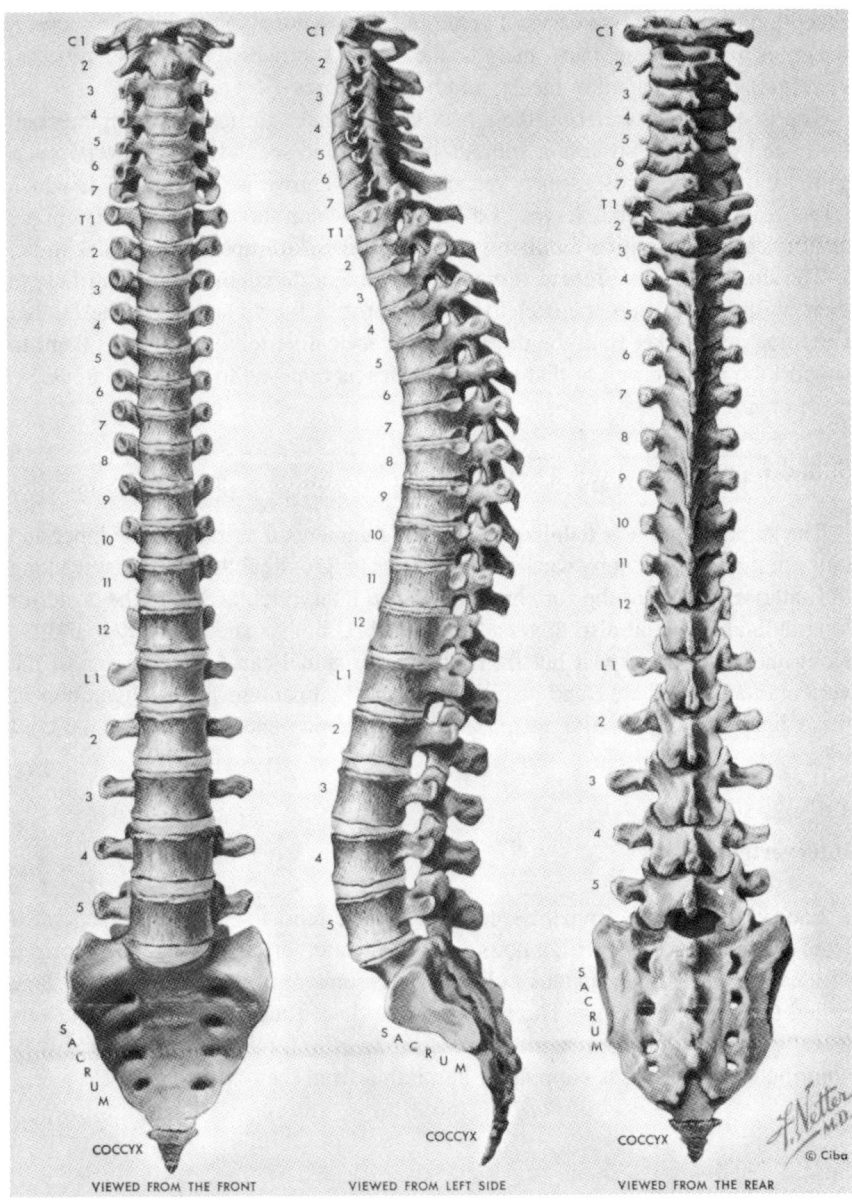

Figure 1-4 Vertebral Column. *Source:* © Copyright 1983. CIBA-GEIGY Corporation. Reproduced with permission from the *CIBA Collection of Medical Illustrations* by Frank H. Netter, MD. All rights reserved.

exception of the first two cervical vertebrae, which are atypical, and the sacrum, which is fused, these parts include the spinous process, transverse process, vertebral arch, articulating facets, and body (Figures 1-5 and 1-6).

The first cervical vertebra, the atlas, is ring shaped, articulates with the skull base, and does not possess a spinous process. The second cervical vertebra is called the axis and possesses a vertical process known as the odontoid, which arises from its body and serves as a base upon which the atlas sits. This unique anatomical configuration facilitates rotation of the skull upon the cervical spine.

The shapes of the vertebrae vary with each major division, which contribute to their ability to support the skeleton and to protect the spinal cord. The lumbar vertebrae are thicker than the thoracic and cervical vertebrae, allowing them to support the greater weight that portion carries as opposed to the upper areas.

Spinal Ligaments

The spinal column is stabilized by strong ligaments that traverse the inner and outer portions of the bony canal. The anterior longitudinal ligament passes along the anterior surface of the vertebral bodies and intervertebral discs. The posterior longitudinal ligament also traverses the vertebral bodies and intervertebral discs along the posterior aspect but from within the spinal canal. The lamina of the vertebrae are connected and stabilized by the ligamentum flava. Disruption of these ligaments is a major factor in the occurrence and extent of spinal cord injuries.

Intervertebral Discs

Each vertebral body from the second cervical vertebra to the sacrum is separated from the next by a fibrocartilaginous disc. These intervertebral discs are comprised of a central mass, the nucleus pulposus, surrounded by a ring of fibrocartilage called the anulus fibrosus. The intervertebral discs function to cushion the vertebral bodies during movement. Excessive stress or strain to the vertebrae may contribute to these discs slipping or herniating from their positions.

Spinal Cord

The spinal cord itself runs from the first cervical level as it arises from the medulla oblongata to approximately the first and second levels of the lumbar vertebrae, where it terminates as the conus medullaris. The rationale for performing lumbar punctures at the interspace of the fourth and fifth lumbar (L4-5) vertebrae is to avert puncture of the spinal cord.

Review of Neuroanatomy and Neurophysiology 7

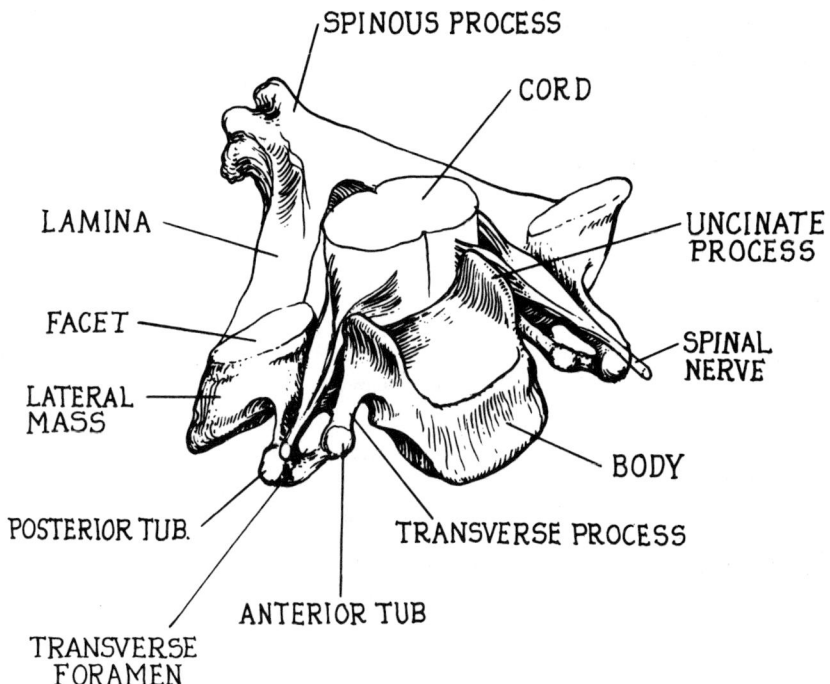

Figure 1-5 Anatomy of Cervical Vertebra. *Source:* Reprinted from *Orthopaedic Neurology: A Guide to Neurologic Levels* by S. Hoppenfield, p. 40, with permission of J.B. Lippincott Company, © 1977.

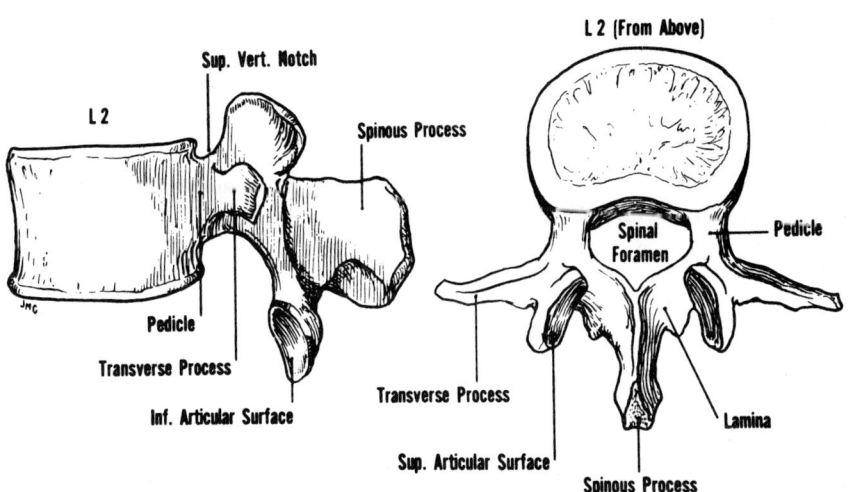

Figure 1-6 Anatomy of Lumbar Vertebra. *Source:* Reprinted from *Essentials of Neurosurgery* by R.R. Smith, p. 122, with permission of J.B. Lippincott Company, © 1980.

MENINGEAL SYSTEM

The three meningeal membranes, the dura, arachnoid, and pia, provide a supportive and protective environment around the brain and spinal cord. Actual or potential anatomical spaces between the meningeal layers are used as clinical reference points. Bleeding that may occur into these spaces is discussed in Chapter 6.

Meningeal Spaces

The epidural, or extradural, space is a potential space between the dura mater and the inner table of the skull. It may become a real space in the event of an epidural (extradural) hematoma, commonly the result of an arterial bleed from the middle meningeal artery.

The subdural space is another potential space lying between the dura mater and the arachnoid membrane. It becomes an actual space, most often as the result of dural-vein bleeding.

The subarachnoid space lies between the arachnoid membrane and the pia mater. A true space, it contains the cerebrospinal fluid (CSF) as well as arteries and veins.

Meningeal Layers

Dura Mater

The dura mater is the thick, fibrous, outermost layer. The exterior layer of the dura mater serves as the periosteum for the cranial bones, while the inner layer contains arteries and veins. At certain points it folds in on itself to form the following anatomical compartments:

- Falx cerebri—longitudinally separates the cerebral hemispheres and forms channels for the superior and inferior sagittal venous sinuses
- Tentorium cerebelli—separates cerebrum from cerebellum and forms the posterior fossa, and encloses the transverse and superior petrosal venous sinuses
- Falx cerebelli—projects between the cerebellar hemispheres and encloses the occipital venous sinuses
- Diaphragma sellae—forms a roof over the sella turcica, in which the hypophysis (pituitary gland) is contained

Within the spinal canal, the dura mater attaches to the filum terminale (a fibrous extension of the spinal cord), coccygeal ligament, and dural nerve-root sleeves.

These attachments assist in maintaining the supportive and protective functions of the meningeal system.

Arachnoid Membrane

The arachnoid membrane, the second meningeal layer, is avascular and loosely envelops the brain. Beneath the arachnoid membrane, CSF circulates in the subarachnoid space. There are several areas where the arachnoid membrane is widely separated from the innermost meningeal layer to form cisterns for the accumulation of CSF. The lumbar cistern, which is the largest, is located below where the spinal cord ends within the spinal canal. The point of spinal cord termination is usually at the level of the first or second lumbar vertebra.

Arachnoid granulations are projections of the arachnoid membrane into the venous sinuses of the brain. These structures allow absorption of the CSF from the subarachnoid space into the venous system once it has circulated through the CNS.

Pia Mater

Pia mater, the innermost and most delicate of the meningeal layers, is closely adherent to the brain parenchyma. Within the spinal canal it continues beyond the end of the spinal cord (conus medullaris), surrounding the filum terminale, and attaches to the dura mater and the coccyx.

CELLULAR COMPOSITION

The nervous system is comprised of two main cell types: glial cells and neurons. The glial cells serve as the support and maintenance cells, while the neuron is the functional unit of the nervous system. There are four main types of glial cells: astrocytes, oligodendrocytes, ependymal cells, and microglial cells. Each cell type is attributed specific functions (Table 1-1).

Table 1-1 CNS Cell Types, Location, and Function

Cell Type	Location and Function
Astroglia	1. Found mostly in white matter
	2. Maintain nourishment and support to the neurons
	3. Contribute to blood-brain barrier formation
	4. Participate in informational storage process
	5. Maintain bioelectrical potential of neurons
Oligodendroglia	1. Produce myelin sheaths
	2. Form white matter
Ependyma	1. Line the ventricular system and the choroid plexuses
	2. Participate in CSF production
Microglia	1. Found throughout the CNS
	2. Phagocytize CNS waste

Gray and White Matter

Nerve cell bodies within the brain and spinal cord are usually located in groups of assorted sizes and shapes called nuclei. Outside the CNS these groups are called ganglia. Exceptions to this classification occur where groups of nerve cell bodies within the CNS are referred to as ganglia. An example of this is the deep brain structures, known as the basal ganglia, which are presented later in this chapter.

Large aggregates of nerve cell bodies and glial cells in the brain and spinal cord constitute gray matter. Nerve fiber collections with the same function are often encased within a myelin covering, which is white in appearance and gives rise to the term *white matter*.

Neuron

The neuron is the basic structural unit of the nervous system and has three major components. The cell body constitutes the main portion of the neuron, from which an axon projects as well as any number of dendrites. Axons carry information away from the neuronal cell body to other neurons or glands, while dendrites conduct impulses to the cell body (Figure 1-7).

The point at which one neuron transmits an impulse to another is the synapse. Transmission of impulses is predicated upon appropriate function of several structures. Presynaptic terminals excrete either an excitatory or inhibitory substance into the synaptic cleft, facilitating a like response on the effector or receiving neuron. These substances are produced within the presynaptic vesicles of the axon's presynaptic terminal. The postsynaptic membrane is the most proximal portion of the effector neuron receiving the impulse to the transmitting neuron.

NEUROTRANSMITTERS

The excitatory and inhibitory substances that facilitate neuronal function are neurotransmitters. The major excitatory neurotransmitter is acetylcholine; others are norepinephrine, dopamine, and serotonin. Gamma-aminobutyric acid (GABA) and glycine are the major inhibitory neurotransmitters. Each neuron secretes only one type of neurotransmitter substance (see Figure 1-7).

Many of the drugs used in treating neurological disorders are based upon their interactions, or lack thereof, with neurotransmitter substances. Mestinon, for example, inhibits the breakdown of acetylcholine by acetylcholinesterase, thus allowing more of this neurotransmitter to be available to facilitate synaptic transmission in individuals with myasthenia gravis.

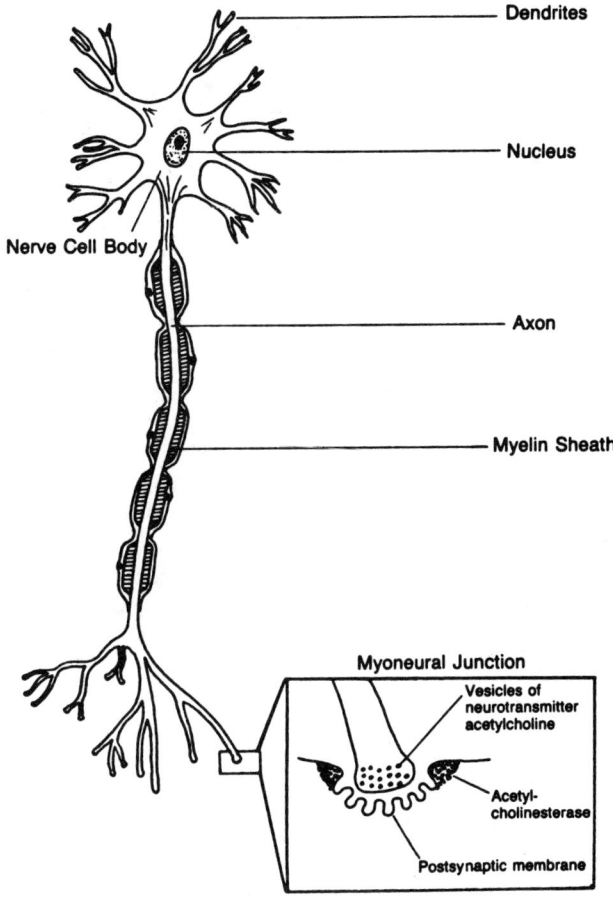

Figure 1-7 Components of the Neuron. *Source:* Reprinted from *Neurological Emergencies: Effective Nursing Care* by J. Raimond and J.W. Taylor, p. 59, Aspen Publishers, Inc., © 1986.

CNS STRUCTURES

Cerebrum

The cerebrum is composed of the cerebral hemispheres, the basal ganglia, the thalamus, and the hypothalamus. The outermost layer of the cerebrum is composed of gray matter organized into raised areas known as gyri and constitutes the cerebral cortex. Sulci, or fissures, form the indentations between the gyri. The left cerebral cortex is credited with the functions involved in sequential analysis and influences the right side of the body (contralateral), while the right manages visuospatial components and influences the left side of the body.

Cerebral Hemispheres

The cerebral hemispheres are divided into lobes: frontal, parietal, temporal, and occipital (Figure 1-8). Each lobe can be further divided into anatomical landmarks that represent specific functional responsibilities (Table 1-2). Organization of the motor area in the precentral gyrus and the sensory area in the postcentral gyrus allows localization to the specific area of the cortex involved, depending upon clinical symptoms.

Through the course of human development, one cerebral hemisphere in each individual becomes more highly developed than the other. It is widely accepted that in most individuals this dominant hemisphere is the left. Both hemispheres are capable of performing similar functions, such as storing memories, analyzing sensory input, recognizing faces, and learning.

Each hemisphere is also fairly specialized for certain mental processes. Language ability, mathematics, abstract reasoning, and symbolisms are attributed to the left cerebral cortex. Information in this hemisphere appears to be processed in analytical, component parts. The right cerebral cortex is more concerned with visuospatial patterns, emotional expressions, and artistic abilities. Information in this hemisphere appears to be processed in a holistic manner as the sensory experiences occur.

Corpus Callosum

Beneath the cerebral cortex lies the corpus callosum, a large area of white matter tracts that enables each portion of one hemisphere to connect with its corresponding portion of the other hemisphere. It essentially allows communication between the two hemispheres (Figure 1-9).

Basal Ganglia

The basal ganglia are groups of subcortical nuclei found deep within the hemispheres (see Figure 1-9). Four distinct nuclei form each basal ganglion:

- caudate nucleus
- globus pallidus
- putamen
- claustrum

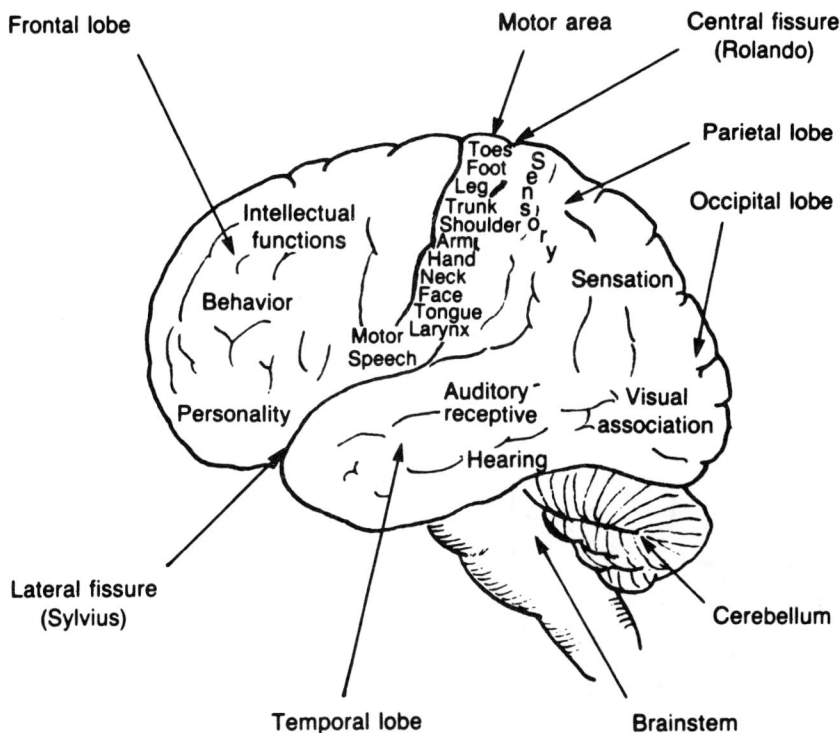

Figure 1-8 Functional Areas of the Cerebrum. *Source:* Reprinted from *Neurological Emergencies: Effective Nursing Care* by J. Raimond and J.W. Taylor, p. 66, Aspen Publishers, Inc., © 1986.

Table 1-2 Cerebral Hemisphere Functions

Lobe	Major Functions
Frontal	Voluntary movement
	Language expression
	Cognition
	Long-term memory
Parietal	Sensory integration
	Sensory interpretation
	Spatial perceptions
Temporal	Hearing
	Short-term memory
	Interpretation of memory
	Language comprehension
Limbic	Behavioral expression
	Integration of recent memory
Occipital	Vision
	Visual interpretation

14   QUICK REFERENCE TO NEUROLOGICAL CRITICAL CARE NURSING

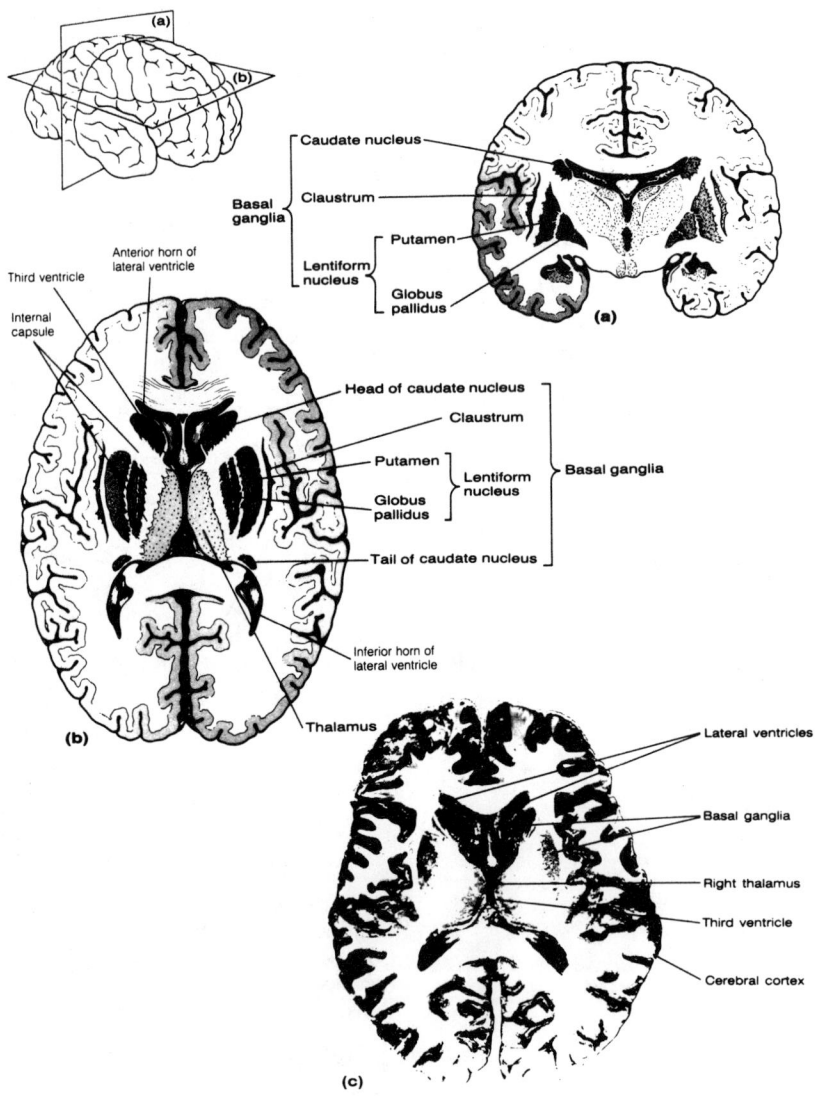

Figure 1-9 Cross Sections of Deep Brain Structures: (a) Frontal Section, (b) Transverse Section, (c) Photograph of a Transverse Section. *Source:* Reprinted from *Human Anatomy and Physiology,* 3rd ed., by A.P. Spence and E.B. Mason with permission of Benjamin/Cummings Publishing Company, © 1987.

These structures facilitate sensory integration between the thalamus and the cerebral cortex to orchestrate fine motor control. The substantia nigra is a specialized area of gray matter found in the midbrain of the brain stem, which is necessary for normal basal-ganglia function.

Internal Capsules

The internal capsules are a collection of white matter pathways ascending to and descending from the cerebral cortex of each hemisphere (see Figure 1-9). They constitute a conversion point for all afferent and efferent fiber tracts. Pathology to the internal capsule area is clinically significant in that it represents disruption of the connecting fibers between the brain and spinal cord. In most cases the individual will have major motor and sensory deficits.

Diencephalon

The diencephalon is a deep portion of the cerebral hemispheres that connects with the midbrain of the brain stem (Figure 1-10). It is comprised of four major structures: the epithalamus, the thalamus, the hypothalamus, and the subthalamus.

Epithalamus

This is the most dorsal part of the diencephalon. It includes the pineal body, which is believed to be involved in growth and development, and structures that connect with the limbic system. In the adult the calcified pineal gland serves as a midline landmark in the interpretation of skull radiographs and brain-imaging techniques. The limbic system is comprised of a group of structures that interact with each other to regulate emotional behavior.

Thalamus

The thalami are paired gray matter structures also located deep within the cerebrum. Projection pathways connect with other portions of the hemispheres, and they connect structurally to the midbrain. The thalamus is referred to as a sensory relay station in that all sensory pathways except olfaction synapse here. It is the last point at which afferent stimuli are integrated before ascending to the cerebral cortex. The capability of the thalamus to connect with other portions of the brain is such that it plays a role in conscious recognition of pain, sleep-wake cycles, attention, and emotions.

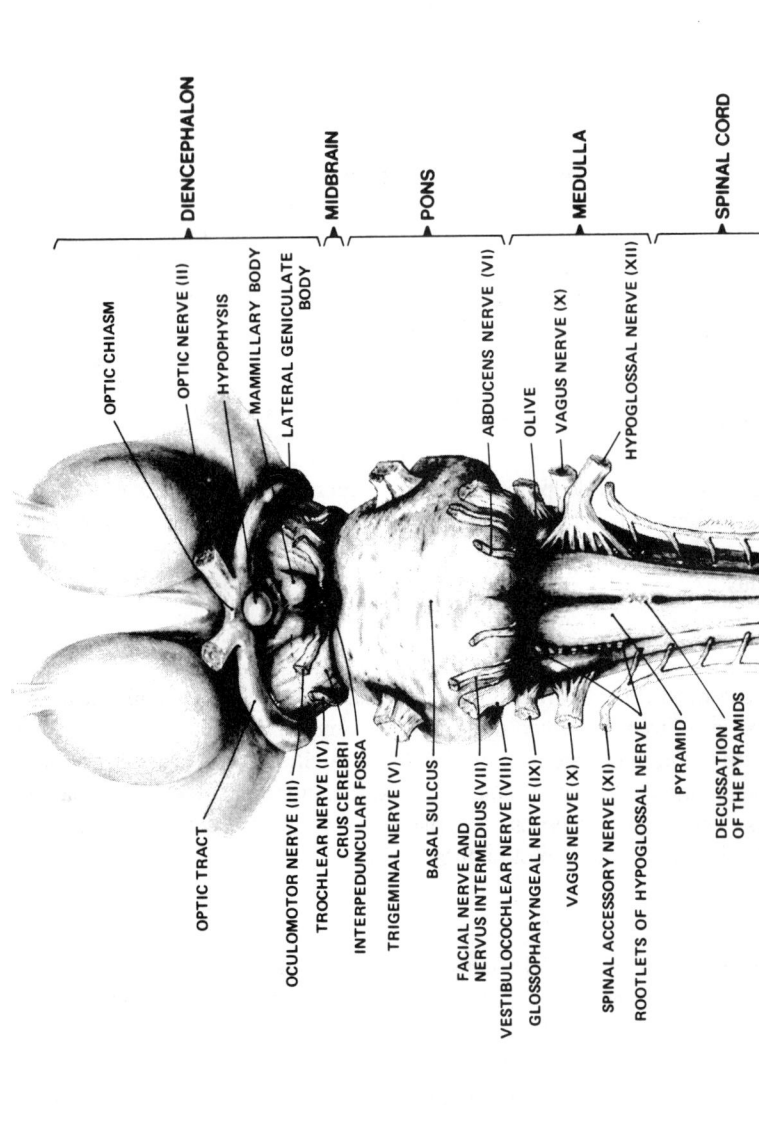

Figure 1-10 Anterior View of the Diencephalon and Brain Stem. *Source:* Reprinted from *Manter and Gatz's Essentials of Clinical Neuroanatomy and Physiology*, 6th ed., by S. Gilman and S. Newman, p. 68, with permission of F.A. Davis Company, © 1982.

Hypothalamus

The hypothalamus comprises the base of the diencephalon and acts to modulate influences from autonomic centers. Its functions include

- coordination of autonomic nervous system function
- regulation of temperature
- regulation of water metabolism
- regulation of hormonal secretions
- mediation of affective behavior
- contribution to sleep-wake cycle maintenance
- regulation of appetite

Pituitary Gland. The hypophysis, or pituitary gland, is connected to the hypothalamus by the pituitary or hypophyseal stalk. It sits within the sella turcica at the base of the brain, and its secretions are controlled by the hypothalamus. Divided into lobes, the anterior portion of the pituitary secretes hormones related to metabolic and sexual functions, while the posterior pituitary secretes only two hormones (Table 1-3). Collectively these hormones function to maintain homeostasis of the body environment.

Subthalamus

Located lateral to the hypothalamus, the subthalami contribute to the function of the basal ganglia by integrating fine motor control.

Table 1-3 Pituitary Hormones and Their Functions

Hormones	Function
Anterior Pituitary	
Growth hormone	Accelerates body growth
Thyroid-stimulating hormone	Stimulates thyroid growth and secretion
Adrenocorticotropin	Stimulates adrenal growth and secretion
Luteinizing hormone	Stimulates ovulation
	Stimulates testosterone production
Prolactin	Maintains corpus luteum and stimulates milk secretion
Follicle-stimulating hormone	Stimulates growth of ovarian follicles
	Stimulates estrogen secretion
	Stimulates spermatogenesis
Posterior Pituitary	
Oxytocin	Stimulates contraction of uterine smooth muscle
Antidiuretic hormone	Regulates water content of the body

Brain Stem

The brain stem is divided into three major divisions: the midbrain, the pons, and the medulla (see Figure 1-10). It serves as the point of origin for cranial nerves III through XII. All ascending (sensory input) and descending (motor) pathways travel through this area. Connecting nerve fibers facilitate transmission of information to and from the cerebellum. Vital reflex centers are located here, such as the centers for the control of respiration and heart rate. This structure also contains part of the reticular activating system, a physiologic network that contributes to maintaining consciousness.

Midbrain

This small area connects the diencephalon with the pons. The roof of the midbrain, known as the corpus quadrigemina, is comprised of the superior colliculi and the inferior colliculi. These structures are associated with the visual and auditory systems respectively. The nuclei of cranial nerves III and IV originate in the midbrain. The cerebral aqueduct traverses through the midbrain to the fourth ventricle.

Pons

Located between the midbrain and medulla, the pons contains components of many afferent and efferent pathways that connect the cerebrum with spinal cord levels of the nervous system. Nerve tracts known as the cerebellar peduncles serve as pathways to and from the cerebellum. The nuclei of cranial nerves V through VIII are found within the pons.

Medulla

The lowest level of the brain stem, the medulla oblongata, is continuous with the spinal cord at the level of the foramen magnum. The foramen magnum is a large opening in the anterior portion of the occipital bone that allows the cranial contents to interconnect with the spinal cord. Nuclei of cranial nerves IX through XII are located within the medulla. Decussation, or crossing, of the corticospinal tracts occurs in the basilar area. Additionally a number of other tracts course through the medulla.

Reticular Activating System

The reticular activating system (RAS) is a diffuse physiological network that extends throughout the brain stem to the cerebral cortex. It is generally believed to contribute to control of the sleep-wake cycle, consciousness, and attentiveness. The brain stem portion is thought to control sleep-wake cycles, while the thalamic portion is thought to convey impulses activating cerebellar input over movement and coordination.

Cerebellum

Found in the posterior fossa, the cerebellum contains both gray and white matter. It is connected to the brain stem by the superior, middle, and inferior cerebellar peduncles, which receive input from the spinal cord and brain stem and convey it to deep nuclei within the cerebellum (see Figure 1-8). The cerebellum is associated with the coordination of muscle groups to maintain posture, equilibrium, coordination, fine motor control, and correction of movement. While the right and left cerebral cortices influence the contralateral side of the body, cerebellar influence is ipsilateral (same side).

SPINAL CORD

The spinal cord is caudal extension of the medulla oblongata (see Figure 1-10). Beginning at the first cervical vertebra (the atlas), the cord descends to about the level of the first lumbar vertebra. At this point the lower end of the cord is tapered to a conelike structure called the conus medullaris. The cord is secured to ligaments at the coccygeal level through a non-neural, threadlike extension called the filum terminale (Figure 1-11). The meningeal system within the cranial cavity is continuous within the spinal canal to help support and protect the spinal column.

Spinal Nerves

Thirty-one pairs of nerves exit from the cord. Each nerve has a dorsal, or anterior, root through which efferent, or motor, impulses exit the cord and a ventral, or posterior, root through which afferent, or sensory, impulses enter the cord. Spinal nerves are organized as eight cervical, twelve thoracic, five lumbar, five sacral, and one coccygeal. Cervical spinal nerves 1 through 7 leave the spinal canal through the intervertebral foramina above the corresponding vertebrae, while the eighth spinal nerve exits through the foramina below C7. The remaining spinal nerves from T1 downward exit through the foramina directly below the corresponding vertebrae (see Figure 1-11).

20 QUICK REFERENCE TO NEUROLOGICAL CRITICAL CARE NURSING

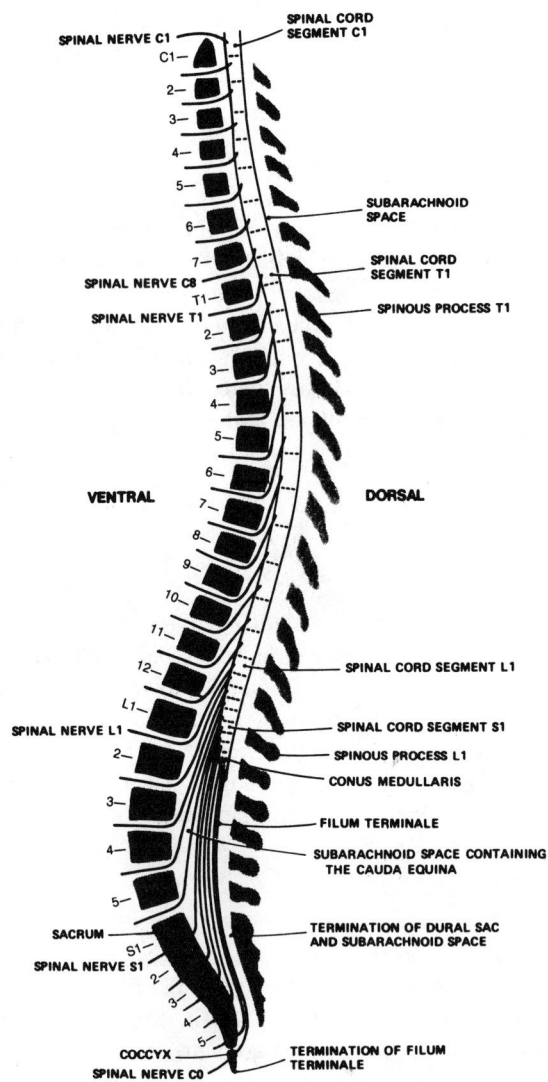

Figure 1-11 Spinal cord In Situ. *Source:* Reprinted from *Manter and Gatz's Essentials of Clinical Neuroanatomy and Physiology*, 6th ed., by S. Gilman and S. Newman, p. 10, with permission of F.A. Davis Company, © 1982.

Segmental Innervation

Each spinal nerve is responsible for transporting sensory input from and carrying motor input to specific regions of the body. Sensory and motor innervation can be specifically localized from the body to the responsible portion of the spinal cord and is illustrated by dermatomes (Figure 1-12).

Organization of Spinal Cord Tracts

A cross section of the spinal cord reveals a butterfly-shaped area of gray matter within a surrounding area of white matter. The gray matter represents neurons and glial cells, while the white matter depicts bundles of myelinated and unmyelinated nerve fibers arranged in tracts that travel the long axis of the spinal cord. The amount of white matter varies at different levels of the cord; it is greatest in the cervical area, where the number of nerve fiber tracts is at its highest (Figure 1-13).

Motor System

Motor output is the result of descending pathways from the CNS. Impulses travel from the precentral gyrus of the frontal lobe, through the posterior limb of the internal capsule, the cerebral peduncle, and the anterior portion of the pons to the pyramids of the medulla where the fibers decussate, or cross. The motor neurons receive input from the basal ganglia, cerebellum, brain stem, and other structures as they descend. From this point the neurons descend to the appropriate level of the spinal cord from which they exit. The motor neurons are organized into specialized pathways, or tracts, and have specific anatomical locations within the spinal cord (Figure 1-14).

Upper and Lower Motor Neurons

Upper motor neurons are those neurons that originate in the cerebral cortex and remain entirely within the CNS. The neuron's point of departure from the anterior horn of the spinal cord out to its final connection with the innervated muscle is referred to as a lower motor neuron. Motor control and subsequent interventions over muscle groups vary according to whether an injury has produced an upper or lower motor-neuron lesion.

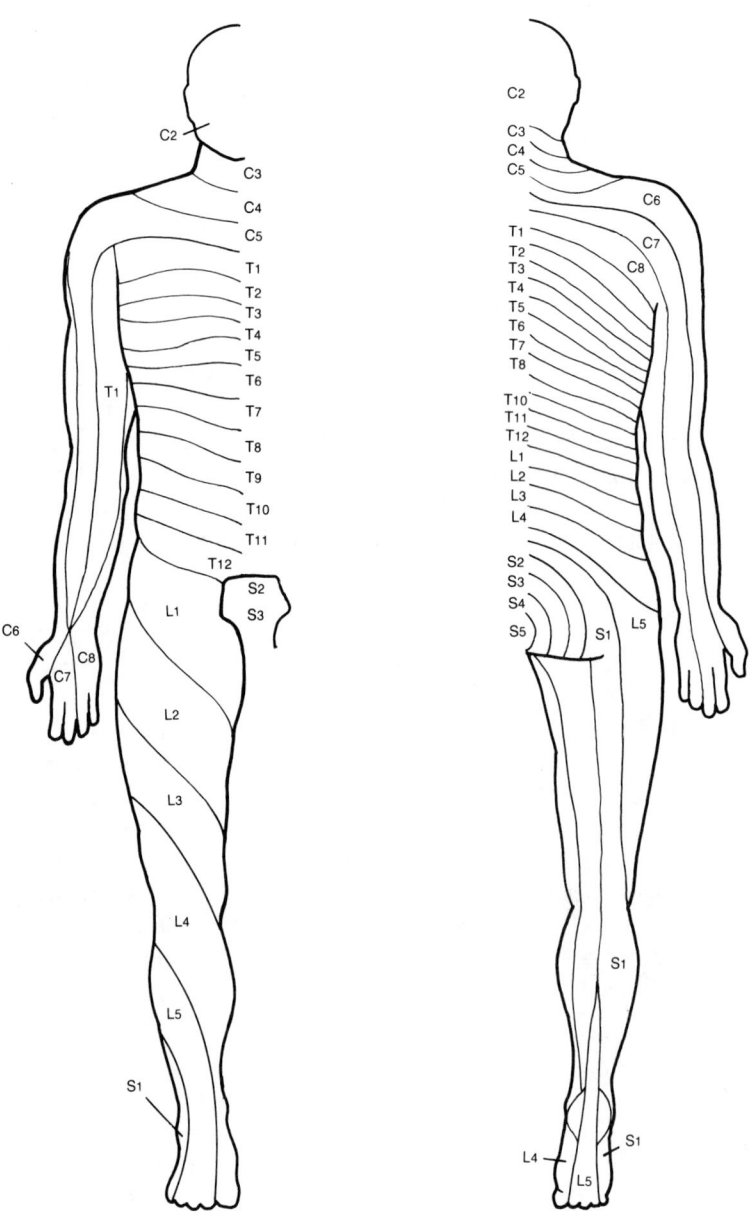

Figure 1-12 Dermal Segmentation.

Spinal cord

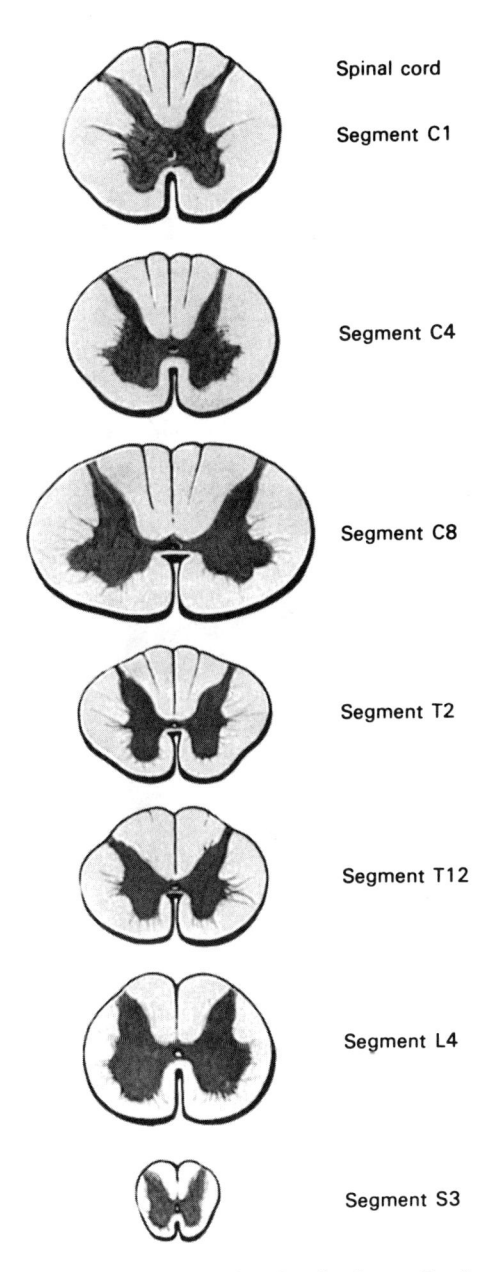

Segment C1

Segment C4

Segment C8

Segment T2

Segment T12

Segment L4

Segment S3

Figure 1-13 Cross Section of the Cord at Various Levels. *Source:* Reprinted from *Human Neuroanatomy*, 7th ed., by M.B. Carpenter, p. 218, with permission of Williams & Wilkins Company, © 1976.

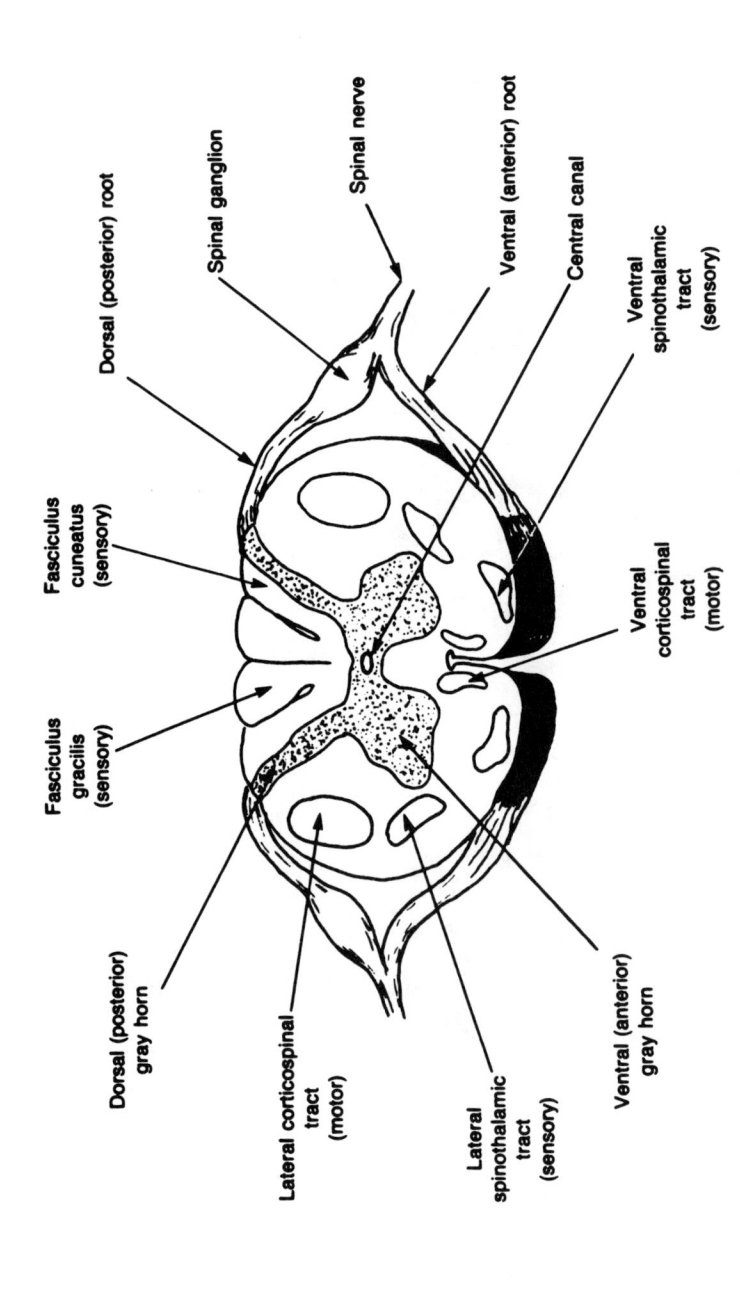

Figure 1-14 Organization of Select Motor and Sensory Tracts within the Spinal Cord. *Source:* Reprinted from *Neurological Emergencies: Effective Nursing Care* by J. Raimond and J.W. Taylor, p. 78, Aspen Publishers, Inc., © 1986.

Major Descending Pathways

The major descending pathways of the spinal cord are as follows:

- Corticospinal tract—This tract facilitates voluntary motor control. Approximately 90% of these fibers cross in the medulla and descend as the lateral corticospinal tract. The remaining 10% descend uncrossed as the anterior corticospinal tract. Fibers originate in the cerebral cortex and synapse at all levels of the spinal cord.
- Corticobulbar tract—Fibers originate in the cerebral cortex and terminate with the motor nuclei of cranial nerves V, VII, IX, X, XI, and XII in the brain stem.
- Corticorubrospinal tract—Fibers originate in the cerebral cortex and terminate in the spinal cord. This tract facilitates flexor motor neurons and inhibits extensor motor neurons.
- Vestibulospinal tracts—These tracts originate in the brain stem to mediate postural balance.
- Reticulospinal tracts—These tracts also originate in the brain stem. The medial tract exerts excitatory influences on muscle tone, while the lateral tract exerts inhibitory influences. The latter also influences respiration, circulation, pupillary dilation, and sweating.
- Tectospinal tract—This tract originates within the tectum, which is part of the midbrain, and serves to mediate audiovisual reflexes.

Major Ascending Pathways

Various receptors located throughout the body convey a variety of sensory impulses to the CNS, where they may be integrated among spinal reflexes or transmitted to higher cortical areas. The receptors are

- Proprioceptors—transmit position sense, movement, and muscle coordination
- Exteroceptors—convey sensations of touch, light pressure, sound, light, pain, temperature, and odor
- Interoceptors—transmit information from the visceral organs, such as pain and cramping
- Chemoreceptors—sense chemical activations at the cellular level

The sensory neurons are organized into specialized pathways, or tracts, and have specific anatomical locations within the spinal cord (see Figure 1-14).

Anterolateral System

This system is comprised of the three pathways that convey sensations of pain and temperature: anterior and lateral spinothalamic and spinoreticulothalamic. These impulses cross to the opposite side of the spinal cord soon after entering it.

Posterior (Dorsal) Columns

These pathways are located in the posterior or dorsal portion of the cord and are comprised of two major sensory tracts: the fasciculus gracilis and fasciculus cuneatus. The fasciculus gracilis carries sensory fibers from the leg, while sensory fibers from the arm are conveyed via the fasciculus cuneatus. Unlike the anterolateral system, impulses within these tracts do not cross to the opposite side of the cord until they reach the medulla. Proprioceptive information from the extremities concerning position and movement, deep pressure, two-point discrimination, vibration, and touch is conveyed by these pathways.

Spinocerebellar Tracts

The anterior and posterior spinocerebellar tracts convey proprioceptive information necessary for movement coordination by the cerebellum.

CEREBRAL VASCULATURE

Arterial System

Blood flow to the head is provided by the carotid and vertebral arteries. Exiting the aortic arch, the common carotids ascend to about the level of the jaw, where they bifurcate into the internal and external carotid arteries. They carry vascular supply to the face, scalp, and anterior brain. The vertebral-basilar system originates from the subclavian artery and supplies the posterior cerebrum, cerebellum, and brain stem.

Circle of Willis

Within the subarachnoid space at the base of the brain, the two internal carotid and the basilar arteries bifurcate into a formation called the circle of Willis, from which project the major cerebral vessels (Figure 1-15). Three paired, main branches arise from this arterial configuration: the middle cerebral artery, the anterior cerebral artery, and the posterior cerebral artery.

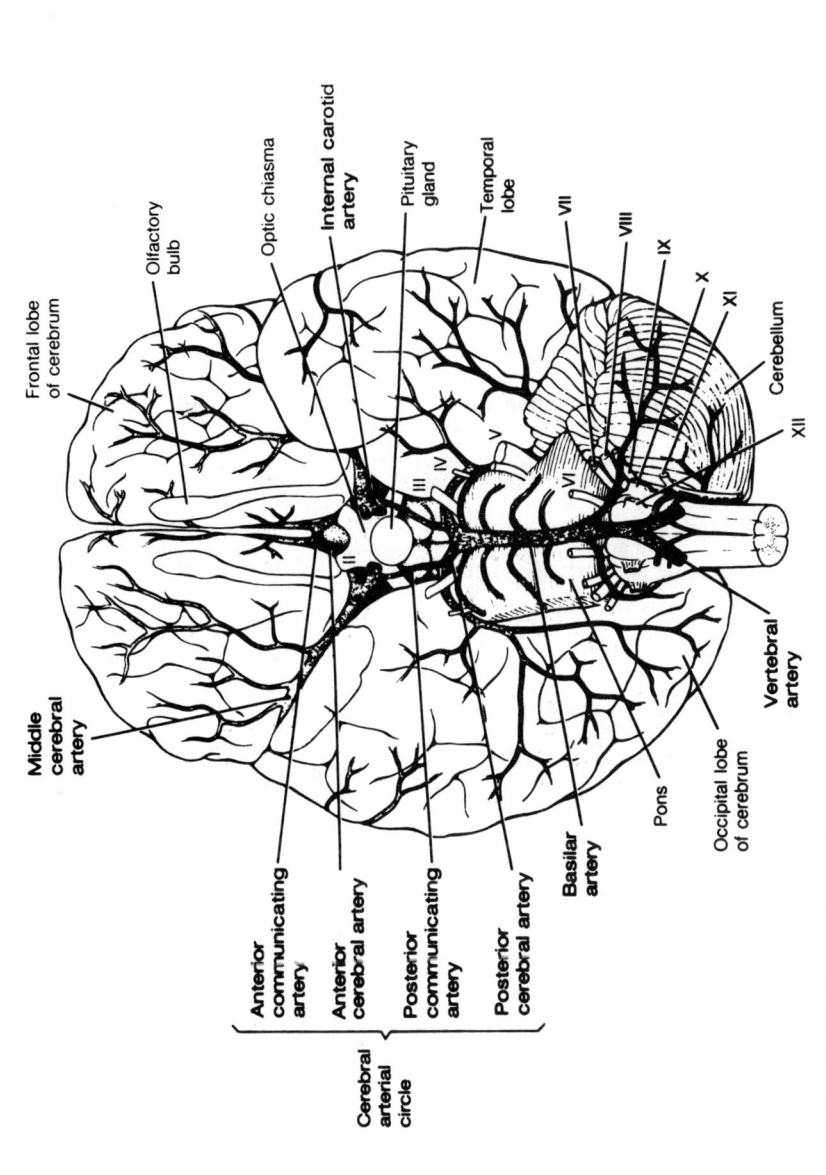

Review of Neuroanatomy and Neurophysiology   27

Figure 1-15 Circle of Willis. *Source:* Reprinted from *Human Anatomy and Physiology*, 3rd ed., by A.P. Spence and E.B. Mason with permission of Benjamin/Cummings Publishing Company, © 1987.

The middle cerebral arteries are direct extensions of the internal carotid arteries. Two anterior cerebral arteries arise from the internal carotid arteries, pass below the optic nerve, and project to the anterior portion of the hemispheres. They are joined at the circle of Willis by the anterior communicating artery. Two posterior communicating arteries also arise from the internal carotid arteries and anastomose with the posterior cerebral arteries as they bifurcate from the basilar artery.

Smaller cortical arteries arise from the main branches and penetrate the pia mater to the cerebral cortex. The areas of the brain supplied by the circle of Willis vessels are summarized in Table 1-4.

Venous System

Venous drainage within the brain varies from other body systems in that

- venous flow does not correspond to arterial flow
- the veins contain no valves
- there is a unique network of venous sinuses lying within the dura

Table 1-4 Blood Supply to the Brain

Cerebral Vessel	Target Areas
Middle cerebral artery	First major branch off the internal carotid Lateral surfaces of cerebral hemispheres Penetrates deep central structures
Anterior cerebral artery	Exits from internal carotid and connected by anterior communicating artery Medial surfaces of frontal and parietal lobes Penetrates central structures
Posterior cerebral artery	Usually a branch of the vertebro-basilar system; may arise from internal carotid system Connected together by posterior communicating artery as it bifurcates from internal carotid Supplies inferior and medial surfaces of the temporal and occipital lobes
Vertebro-basilar system	Vertebral arteries unite at upper area of medulla to form singular basilar artery Supplies the brain stem and cerebellum

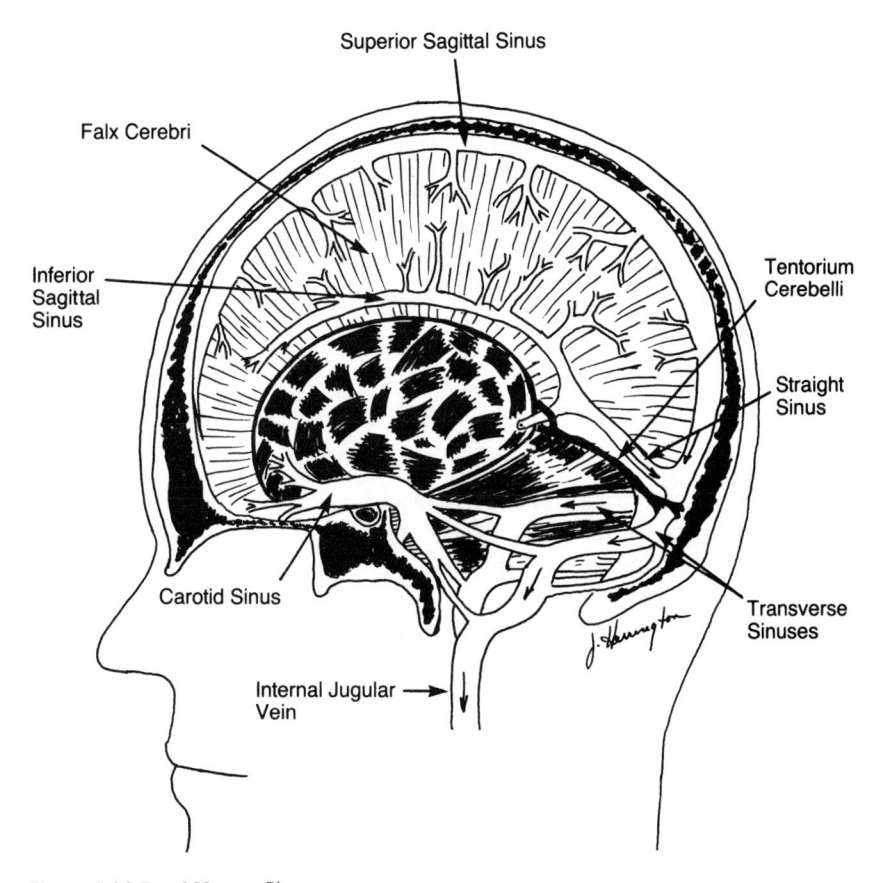

Figure 1-16 Dural Venous Sinuses.

The dural sinuses are formed by the periosteal and meningeal layers of the dura and drain into the internal jugular vein (Figure 1-16).

- The superior sagittal sinus drains venous blood from the rostral portions of the brain as well as CSF.
- The cavernous sinus receives venous return from the inferior portions of the brain, including the eye.
- The transverse sinus collects venous blood from the posterior portion of the brain.

Spinal Vasculature

Major arterial blood supply to the spinal cord is delivered by offshoots from the vertebral arteries. The anterior spinal artery travels the length of the cord along its ventral portion (closest to abdomen and thorax), while two posterior spinal arteries traverse the cord along the dorsal roots. These major blood vessels receive feeder vessels from each segment of the spinal cord and from the lateral spinal arteries.

Intradural and extradural veins provide venous drainage for the spinal cord. These veins communicate with other venous vessels from the neck down through the pelvis.

CSF

The CSF functions to support and to protect the CNS. It is primarily produced by the choroid plexuses of the ventricles, which lie deep within the hemispheres and brain stem, although smaller portions are produced by ependymal cells and blood vessels supplying the pia mater.

CSF circulation flows from the lateral ventricles in each hemisphere through the interventricular foramina into the third ventricle. At this point the CSF flows through the cerebral aqueduct into the fourth ventricle in the brain stem and exits the brain into the subarachnoid space surrounding the brain and spinal cord (Figure 1-17).

Absorption of CSF occurs through arachnoid granulations that project into the dural venous sinuses. Obstruction to CSF flow or absorption will result in dilation of the ventricles, or hydrocephalus. CSF volume norms and usual characteristics are described in Tables 1-5 and 1-6.

PERIPHERAL NERVOUS SYSTEM

All neurons not part of the CNS (brain and spinal cord) are neurons of the PNS. Included in the PNS are the cranial nerves, spinal nerves (see "Spinal Nerves," this chapter), and the ANS.

Cranial Nerves

There are twelve pairs of cranial nerves, each with a specific function. Figure 1-18 demonstrates the relationship of cranial nerves II through XII to the brain stem. Cranial nerve I is located anteriorly and superiorly to the brain stem. The

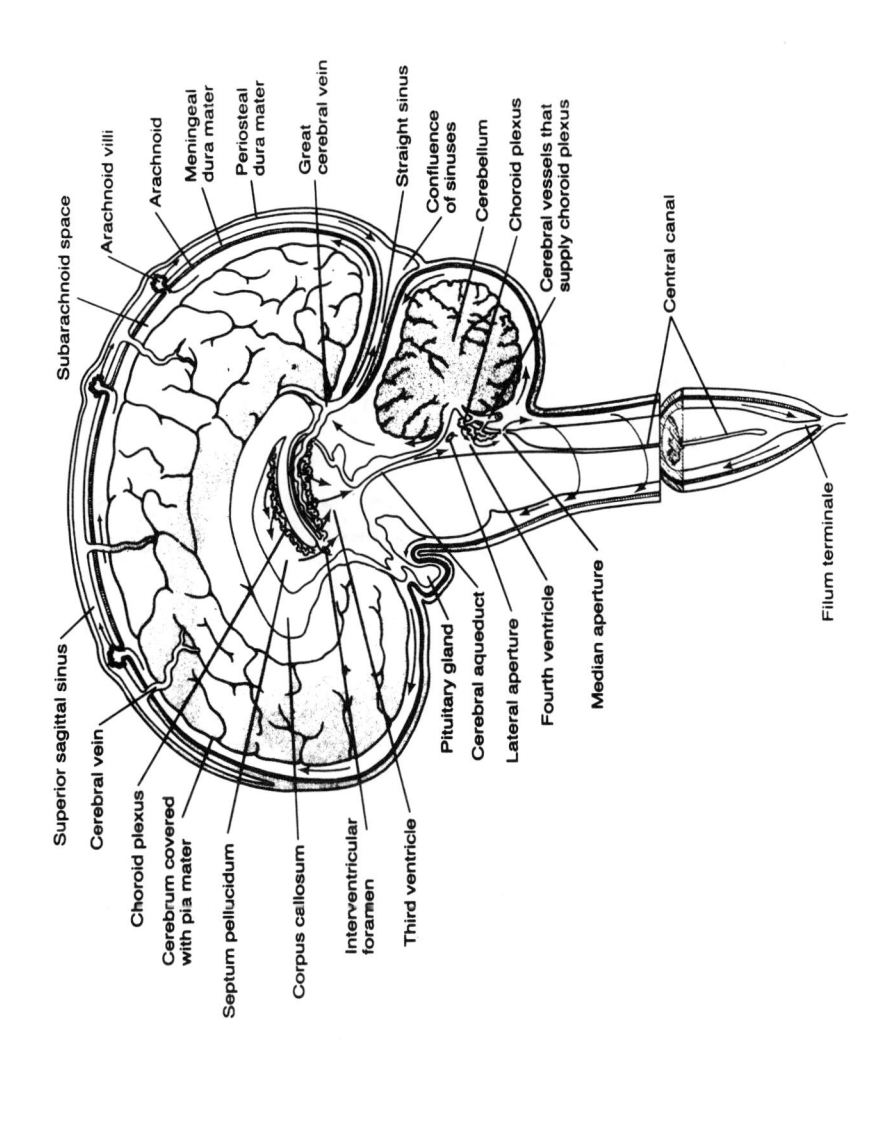

Review of Neuroanatomy and Neurophysiology 31

Figure 1-17 CSF Flow. *Source*: Reprinted from *Human Anatomy and Physiology*, 3rd ed., by A.P. Spence and E.B. Mason with permission of Benjamin/Cummings Publishing Company, © 1987.

Table 1-5 CSF Volumes

Production Influenced By:	Cerebral metabolism
	Hydrostatic forces
	Serum osmolality
Daily Production:	500 mL (20 mL/hour)
Average Total System Volume:	About 150 mL
Ventricles:	25 mL
Lumbar cistern:	90 mL
Subarachnoid space:	35 mL

Table 1-6 Normal Characteristics of CSF

Color:	Clear
Pressure:	70–200 mm water
Specific gravity:	1.005–1.009
Protein count:	15–45 mg/100 mL
Glucose content:	60–80 mg/100 mL or two thirds of serum glucose
Cell count:	0–10 lymphocytes only
Chloride count:	116–130 mEq/L (greater than serum content)

cranial nerves, their points of origin, and their functions are listed in Table 1-7. Methods of assessing each cranial nerve are described in Chapter 2.

Autonomic Nervous System

The autonomic nervous system serves as a regulatory mechanism for the body's internal organs by virtue of the opposing functions of its two divisions: the sympathetic nervous system and the parasympathetic nervous system (Figure 1-19). It is comprised of motor neurons that are categorized as either

- Preganglionic—the presynaptic neuron located within the brain stem or spinal cord, or
- Postganglionic—the postsynaptic neuron located within the ganglia to the visceral organ to be innervated.

Sympathetic Nervous System

Activated by "flight-or-fight" situations, it is also called the thoracolumbar system, reflecting the origin of its preganglionic fibers (T1 through L2). After leaving the spinal cord through the ventral roots, the preganglionic fibers synapse with the postganglionic fibers and form a chain along the spinal cord. The long postganglionic fibers then travel to the appropriate effector organ.

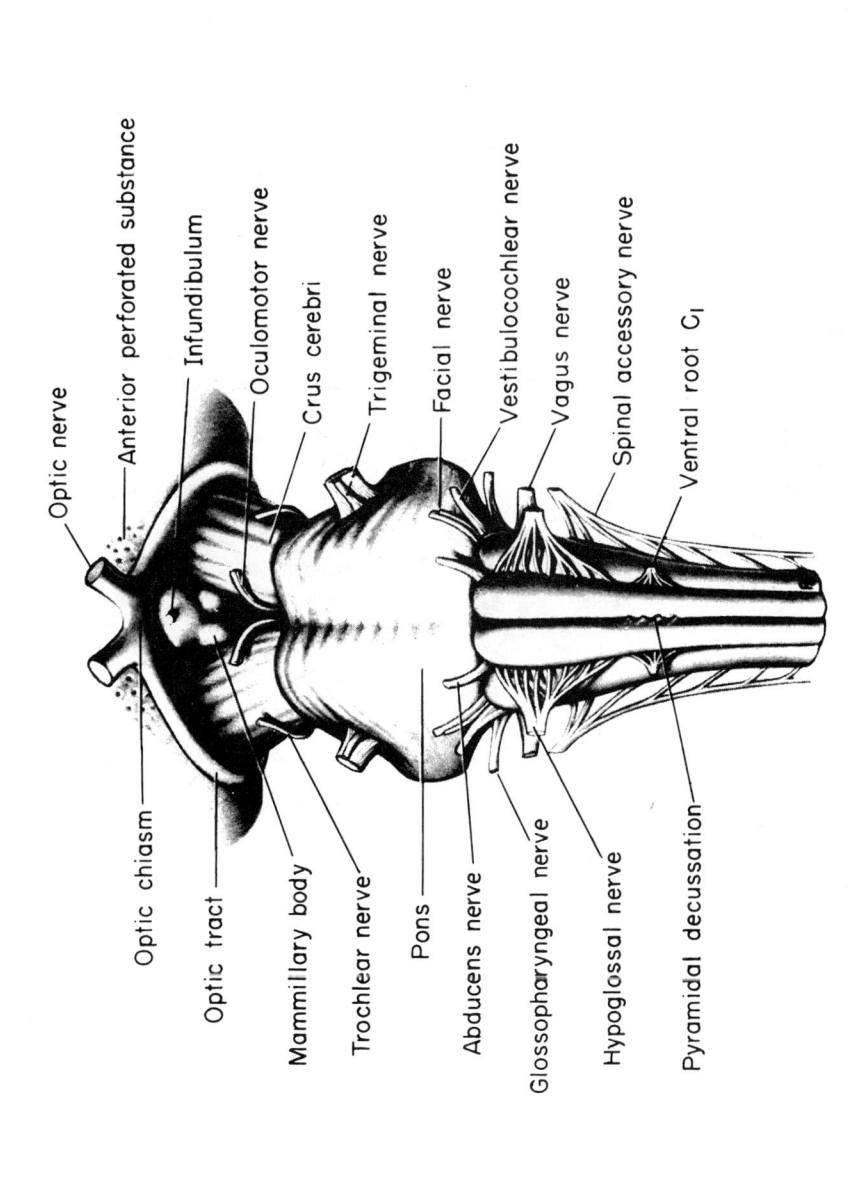

Review of Neuroanatomy and Neurophysiology   33

Figure 1-18 Cranial Nerves II through XII in Relation to the Brain Stem. *Source:* Reprinted from *Human Neuroanatomy*, 7th ed., by M.B. Carpenter, p. 38, with permission of Williams & Wilkins Company, © 1976.

Table 1-7 Cranial Nerve Origins and Functions

Cranial Nerve	Origin	Function
I, Olfactory	Mucous membranes of nasal septum	Sense of smell
II, Optic	Retina	Visual sense
III, Oculomotor	Midbrain	Up, down, and inner eye movement; opens eyelid; pupillary constriction
IV, Trochlear	Midbrain	Down and outward eye movement
V, Trigeminal	Pons	Scalp, facial, and nasal and oral mucous membrane sensation; mastication muscles
VI, Abducens	Pons	Lateral eye movement
VII, Facial	Pons	Facial expression muscles; closes eyelid; salivary and lacrimal gland secretions; taste to anterior two thirds of tongue
VIII, Acoustic	Pons	Sensations of hearing and equilibrium
IX, Glossopharyngeal	Medulla	Pharyngeal muscles and sensation; taste to posterior tongue; parotid gland secretion; carotid sinus sensation
X, Vagus	Medulla	Motor and sensory innervation of pharynx and larynx; motor innervation to thorax and abdomen; autonomic innervation for cardiac and respiratory reflexes
XI, Spinal accessory	Medulla	Motor innervation of sternocleidomastoid and trapezius muscles
XII, Hypoglossal	Medulla	Tongue movement

Norepinephrine is the neurotransmitter released from the postganglionic fibers and gives rise to the name "adrenergic" system. The preganglionic neurotransmitter released is acetylcholine.

Parasympathetic Nervous System

The parasympathetic system is concerned with promoting and maintaining those activities necessary for normal body functions. It arises from regions of the brain stem and sacral spinal cord and is otherwise referred to as the craniosacral division. While cranial division fibers exit with those of cranial nerves III, VII, IX, and X, the sacral division fibers exit with the sacral spinal nerves. In contrast to the sympathetic system, the long preganglionic fibers of the parasympathetic

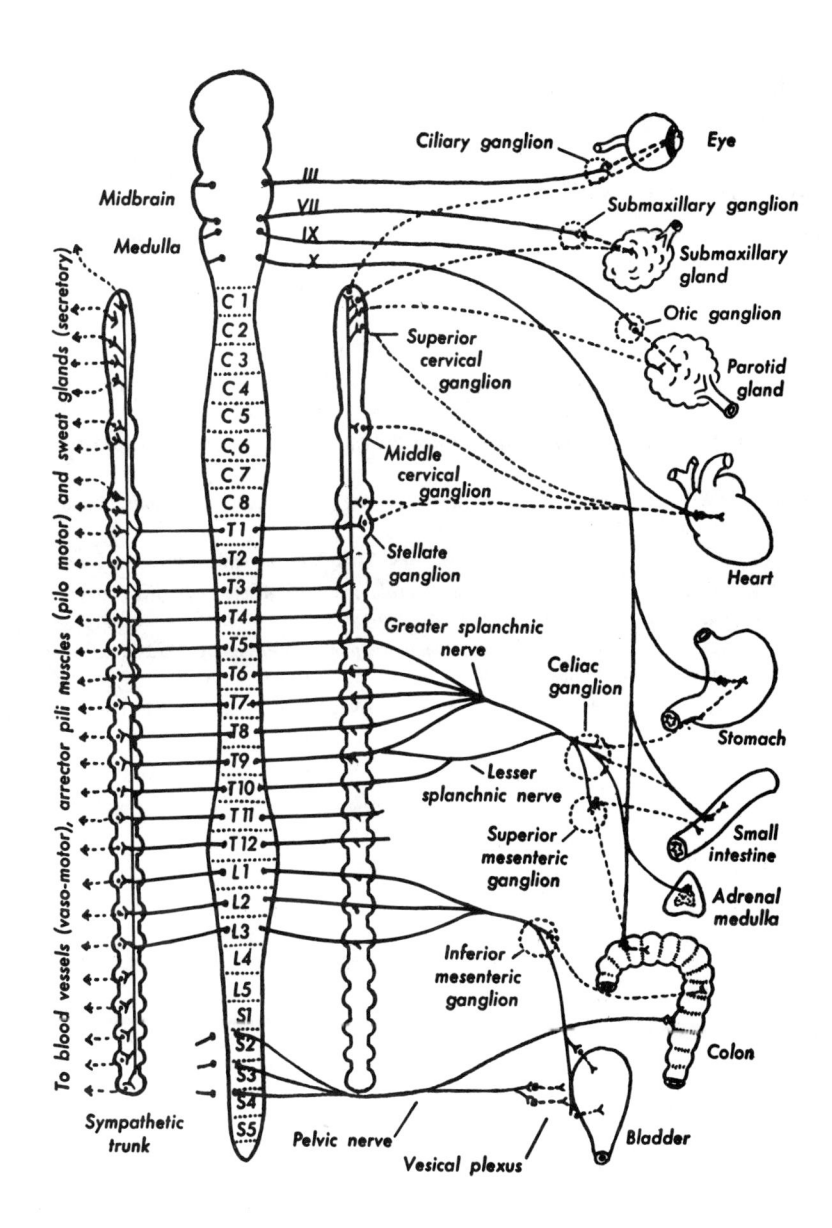

Figure 1-19 Schematic of the ANS. *Source:* Reprinted from *Human Neuroanatomy*, 7th ed., by M.B. Carpenter, p. 192, with permission of Williams & Wilkins Company, © 1976.

system travel to within close distance of the specific effector organ to synapse with the short postganglionic fibers. Acetylcholine is the neurotransmitter released from the preganglionic and postganglionic fibers and gives rise to the name "cholinergic" system.

SUGGESTED READINGS

American Association of Neuroscience Nurses. *Core Curriculum for Neuroscience Nursing*. Edited by Marilyn M. Ricci. Park Ridge, IL: American Association of Neuroscience Nurses, 1984.

Boss, Barbara J., and Ann Coghlan Stowe. "Neuroanatomy." *Journal of Neuroscience Nursing* 18(1986):214–30.

Carpenter, Malcolm B. *Human Neuroanatomy*. Baltimore: Williams & Wilkins, 1976.

Gilman, Sid, and Sarah S. Newman. *Manter and Gatz's Essentials of Clinical Neuroanatomy & Neurophysiology*. 6th ed. Philadelphia, PA: F.A. Davis Company, 1982.

Goldberg, Stephen. *Clinical Neuroanatomy Made Ridiculously Simple*. Miami: MedMaster, Inc, 1983.

Leech, Richard W., and Robert M. Shuman. *Neuropathology: A Summary for Students*. Philadelphia: Harper & Row, 1982.

Noback, Charles R. *The Human Nervous System*. New York: McGraw-Hill, 1967.

Raimond, Jeanne, and Joyce Waterman Taylor. *Neurological Emergencies: Effective Nursing Care*. Rockville, MD: Aspen Publishers, 1986.

Spence, Alexander P., and Elliott B. Mason. *Human Anatomy and Physiology*. 3rd ed. Menlo Park, CA: Benjamin/Cummings Publishing, 1987.

Willis, William D. Jr., and Robert G. Grossman. *Medical Neurobiology*. 2nd ed. Saint Louis: Mosby, 1977.

2

Neurological Assessment

The ability of critical care nurses to perform a neurological assessment accurately and swiftly provides great advantage in determining baseline neurological function and in identifying nervous system abnormalities. When performing a neurological assessment, following a systematic format facilitates completion and minimizes omission of certain assessment strategies.

Realistically it is not possible to perform a full assessment on every person each time patient condition is evaluated. It is possible, however, to complete a modified assessment on each individual with specific emphasis on the components of the nervous system that are dysfunctional and/or on major structures that delineate overall nervous system function. This chapter will present an overview of the neurological examination and an assessment of neurological signs in the conscious and unconscious patient, including methods and interpretation of abnormal findings.

OVERVIEW OF THE NEUROLOGICAL EXAMINATION

The neurological examination can be divided into the following components:

- general cerebral function, including level of consciousness and cognition
- motor function
- sensory function
- cerebellar function
- cranial nerve function

GENERAL CEREBRAL FUNCTION

In assessing cerebral function, some general considerations to evaluate include

- behavior and appearance
- mood/affect

- content and flow of speech
- overall cognitive capabilities

In the responsive patient, observation of actions, posture, and facial expressions, as well as attention to conversational responses provide data regarding general cerebral function.

Orientation

To assess orientation, consider the following areas:

- Person—the patient's ability to identify own name, names of family members, and/or health care personnel
- Time—the patient's ability to identify date, day, month, year, and appropriate seasonal events
- Place—the patient's ability to identify current location, home address

Memory

Assessment of memory can be evaluated as follows:

- Remote—Ascertain by asking questions relative to age, date of birth, date of parents'/children's births.
- Intermediate—Ascertain by asking questions pertaining to current events of the past three to five years.
- Recent—Ascertain by having the patient delineate events that precipitated current hospitalization.

Attention and Immediate Recall

To assess attention and immediate recall, consider the following:

- Serial sevens—Request patient to count backward by 7.
- Word repetition—Give the patient a list of three to five words (objects/names/dates) to remember and ask the patient to repeat them at specific intervals (three to five minutes).

Abstract Reasoning

Evaluate the patient's ability to reason abstractly by asking for interpretation of several common proverbs. For example:

- People who live in glass houses should not throw stones.
- The early bird catches the worm.
- A stitch in time saves nine.

Judgment

Query the patient regarding the reason for the hospitalization. The answers will provide information relative to the patient's insight into the current situation.

Specific Cognitive Function

By evaluating functions related specifically to cognition, the nurse can determine which, if any, structural areas are dysfunctional.

Aphasia

The inability to understand or express one's own language is referred to as aphasia. Difficulty in understanding or expressing one's language is known as dysphasia. The terms used to qualify aphasia are many and may originate from the anatomical source of the lesion or may reflect the resulting functional deficit. Fluency of speech is a descriptive factor often referred to in classifying the aphasias and is used below to summarize the types of aphasias.

- Nonfluent (expressive or motor) aphasia is the inability to speak one's language or to express it in writing (agraphia). These dysfunctions are caused by lesions in Broca's area of the frontal lobe for motor speech or in the posterior frontal lobe area for writing. Deficits may range from slight difficulty in articulating speech to almost complete loss of speech.

  These individuals produce speech very haltingly, often omitting words or repeating the same words. Since the person can comprehend spoken and written language, he or she becomes easily frustrated. Evaluation of these functions is made by giving the patient commands which range from simple to complex. Motor speech is tested by asking the individual open-ended questions such as "Tell me about your family," while the presence of agraphia can be tested by asking the patient to write his or her name and address. One can expect that the difficulties a patient has with motor speech will also be reflected in writing, since the motor fibers for speech and writing are closely associated anatomically.

- Fluent (receptive or sensory) aphasia is the inability to understand spoken and/or written language. Pathology in Wernicke's area of the temporal lobe produces the inability to understand the spoken word, while lesions in the occipital area may produce alexia, or inability to understand the written word. Pathways that permit associations of spoken words with other areas of the brain are impaired. Broca's area remains intact, so the person can speak.

  These individuals articulate well and convey normal intonation, but the content of their speech has little or no meaning. The severity may range from slight distortions to unintelligible speech. Incorrect or nonsensical words may be used, known as paraphasias, and the individual is often unaware of the substitutions. Fluent aphasia is evaluated by giving the patient a series of commands to obey, ranging from simple to complex. The fluent aphasic is unable to comprehend the spoken word or to repeat words.

Alexia is evaluated by having the patient follow the same range of commands that must be read from paper or cards. The patient's writing will reflect the same errors as speech.

- Global aphasia occurs when there is widespread pathology to both the Broca's and Wernicke's speech areas. These individuals demonstrate difficulty in expressing and understanding language. The severity is such that the individual may be unable to communicate at all.

Agnosia

Agnosia is the inability to recognize common objects through the senses of sight, touch, and sound.

- Visual agnosia is evaluated by asking the patient to name objects held within the line of vision, such as a pen, tie, cup; or to name objects that are pointed to in pictures.
- Tactile agnosia is the inability to recognize objects that are placed into the patient's hands while his or her eyes are closed. Examples of objects that might be used are a pen, comb, set of keys. The inability represents a lesion in the parietal lobe.
- Auditory agnosia is the inability to recognize environmental sounds, such as a door closing, telephone ringing, or traffic. It represents a lesion in the temporal lobe.
- Prosopagnosia represents the inability to recognize famous faces and is due to right-hemisphere damage.
- Visuospatial agnosia is difficulty negotiating within familiar surroundings or manipulating objects or clothing due to poor spatial relationships. It is attributed to lesions of the nondominant parietal lobe.

Apraxia

The inability to perform a skilled motor act in the absence of paralysis is termed apraxia. Normal execution requires that the act be understood, the directions be remembered, and that motor strength is available. Its presence signifies dysfunction in the brain's ability to integrate a variety of cortical areas to complete the task at hand.

In assessing for fluent aphasia, one must rule out ideomotor apraxia when giving commands to be followed; this type of apraxia exists if the individual cannot carry out a command to verbal stimuli (pick up the glass) but then proceeds to execute the same action spontaneously. It usually represents a lesion in the dominant parietal lobe. As with the agnosias, there are a variety of apraxic states.

- Constructional apraxia is difficulty in the ability to perceive spatial relationships. It is assessed by having the patient draw a clock and insert the numbers appropriately, draw a map of the United States, and/or draw geometric figures. It occurs with lesions to either parietal lobe.
- Dressing apraxia is the inability to correctly manipulate articles of clothing. The patient may dress incorrectly or fail to dress one side of the body. It occurs with lesions of the nondominant parietal lobe.
- Ideational apraxia is the inability to execute complex acts as a single motion. Common objects may be recognized but incorrectly used (eg, comb, toothbrush, pen). It is associated with lesions of the dominant parietal lobe.

MOTOR FUNCTION

Motor function involves the integration of a number of different anatomical structures within the central and peripheral nervous system as well as the musculoskeletal system. Several components of the motor examination can be evaluated in the unconscious patient as well.

Gait and Posture

Gait and posture essentially represent a composite of all motor activity. For gait, assess smoothness and rhythm and the ability to tandem walk. To evaluate posture, assess the ability to stand with eyes open and closed and then the ability to stand on one leg with eyes open and closed.

Dysfunctions of Gait

To assess dysfunctions of gait, consider the following:

- Spastic—signifies corticospinal tract lesion, such as with a stroke. The leg is held in stiff posture, is moved slowly, and the toes and lateral aspect scrape the floor as the leg is moved.
- Steppage—signifies peripheral nerve injury, which results in foot drop or the inability to dorsiflex the foot. Because the foot must be lifted abnormally high with each step, there is a distinct slapping sound as it hits the floor.

- Ataxic—represents cerebellar and/or dorsal column lesions. The feet are placed far apart (broad based), and the steps are unsteady and staggering.
- Propulsive—also called festinating; significant for basal ganglia dysfunction (Parkinson's disease). Trunk is bent over, and the steps are short and shuffling; as the walker gains momentum, there is the appearance that a fall might occur if not assisted.
- Waddling—due to proximal muscle weakness, as seen in muscular dystrophy. Muscle weakness does not allow stabilization on the weight-bearing hip, causing the opposite pelvis to drop and the trunk to incline, thus producing the waddle.

Dysfunctions of Posture

To assess dysfunctions of posture, consider the following:

- Loss of standing balance with eyes open and closed is attributed to cerebellar and posterior column dysfunction.
- Loss of standing balance with eyes closed only is due to posterior column dysfunction. The cerebellum helps to provide visual correction when the eyes are open.

Muscle Size

Assessment of muscle size should include evaluation of truncal, intercostal, abdominal, and extremity muscle groups for symmetry. It may be affected by such variables as sex, age, nutrition, and physical condition.

Abnormalities in Muscle Size

Abnormalities in muscle size are classified as follows:

- Atrophy—loss of muscle bulk due to peripheral nerve injuries or disuse associated with corticospinal tract lesions
- Hypertrophy—compensatory response to weakness of other muscle groups or deliberate muscle building

Muscle Tone

Muscle tone is evaluated by palpating the muscle for firmness and placing it through passive range of motion.

Dysfunctions

Consider the following when assessing dysfunctions in muscle tone:

- Hypotonia or atonia—appear as flaccid or "rag doll" in tone; is due to cerebellar and proprioceptive impairment and is seen initially with acute hemispheric and spinal cord lesions
- Spasticity—resistance to passive movement, which may suddenly decrease as muscle is placed through motion
- Rigidity—steady resistance seen with diffuse hemispheric lesions. Cogwheel or rhythmic rigidity is characteristic of Parkinson's disease; postural rigidity such as decortication and decerebration is seen with deep cerebral and brain stem injuries

Strength

It is important to determine which hand is dominant for strength assessment. Extremities are evaluated against gravity and resistance and with gravity eliminated. Strength is usually evaluated on a 0- to 4- or 0- to 5-point scale.

- 0—No movement or evidence of muscle contraction
- 1—No movement; some evidence of muscle contraction
- 2—Movement with gravity eliminated
- 3—Movement against gravity
- 4—Movement against some resistance
- 5—Movement against full resistance

The patient should be observed performing motor activities and moving to a sitting from a lying position to assess abdominal musculature.

Dysfunctions

Consider the following when assessing dysfunctions of strength:

- Unilateral paresis/paralysis—due to a muscle-specific peripheral nerve injury
- Hemiparesis/hemiplegia—seen with injury to the contralateral corticospinal tract
- Bilateral paresis/plegia—associated with spinal cord lesions, Guillain-Barré syndrome
- Generalized weakness—may be indicative of myasthenia gravis or electrolyte disturbances

Involuntary Movements and Coordination

Assess the patient's ability to coordinate movement by demonstrating rapid, alternating movements and pointing. The patient's ability to maintain balance and gait also tests for coordination. Disorders of coordination and tremors reflect lesions of the cerebellum and posterior columns. The dysfunctions demonstrated include ataxia, intention tremor, nystagmus, dysarthria, and dysmetria (past pointing).

Reflexes

Reflexes are involuntary responses to stimuli that essentially act as protective mechanisms for the body. While some reflexes may be overcome by cortical inhibition, others are solely dependent upon the reflex arc that exists between the point of stimulus and the corresponding spinal cord level. Evaluation is made of the deep tendon reflexes (DTRs) and superficial reflexes; the presence of pathological reflexes is assessed.

DTRs are also referred to as muscle-stretch or extensor reflexes. They are elicited by tapping a tendon associated with a specific muscle group. Superficial or cutaneous reflexes produce movement within specific muscle groups when the skin associated with them is stimulated. Pathological reflexes are demonstrated when there is pathology of the nervous system.

It is helpful to understand the appropriate reflex response in assessing spinal cord injuries, determining the extent of cortical involvement, and initiating appropriate treatment interventions. Deep tendon and superficial reflexes are outlined in Tables 2-1 and 2-2.

Pathological reflexes exist when a lesion interrupts the normal motor circuitry. Common pathological reflexes are listed below.

- Babinski's response—Assessment for a Babinski's response should be part of each neurological assessment. It involves superficial testing for plantar flexion of the toes, which is the normal response. A positive Babinski's sign exists when the great toe dorsiflexes (comes up) and the other toes fan out. Presence of this response reflects pathology within the corticospinal motor system.
- Grasp reflex—Stimulation of the palm causes the patient to grasp the examiner's fingers and to maintain the hold against resistance. It is similar to the normal grasp reflex seen in infants. Its presence indicates bilateral cerebral pathology or massive frontal lobe pathology if occurring unilaterally.

Table 2-1 Deep Tendon (Stretch) Reflexes

Reflex	Response	Spinal Cord Segment
Biceps	Elbow flexion	C5-6
Triceps	Elbow extension	C6-8
Patellar	Knee extension	L2-4
Achilles	Foot extension	S1-2

Test by tapping the tendon innervating the relaxed muscle.

Table 2-2 Superficial Reflexes

Reflex	Testing Method	Absence
Abdominal	Stimulate abdomen above and below umbilicus: navel should move toward stimulus	T8-12 lesion
Cremasteric (males)	Stimulate inner surface of thigh: ipsilateral testicle should elevate	L1-2 lesion
Bulbo-cavernosus	Stimulate foreskin or glans: muscle at base of penis should contract	S3-4 lesion
Anal sphincter	Stimulate perianal skin with gloved finger in rectum: anal sphincter should contract	S3-5 lesion
Plantar	Stimulate lateral aspect of foot from heel to great toe: toes should flex	Corticospinal tract lesion

SENSATION

Sensation is assessed in the conscious patient by introducing various stimuli to different portions of the body with the eyes closed. The degree to which sensation is evaluated will depend upon the severity of the patient's condition. In the unconscious patient, sensation is assessed by introducing noxious or painful stimuli. The sensory modalities evaluated include the following:

- Light touch—Stimulate distal and proximal portions of each extremity and the trunk. The patient is asked to tell the examiner when and where the stimulus is felt.
- Pain—A safety or common pin is used to touch the extremities and trunk, alternating between the sharp and dull ends of the pin. The patient is asked to tell the examiner when and where the stimulus is felt and whether the sensation is sharp or dull. In spinal cord-injured patients, this test of sensation is crucial in helping to localize the level of the spinal cord lesion.
- Proprioception—Distal portions of the fingers and toes are moved up and down. The patient is asked to tell the examiner in which position the digit being examined is placed. Loss of proprioceptive ability can occur to the extent that the patient is unable to discern where body parts are in space.

CEREBELLAR FUNCTION

Assessment of the cerebellum focuses on the ability to coordinate movement and to maintain normal muscle tone and equilibrium. Tests to evaluate cerebellar function are presented in relation to the dysfunctions associated with them.

Coordination of Movement

The ability of the patient to perform voluntary movements smoothly and without error is the norm. Dysfunctions include the following:

- Ataxia—the presence of uncoordinated voluntary muscle actions; may be most noticeable when reaching for objects (jerking) or when walking
- Dysarthria—slurred or halting speech
- Involuntary movements—assessment for intention and resting tremors, athetotic and choreoathetotic movements
- Dysdiadochokinesia—inability to perform rapid, alternating movements. The patient is asked to rapidly supinate, then to pronate hands and forearms.
- Cerebellar nystagmus—jerky eye movements when attempting to visualize a field to the side of the head; may require several attempts to focus
- Disequilibrium—inability to maintain equilibrium with eyes closed, visual correction provided with eyes open. Patient is asked to stand with feet together, with eyes open first, then closed. Cerebellar lesions will result in the patient leaning toward the affected cerebellar hemisphere, which is referred to as a positive Romberg's sign.
- Dysmetria—inability to correctly measure the distance to an object. The patient is asked to touch his or her index finger to the examiner's index finger, then bring it back to his or her nose. The procedure is repeated several times, with the examiner's finger moving to different positions each time. The patient may past point or stop short of the target.

CRANIAL NERVES

Assessment of cranial nerve function should be part of every neurological examination. The origin of the cranial nerves and their functions were presented in Chapter 1. Table 2-3 illustrates testing methodologies and dysfunctions of the 12 cranial nerves.

Table 2-3 Cranial Nerve Testing and Dysfunction

Cranial Nerve	Testing Method	Dysfunction
I, Olfactory (Sensory)	Identification of familiar scents (coffee, peppermint)	Loss of the sense of smell
II, Optic (Sensory)	Have patient read printed material. With one eye closed and the head stationary, move a pen or finger through all four quadrants of the visual field. Repeat procedure to other eye.	Decrease or loss of visual acuity; impairment of visual fields
III, Oculomotor (Motor)	Have patient keep head stationary and follow examiner's pen or finger as it is moved up, down, in, and out. Cranial nerves III, IV, and VI control extraocular eye movements (EOMs) and are examined together. Evaluate ability to open eyelids.	Paresis or paralysis of superior rectus, inferior rectus, medial rectus, and inferior oblique eye muscles; ptosis of eyelid
	Evaluate direct and consensual pupillary constriction. Bring object from distance of two feet to within inches from eye.	Decreased or loss of pupil constriction; loss of accommodation reflex if pupil does not constrict as object approaches
IV, Trochlear (Motor)	When assessing EOMs, observe for down-and-out eye movement.	Paresis or paralysis of superior oblique eye muscle
V, Trigeminal (Motor and sensory)	Test response to facial sensation with eyes closed. Apply cotton wisp to sclera to assess corneal reflex.	Decreased or loss of facial sensation; decreased or absent corneal reflex
	Ask patient to open and close jaw.	Decreased innervation to muscles of mastication
VI, Abducens (Motor)	When assessing EOMs, assess for lateral eye movement.	Paresis or paralysis of lateral rectus eye muscle
VII, Facial (Motor and sensory)	Ask patient to smile, frown, close eyelids against resistance.	Decreased or loss of facial muscle innervation
	Identification of familiar tastes on anterior tongue (sugar, salt) is often deferred.	Loss of taste to anterior tongue
VIII, Acoustic (Sensory)	Evaluate grossly by determining when watch ticking or whispered word is heard.	Decreased hearing

Table 2-3 continued

Cranial Nerve	Testing Method	Dysfunction
	Have patient stand with feet together; evaluate ability to maintain posture and to balance with eyes open and closed.	Pathology to vestibular portion of nerve
IX, Glossopharyngeal (Motor and sensory)	Assess for identification of familiar tastes on posterior tongue. The motor portion is tested together with the vagus; assess gag reflex and swallowing ability.	Loss of taste to posterior tongue Decreased or absent gag reflex, dysphagia
X, Vagus (Motor and sensory)	Assess phonation and symmetry of uvula.	Hoarseness, deviation of uvula
XI, Spinal Accessory (Motor)	Ask patient to turn head and shrug shoulders with and without resistance.	Decreased or loss of neck muscle innervation
XII, Hypoglossal (Motor)	Ask patient to stick out tongue and assess for symmetry.	Loss of tongue movement

NEUROLOGICAL ASSESSMENT

The purposes of neurological assessment are to

- determine the patient's baseline neurological status
- identify deviations from normal nervous system function
- determine the effect of the deviations on the functional capabilities of the individual
- Identify life-threatening events (increased intracranial pressure [ICP])

Factors evaluated when performing neurological assessment include

- level of consciousness
- motor and sensory function
- pupillary size and reaction to light
- eye movements
- vital signs

Neurological assessment in an emergency situation and in critical and acute care settings is frequently based upon use of the Glasgow Coma Scale, described below. Level of consciousness and motor function can be readily assessed using this scale.

Glasgow Coma Scale

The Glasgow Coma Scale (GCS) was developed in 1974 by Teasdale and Jennett at the University of Glasgow to assess neurological function in comatose patients.[1] The scale is based upon the patient's best response in each of three categories: eye opening, motor response, and verbal response.

The patient's response is assigned a numerical value for each category. The lowest score possible is 3, indicating profound coma, while the highest score of 15 reflects an alert and oriented individual. A score of 8 or below can be considered to define coma.[2] The scale serves as an objective measure of neurological function. The categories, responses, and corresponding numerical values of the GCS are listed in Table 2-4.

Slight modification of the scale has occurred, and it remains a popular tool in assessing neurological status. Many institutions have incorporated the components of the GCS as a part of vital sign sheets, which enables graphic representation of an individual's neurological status at any point in time. Exhibit 2-1 displays an example of such a neurological assessment sheet.

In some instances patient condition may preclude the ability to assess the patient's eye opening and/or best verbal response. Causes of such instances might

Table 2-4 Glasgow Coma Scale Scoring

Response	Score
Best Eye Opening	
Spontaneous	=4
To voice	=3
To pain	=2
None	=1
Best Motor Response	
Obeys commands	=6
Localizes to pain	=5
Flexion withdrawal	=4
Abnormal flexion	=3
(decorticate rigidity)	
Extension	=2
(decerebrate rigidity)	
Flaccidity	=1
Best Verbal Response	
Oriented	=5
Confused	=4
Inappropriate	=3
Incomprehensible	=2
None	=1

Source: Adapted from "Assessment of Coma and Impaired Consciousness" by G. Teasdale and B. Jennett, *Lancet,* Vol. 7, pp. 81-84, with permission of The Lancet, © 1974.

Exhibit 2-1 Neurological Assessment Flow Sheet.

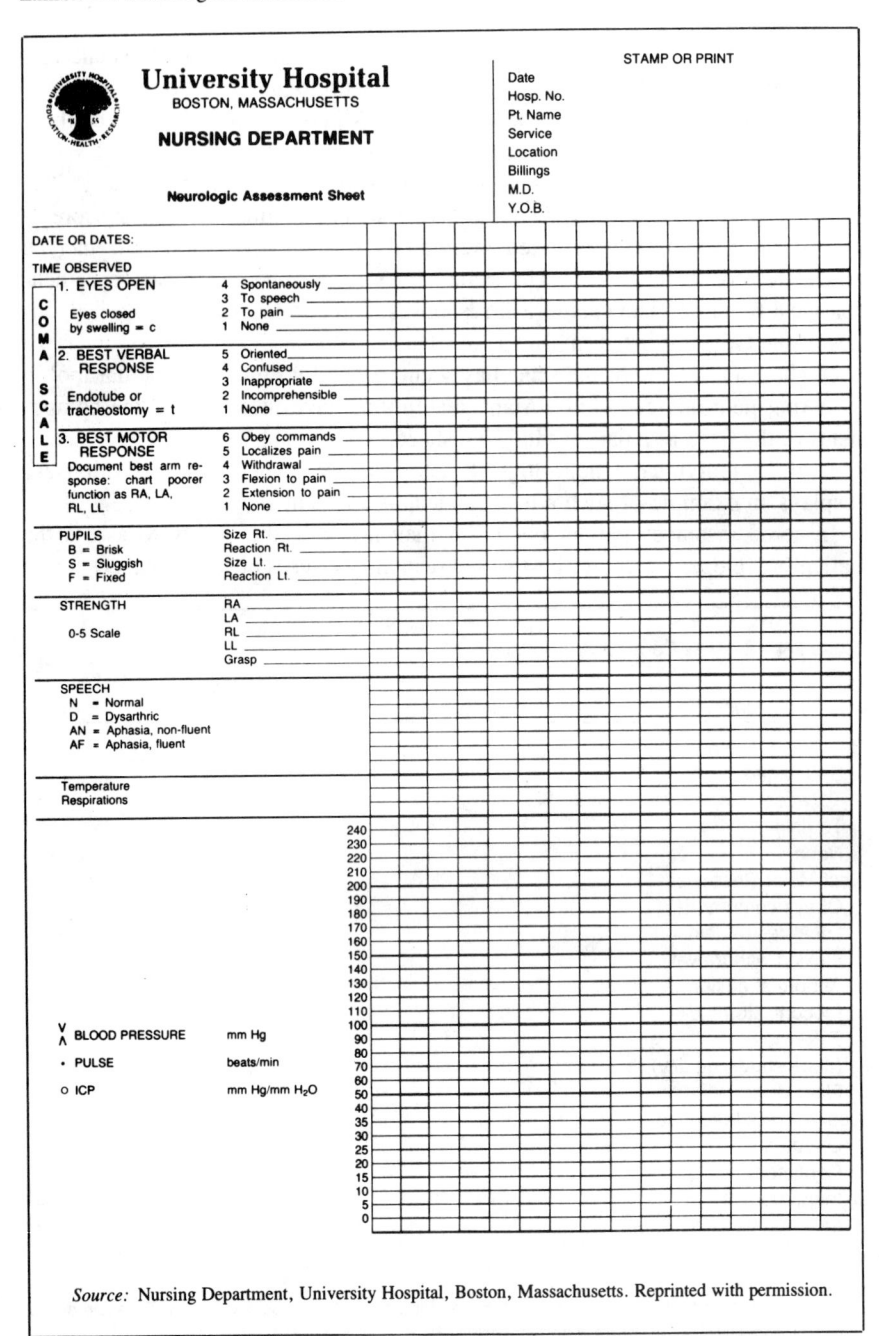

University Hospital
BOSTON, MASSACHUSETTS

NURSING DEPARTMENT

Neurologic Assessment Sheet

STAMP OR PRINT
Date
Hosp. No.
Pt. Name
Service
Location
Billings
M.D.
Y.O.B.

DATE OR DATES:

TIME OBSERVED

COMA SCALE

1. EYES OPEN
 - 4 Spontaneously
 - 3 To speech
 - 2 To pain
 - 1 None
 Eyes closed by swelling = c

2. BEST VERBAL RESPONSE
 - 5 Oriented
 - 4 Confused
 - 3 Inappropriate
 - 2 Incomprehensible
 - 1 None
 Endotube or tracheostomy = t

3. BEST MOTOR RESPONSE
 Document best arm response: chart poorer function as RA, LA, RL, LL
 - 6 Obey commands
 - 5 Localizes pain
 - 4 Withdrawal
 - 3 Flexion to pain
 - 2 Extension to pain
 - 1 None

PUPILS
B = Brisk
S = Sluggish
F = Fixed
 Size Rt.
 Reaction Rt.
 Size Lt.
 Reaction Lt.

STRENGTH
0-5 Scale
 RA
 LA
 RL
 LL
 Grasp

SPEECH
N = Normal
D = Dysarthric
AN = Aphasia, non-fluent
AF = Aphasia, fluent

Temperature
Respirations

V/A BLOOD PRESSURE — mm Hg
• PULSE — beats/min
○ ICP — mm Hg/mm H_2O

240
230
220
210
200
190
180
170
160
150
140
130
120
110
100
90
80
70
60
50
40
35
30
25
20
15
10
5
0

Source: Nursing Department, University Hospital, Boston, Massachusetts. Reprinted with permission.

include eyes closed by swelling or the presence of an endotracheal or tracheostomy tube. Flow sheets can include specific denotations (such as "c" for closed by swelling or "t" for the presence of an endotracheal or tracheostomy tube), which can be charted indicating the presence of factors that preclude assessment of these parameters (see Exhibit 2-1).

Level of Consciousness

Level of consciousness is the ability of the patient to interact appropriately within the context of the immediate environment. Various levels of alterations can occur, ranging from full consciousness to profound coma. Some of the common terminology is described below.

Full Consciousness

The individual is alert and cognizant of the environment and able to appropriately identify person, time, and place.

Confusion

The confused individual is unable to appropriately maintain orientation in the environment or may misinterpret environmental stimuli. Memory disturbances, inability to follow commands, poor attention patterns, and daytime drowsiness followed by nocturnal agitation may be present.

Delirium

Delirium is manifested by disorientation, fear, agitation, and sensory disturbances such as hallucinations and delusions. The patient displays behavior that is loud, offensive, and suspicious. Distortion of environmental stimuli such that the patient fears for personal safety often is present.

Lethargy

The lethargic individual is one who, with stimulation, can be easily aroused and appropriately responsive to the environment. The individual falls back into a sleepy state when the stimulation is halted. Obtunded, drowsy, and somnolent are terms used synonymously for lethargy.

Stupor

A stuporous individual is one who is unresponsive and requires vigorous, noxious (painful) stimuli to achieve arousal. Once aroused the patient may purposefully withdraw from the source of the stimulus, demonstrate confused and agitated behavior, and/or be unable to follow commands or to answer questions.

Coma

A comatose individual is one who is unresponsive and cannot be aroused. The degree to which coma is present may vary. Comatose states may occur due to structural processes within the intracranial compartment or due to metabolic processes that disrupt normal metabolic mechanisms.

- Semicoma—The individual does not move spontaneously and is unresponsive. The administration of noxious stimuli (nailbed pressure, supraorbital pressure, vigorous shaking) may elicit stirring or moans and the attempt to withdraw the stimulated body part from the source of the stimulus. Cranial nerve reflexes (pupillary, corneal, and pharyngeal) and deep tendon reflexes are intact. The plantar reflex (Babinski's response) may be present or absent. Abnormal posturing may or may not be present.
- Coma—The individual is unresponsive and will not moan or stir to noxious stimuli nor attempt to withdraw from the stimulus. Cranial nerve reflexes are absent or greatly diminished; deep tendon and plantar reflexes are absent.

Recovery from coma generally occurs in stages and is referred to as "lightening," with the reference being to the patient's ability to respond to stimuli.

Motor and Sensory Function

Motor strength and sensory function can be assessed, as described earlier in this chapter, in patients able to obey commands and to communicate. Motor function is assessed in patients with a depressed level of consciousness by evaluating their response to the administration of noxious stimuli.

Common methods of administering noxious stimuli include

- applying pressure to the nailbed of a finger or toe
- applying pressure with the examiner's thumbs to the supraorbital ridge above the eyes
- rubbing the sternum

Patients in stuporous states may purposefully withdraw the body or body part from the source of the stimulus, while those in coma may demonstrate one or more of several abnormal motor responses. Figure 2-1 demonstrates motor responses to noxious stimuli in comatose patients.

Neurological Assessment 53

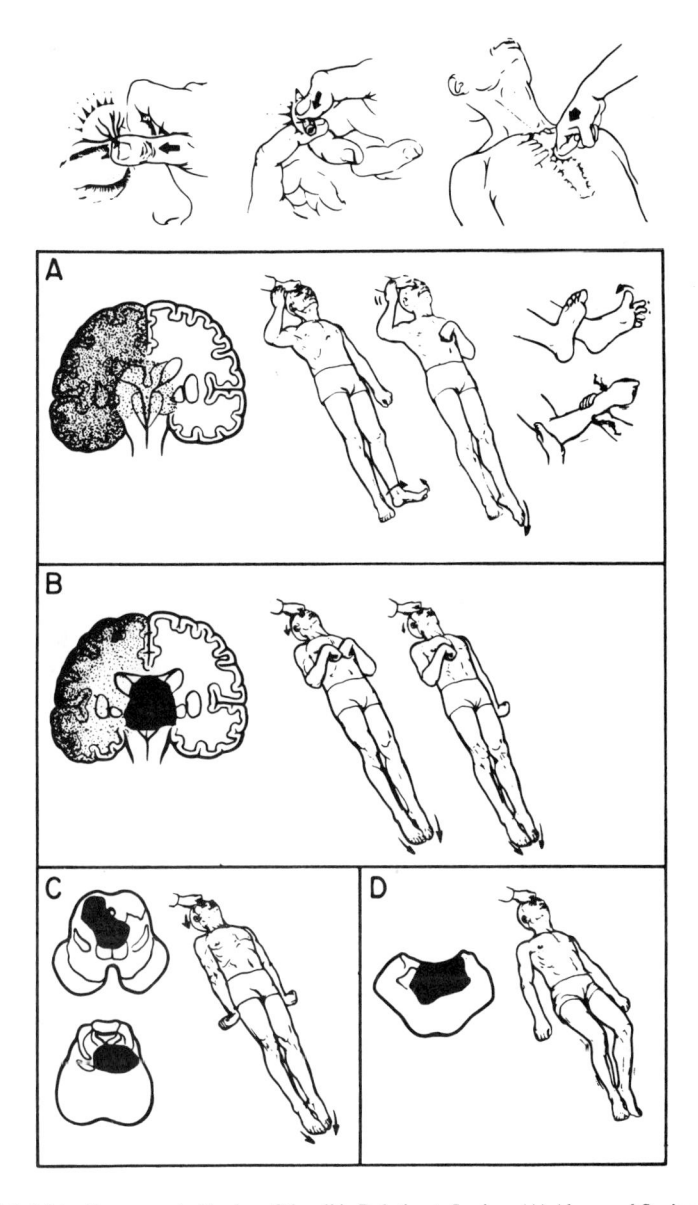

Figure 2-1 Motor Responses to Noxious Stimuli in Relation to Lesion. (A) Abnormal flexion response on the left due to right hemisphere damage. (B) Abnormal flexion and extension responses due to involvement of the hemisphere and deeper supratentorial regions. (C) Fully developed decerebrate rigidity with opisthotonos from diencephalic and midbrain involvement. (D) Abnormal arm extension with leg flexion, indicating pontine damage. *Source:* Reprinted from *The Diagnosis of Stupor and Coma,* 3rd ed., by F. Plum and J.B. Posner, p. 66, with permission of F.A. Davis Company, © 1983.

Abnormal Motor Responses

Individuals with decreased levels of consciousness and who are unresponsive to verbal stimuli can have the intactness of their motor system assessed by applying external stimuli to various body parts and observing the motor response.

- Decorticate rigidity (abnormal flexion of the arm with extension of the leg)—Fully developed, decortication is demonstrated by adduction of the upper extremities with flexion of the arms, wrists, and fingers with extension and internal rotation of the lower extremities. It may be produced by applying noxious stimuli or may occur without stimuli. This abnormal posture (or posturing, as it is often termed) represents interruption of the corticospinal pathways within the cerebrum.
- Decerebrate rigidity (abnormal extension of the arm and leg)—Decerebration is demonstrated by extension and adduction of the arms with flexion of the fingers and extension of the legs with plantar flexion of the toes. In its truest form, opisthotonos (arching of the back) is also demonstrated. Like decortication, decerebration is an abnormal posturing that can occur with or without stimuli. It represents corticospinal tract interruption at the level of the diencephalon that extends to involve portions of the upper brain stem.
- Flaccidity—Absence of motor responses to noxious stimuli reflects depression of the motor mechanisms within the pons and medulla, or peripheral nerve denervation.

Pupillary Responses

Examination of pupils is an integral component of neurological assessment, as they provide information relative to the integrity of the intracranial environment. Pupils should be assessed for size and shape, their reaction to direct light, and in comparison to each other.

Pupils should be round and approximately the same size and should constrict briskly when bright light is shone upon them. The pupil that did not have the light directly applied should also constrict, producing a consensual light response. Pupils that are sluggish, nonreactive, or fixed reflect processes within the intracranial compartment producing increased ICP, or localized tissue compression.

The use of mydriatic or miotic agents in the patient's eyes needs to be known prior to pupil examination. Mydriatics (atropine) cause pupillary dilation, while miotics (pilocarpine) cause pupillary constriction. Pupillary responses in

Neurological Assessment   55

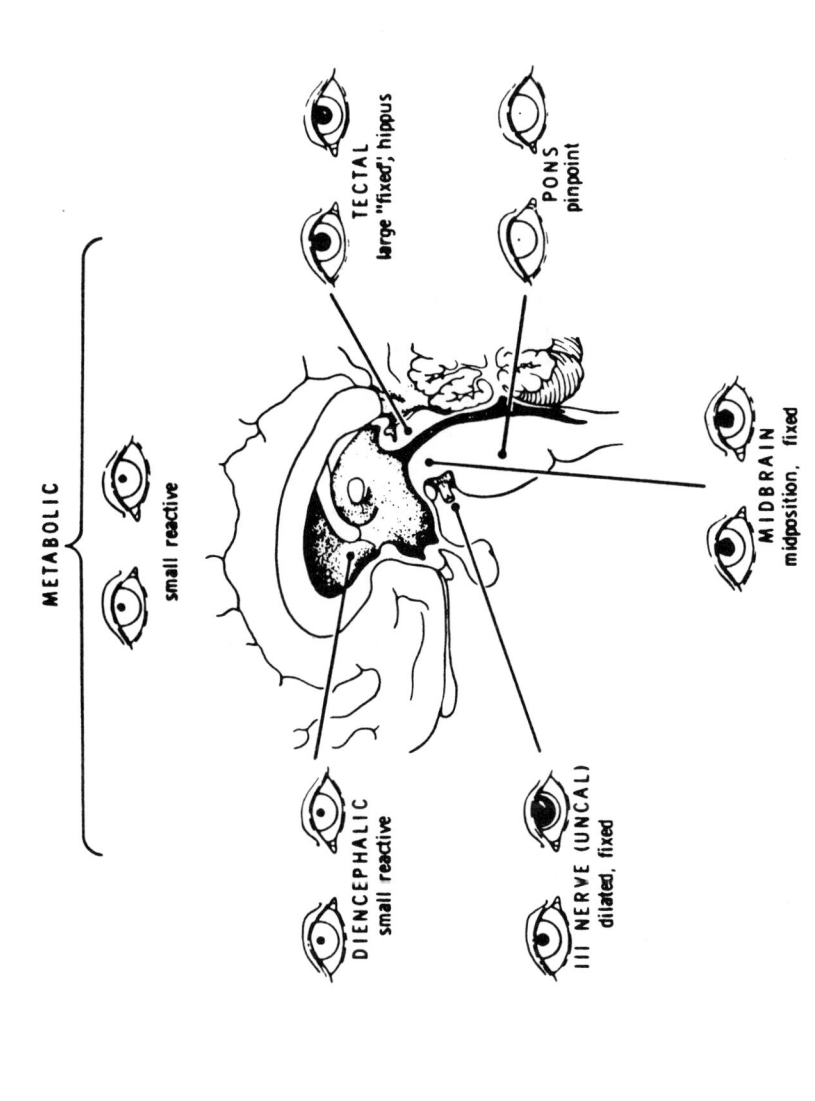

Figure 2-2 Pupillary Responses Based upon the Location of Pathology. *Source:* Reprinted from *The Diagnosis of Stupor and Coma*, 3rd ed., by F. Plum and J.B. Posner, p. 46, with permission of F.A. Davis Company, © 1983.

comatose individuals are summarized in Figure 2-2. Other references to pupillary discrepancies not associated with coma are

- Anisocoria—inequality in pupillary size; may occur as patient's normal baseline
- Hippus—initial constriction of the pupil to direct light, then a rhythmic contraction and dilation of the pupil independent of light stimulus or visual focus. It may be baseline for the patient or may represent midbrain damage.
- Adie's (tonic) pupil—loss of parasympathetic influence to constrict the pupil, allowing the sympathetic influence to maintain it dilated. Prolonged direct light stimulation may cause it to slowly constrict. The response may occur with oculomotor nerve injuries independent of diffuse intracranial processes or following a viral infection.
- Argyll Robertson pupil—small, unequal, and irregular shaped pupils that do not respond to light and are associated with latent syphilis
- Amaurotic (blind) pupil—The blind pupil will not respond to direct light, and the unaffected pupil will not demonstrate a consensual light response. The consensual light reflex will be present in the blind pupil in response to direct light shone in the unaffected eye.

Eye Movements

Assessment of eye movements, known as EOMs, also provides data relative to central nervous system (CNS) function. EOMs are evaluated differently in conscious patients than in unconscious patients. Both methods are presented below.

Conscious Person

In the conscious person EOMs are evaluated by asking the patient to maintain the head in a neutral position, then to follow the examiner's finger or pen as it is moved through the range of ocular motion. The range of ocular motion includes upward, medially, laterally, downward, upward and out, and downward and out. Normal eye movement is displayed by conjugate gaze (eyes move together) in all directions, without the occurrence of nystagmus (beating movements of the eyeball).

Gross assessment of visual fields can be made at the same time. Normal visual field extensions are 60 degrees nasally, 100 degrees temporally, and 130 degrees vertically. This assessment may reveal functional defects anywhere along the visual pathway (retina, optic nerve, optic tract, lateral geniculate body, geniculocalcarine tract, or occipital lobe).

The left visual field falls on the right half of each retina and projects to the right side of the brain; the converse is true of the right visual field. Some specific visual field defects are listed below.

- Blindness—in one or both eyes, due to a lesion of the retina, optic nerve, or globe itself
- Bitemporal hemianopsia—loss of the temporal half of each visual field due to a lesion of the optic chiasm involving the visual fibers crossing to the opposite side; often seen with pituitary area tumors
- Homonymous hemianopsia—loss of vision in the same half of both visual fields (may be right or left) due to a lesion of the visual pathways after they have crossed at the optic chiasm; seen with stroke
- Quadrantopsia—loss of the one fourth of the visual field in each eye due to lesion involving part of the optic radiations. The visual loss may be in any one of the four visual field quadrants.

Unconscious Person

Assessing EOMs in the comatose patient requires that the oculocephalic (doll's eye phenomenon) and/or oculovestibular reflexes be evaluated.

- Oculocephalic reflexes are demonstrated by holding the patient's eyelids open and briskly rotating the head from side to side or by briskly flexing and extending the neck. Cervical spine injuries should always be disproved before attempting oculocephalic reflexes in the unconscious patient.

  Absent doll's eyes reflects compression in the midbrain-pontine area, where the cranial nerves for eye movement (III, IV, and VI) originate, while positive doll's eyes reflect supratentorial causes for the coma. The vestibular portion of cranial nerve VIII is also involved in the execution of this reflex in that information regarding head position is transmitted through this neural pathway.

  Doll's eyes are present, and the response is positive or normal when the eyes move conjugately in the direction opposite the rotation of the head or upward when the neck is flexed. There may be eye movement that is dysconjugate or asymmetrical in nature, that is, the eyes do not move together. Negative, or absent, doll's eyes exist when the eyes follow the rotation of flexion and extension of the head. Figure 2-3 demonstrates eye movements in the comatose patient.

- Oculovestibular reflexes are demonstrated by the injection of ice water into the external ear canal of the comatose individual. Although not performed as easily as the doll's eye phenomenon and generally performed by physicians, it is used as a measure of brain stem function. Intactness of the tympanic membrane must be determined prior to performing the procedure; it is contraindicated in the presence of a perforated eardrum.

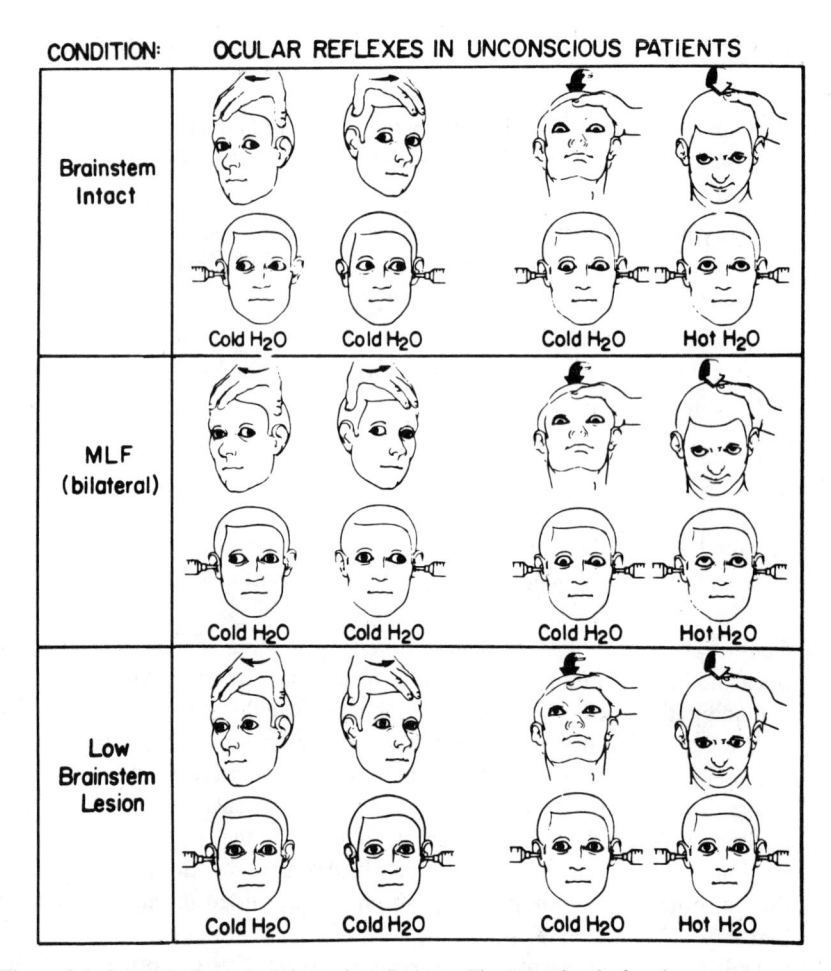

Figure 2-3 Ocular Reflexes in Unconscious Patients. The upper level of each segment represents oculocephalic responses based upon the level of the pathology, while the lower level represents oculovestibular responses to the same pathological lesion. The medial longitudinal fasciculus (MLF) is a bundle of several tracts extending from the midbrain to the cervical spinal cord. It influences reflex movements of the head and neck in response to stimulation of visual and vestibular pathways.
Source: Reprinted from *The Diagnosis of Stupor and Coma,* 3rd ed., by F. Plum and J.B. Posner, p. 55, with permission of F.A. Davis Company, © 1983.

Stimulation of the semicircular canals transmits information from the acoustic nerve to the oculomotor (third) and abducens (fourth) nerves. Intact pathways are assumed when the eyes move conjugately and slowly toward the irrigated ear, then return rapidly toward the ear not irrigated. Figure 2-3 demonstrates oculovestibular responses in comatose patients. Documentation of oculovestibular responses is the same as for oculocephalic responses.

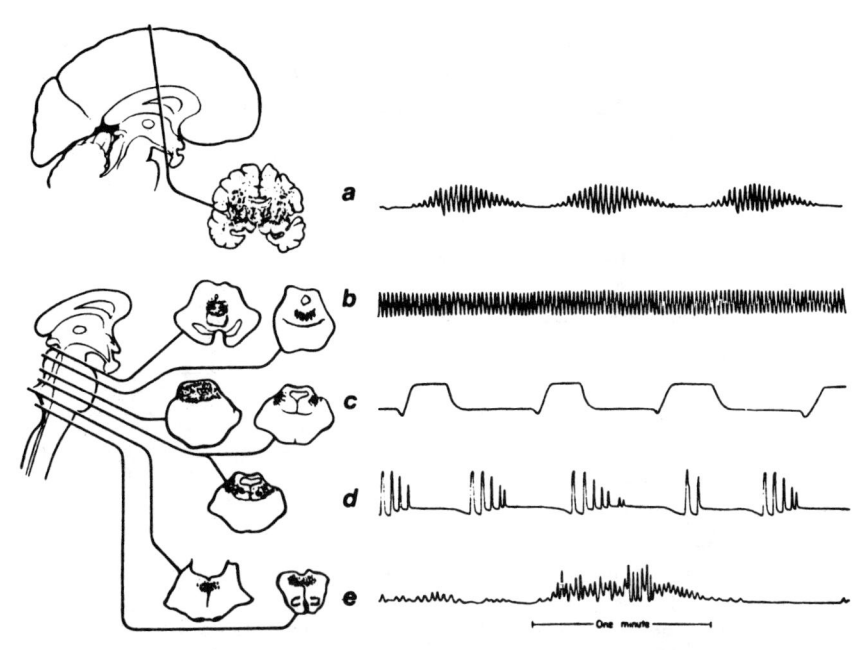

Figure 2-4 Respiratory Patterns Associated with Pathology at Different Levels of the Brain. Pathology is represented by shaded areas: (a) Cheyne-Stokes respirations; (b) central neurogenic hyperventilation; (c) apneustic respirations; (d) cluster respirations; (e) ataxic respirations. *Source:* Reprinted from *The Diagnosis of Stupor and Coma,* 3rd ed., by F. Plum and J.B. Posner, p. 34, with permission of F.A. Davis Company, © 1983.

In comatose individuals, the oculocephalic reflexes are frequently assessed along with the corneal and gag reflexes to evaluate brain stem integrity. These reflexes are all mediated by cranial nerves exiting from the three regions of the brain stem:

1. EOMs from the midbrain (III and IV), and pons (VI)
2. corneal from the pons (V and VII)
3. gag from the medulla (IX and X)

Vital Signs

The influencing control of the CNS over vital functions is tremendous. Alterations in cardiovascular and respiratory status may occur with insults affecting the brain stem reflex centers, and temperature control and endocrine mechanisms may be altered by compromise to the hypothalamic-pituitary axis. The necessity for evaluating vital sign parameters in relation to neurological status is a final, but by no means least, important step in neurological assessment. Specific changes in temperature control, blood pressure, and heart rate with CNS compromise are discussed in Chapters 4 and 6. Respiratory pattern changes vary with the area of the CNS compressed. Figure 2-4 demonstrates respiratory pattern changes.

NOTES

1. Graham Teasdale, and Bryan Jennett. "Assessment of Coma and Impaired Consciousness." *Lancet* 7(1974):81-84.
2. Bryan Jennett, and Graham Teasdale. *Management of Head Injuries* (Philadelphia: F.A. Davis Company, 1981).

SUGGESTED READINGS

American Association of Neuroscience Nurses. *Core Curriculum for Neuroscience Nursing*. Edited by Marilyn M. Ricci. Park Ridge, IL: American Association of Neuroscience Nurses, 1984.

Boss, Barbara J. "Dysphasia, Dyspraxia, and Dysarthria: Distinguishing Features, Part II." *Journal of Neuroscience Nursing* 16(1984):211–216.

Boss, Barbara J. "Memory Impairments: Forgetfulness versus Amnesia." *Journal of Neuroscience Nursing* 20(1988):151–158.

Gilman, Sid, and Sarah S. Newman. *Manter and Gatz's Essentials of Clinical Neuroanatomy & Neurophysiology*. 6th ed. Philadelphia: F.A. Davis, 1982.

Hickey, Joanne. *The Clinical Practice of Neurological and Neurosurgical Nursing*. Philadelphia: J.B. Lippincott, 1981.

Nikas, Diana L., ed. *The Critically Ill Neurosurgical Patient*. New York: Churchill Livingstone, 1982.

Ozuna, Judy. "Alterations in Mentation: Nursing Assessment and Intervention." *Journal of Neuroscience Nursing* 17(1985):66–70.

Plum, Fred, and Jerome B. Posner. *The Diagnosis of Stupor and Coma*. 3rd ed. Philadelphia: F.A. Davis, 1983.

Raimond, Jeanne, and Joyce Waterman Taylor. *Neurological Emergencies: Effective Nursing Care*. Rockville, MD: Aspen Publishers, 1986.

Rudy, Ellen B. *Advanced Neurological and Neurosurgical Nursing*. St. Louis: Mosby, 1984.

Spence, Alexander P., and Elliott B. Mason. *Human Anatomy and Physiology*. 3rd ed. Menlo Park, CA: Benjamin/Cummings Publishing, 1987.

Taylor, Joyce Waterman, and Sally Ballenger. *Neurological Dysfunctions and Nursing Interventions*. New York: McGraw-Hill, 1980.

3

Neurodiagnostic Procedures

A number of diagnostic procedures are commonly used to assist in diagnosing neurological dysfunction and its etiology. Informed consent and, in certain instances, written consent by the patient or other responsible party may be necessary. Intricacies of each procedure can be explained to patients as their condition permits understanding. Issues of concern to critical care nurses are presented with each procedure.

COMPUTED TOMOGRAPHY

Description

Computed tomography (CT) scan is a computer-calculated image that results from absorption of an x-ray beam as it passes through cross sections of bone and tissue in a single plane. The degree to which the beam is absorbed is determined by the density of the bone and cranial contents, which allows differentiation between bone, brain tissue, blood, and cerebrospinal fluid (CSF).

Normal brain appears as isodense areas on CT. Hypodense regions present as very dark areas and may reflect infarction, edema, or necrosis. Increased vascularity, hemorrhage, tumor, or calcified areas are displayed as light, hyperdense regions on this scan. A CT scan may involve injection of a radiopaque contrast medium.

Indications

CT scan may be used for any of the following situations:

- to assess size, shape, and location of intracranial structures
- to diagnose intracranial abnormalities: space-occupying lesions, hematomas, hemorrhages, hydrocephalus, edema, contusions, shift of intracranial structures

- to diagnose intraspinal lesions
- to provide follow-up data on intracranial or intraspinal abnormalities or surgery

Patient Teaching

The patient should be informed of the following regarding CT scan:

- Patient must remain still during scan; sedation may be required for agitated patients.
- Hair must be free of adornments.
- Intravenous (IV) line may be inserted for injection of contrast medium.
- Scan requires twenty to thirty minutes to complete.

Nursing Implications

Nurses should be aware of the following regarding CT scan:

- Agitated patients will require sedation.
- Unstable patients will require nurse or physician escort.
- Assessment for allergies to seafood or iodine is necessary if contrast scan is to be obtained.

MAGNETIC RESONANCE IMAGING

Description

Magnetic resonance imaging (MRI) is a scanning technique that uses magnetic fields and radiofrequency pulses to produce computer-calculated images of organs and tissues from different planes. It is more sensitive than CT in delineating tissues and is better than CT in detecting posterior fossa lesions. This procedure may be contraindicated in patients with metallic implants (cardiac pacemakers, aneurysm clips, ventricular shunts).

Indications

MRI may be used in any of the following situations:

- to differentiate vascular lesions
- to assess tissue abnormalities
- to diagnose brain stem abnormalities
- to diagnose lacunar infarctions
- to localize epileptogenic foci

Patient Teaching

The patient should be informed of the following regarding MRI:

- No ionizing radiation is used.
- Patient may experience claustrophobia with head enclosed in machine.
- MRI requires patient to remain still during scan.
- Procedure requires thirty to ninety minutes to complete.
- Metal objects such as hair adornments, earrings, rings, and watches need to be removed; they may distort the image even though they are not magnetic, and some watches may be affected by the magnetic fields. Some cervical tongs and halo rings may also cause image distortions.

Nursing Implications

Nurses should be aware of the following regarding MRI:

- Assess for claustrophobia prior to scan.
- Assess need for sedation.
- Assist in removing and safeguarding metal articles.

SINGLE-PHOTON EMISSION-COMPUTED TOMOGRAPHY

Description

Single-photon emission-computed tomography (SPECT) is a computer-calculated image derived from emissions of positrons after infusion with a radioactive isotope. Unlike positron emission tomography (PET), which requires an on-line cyclotron to generate the radioisotope, SPECT uses commercially prepared isotopes, which are more readily available. SPECT enables metabolic mapping of brain tissue according to glucose metabolism. It is used to research stroke, epilepsy, migraines, and metabolic brain disorders. Clinically SPECT differentiates depression, Alzheimer's disease, and other types of dementias in the aged.

Indications

SPECT may be used in any of the following situations:

- to delineate blood flow and metabolism
- to differentiate healthy from unhealthy brain tissue
- to localize epileptogenic foci
- to project prognostic indicators and course of rehabilitative treatment

Patient Teaching

The patient should be informed of the following regarding SPECT:

- The amount of radiation absorbed is less than one fourth that absorbed during a brain CT.
- Stimulants should be avoided 24 hours preprocedure.
- Avoid as many medications as possible, as they alter cerebral metabolism.
- Patient must be able to cooperate with the procedure and remain still during the scan.
- IV lines will be in place for isotope infusion and blood specimen collection.
- SPECT requires 60 to 90 minutes to complete.

Nursing Implications

Nurses should be aware of the following regarding SPECT:

- Unstable patients are not appropriate for scan.
- Medications alter metabolism.
- Postural hypotension may occur after the scan.
- Encourage patient to urinate as soon as possible after the scan to clear the isotope from the bladder.

SKULL RADIOGRAPHS

Description

Skull radiographs are radiographic films of the skull taken from different angles. The angles most commonly ordered are

- posteroanterior views
- occipital view (Towne view)
- lateral views
- axial view (base view)
- maxillary sinus view (Water's view)

Skull radiographs are often done routinely after head trauma to rule out skull fractures. Basilar skull fractures are not always demonstrated on skull films; their diagnosis is discussed in Chapter 6.

Indications

Skull radiographs may be used for any of the following situations:

- to assess for skull fractures
- to assess for fractures of facial, orbit, or sinus bones
- to identify areas of calcification

Patient Teaching

The patient should be informed of the following regarding skull radiographs:

- Patient must remain still while films are taken.
- The amount of radiation to which the patient is exposed is not dangerous.

Nursing Implications

No postprocedure care is required.

SPINE RADIOGRAPHY

Description

Spine radiography is comprised of radiographic films of the entire spinal column or of various spinal segments (cervical, thoracic, lumbar, or sacral). Films are taken from the anteroposterior, oblique, and lateral angles; clear views of the upper cervical vertebrae may require taking the radiograph through the patient's open mouth. Tomograms of the spine may be ordered after stabilization to afford clearer images of the individual vertebrae.

Indications

Spine radiography may be used in any of the following situations:

- to assess for fracture, dislocation, or compression of the vertebrae
- to examine for degenerative processes of the spinal column
- to assess for abnormal spinal curvatures

Patient Teaching

The patient should be informed of the following regarding spine radiography:

- Patient must remain still while films are taken.
- The amount of radiation received is not dangerous.

Nursing Implications

Nurses should be aware of the following regarding spine radiography:

- No postprocedure care is required.
- Patients in cervical traction should be accompanied by a nurse or physician to ensure traction stabilization.
- During flexion/extension views of an unstable cervical spine, the physician should be available for manipulation of the neck.

LUMBAR PUNCTURE

Description

Lumbar puncture involves insertion of a hollow needle into the interspace between the L3-L4 or L4-L5 vertebrae to obtain CSF. It is contraindicated in instances where increased intracranial pressure is suspected, as it may precipitate brain stem herniation.

Indications

Lumbar puncture may be used in any of the following situations:

- to obtain CSF for microscopic examination and/or culture and sensitivity
- to measure CSF pressure
- to insert contrast media for diagnostic evaluation
- to administer spinal anesthesia or analgesia

Patient Teaching

The patient should be informed of the following regarding lumbar puncture:

- The procedure requires the patient to lie on his or her side with knees brought up as close as possible to the chest.
- Patient must remain still during the procedure.
- Procedure requires about twenty minutes.
- Patient must remain flat in bed for six to twelve hours as ordered by the physician.

Nursing Implications

Nurses should be aware of the following regarding lumbar puncture:

- Assess neurological status.
- Encourage fluids.
- Provide analgesics for headache as needed.

CISTERNOGRAM

Description

Cisternogram involves insertion of a radioisotope or other contrast media into the subarachnoid space to visualize structures around the base of the brain or upper spinal cord regions. Scans will be taken at specified intervals, depending upon the type of contrast media used.

Indications

Cisternograms may be used in any of the following situations:

- to assess CSF flow
- to assess for obstructive hydrocephalus
- to evaluate presence of CSF leakage through a dural tear
- to evaluate for abnormality of structures at the base of the brain or upper cervical-cord region

Patient Teaching

Patients should be aware of the following regarding a cisternogram:

- The procedure requires lumbar or cisternal (insertion of hollow needle into the cisterna magna at the base of the brain) puncture to inject isotope or other contrast media.
- Patient must remain still during scans.
- Nothing by mouth (NPO) status or a diet of clear liquids only may be required before the test.
- The procedure requires one to two hours to complete.

Nursing Implications

Nurses should be aware of the following regarding a cisternogram:

- Patients having a cisternal puncture will receive an analgesic prior to the procedure.
- Assess neurological status.

- Provide analgesics as needed.
- Patient's activity may be restricted to bed rest for a number of hours, depending upon type of contrast media used.

MYELOGRAM

Description

Myelogram involves injection of contrast media into the subarachnoid space, usually through a lumbar puncture, to visualize spinal cord structures. It may be done with water-based contrast medium such as metrizamide (Amipaque) or with an oil-based medium such as iophendylate (Pantopaque). Patient preparation and postprocedure care differ according to the contrast medium used.

Indications

Myelogram may be used in any of the following situations:

- to assess for areas of partial or complete blockage with the spinal cord
- to aid in diagnosing cause of spinal cord obstruction (herniated intervertebral disc versus tumor)

Patient Teaching

Patients should be informed of the following regarding a myelogram:

- Patient will receive nothing by mouth (iophendylate medium) or be given clear liquids (metrizamide medium).
- Patient will receive lumbar puncture with injection of contrast medium, then radiographs are taken of the spinal area.
- If iophendylate medium is used, as much of the dye as possible is removed once the radiographs are complete.
- The procedure requires one to two hours to complete.

Nursing Implications

Nurses should be aware of the following regarding a myelogram:

- Monitor neurological status.
- Metrizamide contrast may precipitate seizures in patients when the medium ascends to the cranium; such patients may receive prophylactic phenobarbital and should be monitored for seizure activity.
- Activity postprocedure will be restricted to bed rest for six to eight hours with the head elevated thirty to sixty degrees for patients receiving metrizamide contrast, while those who receive iophendylate contrast will need to remain in a flat position eight to twelve hours postprocedure.
- Encourage fluids, monitor intake and output.
- Provide analgesics as needed.
- Avoid administration of phenothiazines to patients receiving metrizamide contrast; these two agents interact to lower the seizure threshold.

CEREBRAL ARTERIOGRAPHY

Description

Cerebral arteriography involves percutaneous puncture of the femoral artery with injection of radiopaque medium to visualize the cerebral vasculature. It may be a four-vessel study, in which the carotids and vertebrals and their branches are examined, or it may be a two-vessel study, in which just the carotid or vertebral arteries are assessed.

Indications

Cerebral arteriography may be used in any of the following situations:

- to visualize vascular abnormalities (aneurysms, arteriovenous malformations)
- to delineate individual vasculature anomalies
- to identify low blood-flow or no blood-flow regions
- to delineate collateral blood flow
- to diagnose space-occupying lesions (brain tumors, abscesses)

Patient Teaching

Patients should be informed of the following regarding cerebral arteriography:

- NPO status or a diet of clear liquids only is required before the procedure.
- Puncture site preparation (shaving of hair, antimicrobial scrub) may be ordered the evening prior to the procedure.
- Patient may experience sensation of extreme warmth or burning when contrast material is injected.
- Patient must remain still during procedure.
- Procedure requires one to two hours for completion.

Nursing Implications

Nurses should be aware of the following regarding cerebral arteriography:

- Monitor neurological and neurovascular status for signs and symptoms of stroke or interrupted vascular integrity at the puncture site.
- Encourage fluids; monitor intake and output.
- Activity will be restricted to bed rest for eight to 10 hours postprocedure. Flexion of the femoral site is to be avoided during this time to prevent disruption of the arterial clot.

DIGITAL SUBTRACTION ANGIOGRAPHY

Description

Digital subtraction angiography is a computerized imaging modality in which a radiopaque contrast medium is systemically injected into the superior vena cava or right atrium. It offers the opportunity to visualize the cerebral vasculature with less invasiveness and expense than conventional arteriography and can be done on an outpatient basis.

A "mask"-image radiograph is taken prior to injection of the contrast medium. This image is later subtracted from the postinjection image by computer to remove obstructions of the cerebral vasculature imposed by bone and tissue. The procedure may be arterial or venous puncture. Arterial puncture requires less contrast medium than venous and provides sharper imaging.

Indications

Digital subtraction angiography may be used in any of the following situations:

- to obtain data about vascular integrity in patients with hypertension and documented carotid bruits who are at high risk for stroke with conventional angiography
- to provide periodic follow-up for patients with documented stenotic or thrombotic carotid artery disease

Patient Teaching

Patients should be informed of the following regarding digital subtraction angiography:

- NPO status or a diet of clear liquids may be required before the procedure.
- Patient may experience sensations of extreme warmth or burning or a metallic taste when contrast medium is injected.
- Patient must remain still during procedure.
- Procedure requires about one hour for completion.
- Patient should avoid strenuous activity with affected extremity if venous puncture.

Nursing Implications

Nurses should be aware of the following regarding digital subtraction angiography:

- Monitor neurological and neurovascular status for signs and symptoms of stroke or disrupted vascular integrity. Antecubital site is often used.
- Encourage fluids; monitor intake and output.
- If an arterial study, activity will be restricted to bed rest for eight to ten hours postprocedure with a femoral puncture. Flexion of the femoral or brachial site is to be avoided during this time to prevent disruption of the arterial clot.

CEREBRAL BLOOD-FLOW STUDIES

Description

Cerebral blood-flow studies measure cerebral blood flow changes over time as quantified by the uptake and clearance time of an inhaled or injected metabolically inert radioisotope, such as xenon 133. The radioisotope is introduced by inhalation or intracarotid injection, and its radioactive emissions are picked up by probes placed external to the skull at predetermined time intervals. In another variant of this procedure, arterial and venous blood samples are drawn at specified intervals after inhalation or injection of the radioisotope.

Indications

Cerebral blood-flow studies may be used in any of the following situations:

- to delineate perfusion to specific brain regions
- to determine collateral blood flow
- to determine effect of stenotic vessels on cerebral perfusion

Patient Teaching

Patients should be informed of the following regarding cerebral blood-flow studies:

- Patient must be able to cooperate during procedure.
- Anxiety can alter saturation curves of the gas; so too can sedative or antianxiety medications.
- Radioisotope is metabolically inert; there is no danger from its radioactive nature.

Nursing Implications

The patient's hemoglobin level must be known. It can alter the gas saturation curve much the same as it does the oxygen saturation curve.

NONINVASIVE CAROTID ARTERY STUDIES

Description

Noninvasive carotid artery studies use Doppler ultrasound techniques in monitoring physiological changes and hemodynamics within the internal and external carotid arteries and extracranial vessels. Studies are classified as direct or indirect: the former monitor the carotid bifurcation while the latter monitor changes and provide hemodynamic data about distal cerebral and orbital circulation (Table 3-1).

Indications

Noninvasive carotid artery studies may be used in any of the following situations:

- to evaluate persons at risk for carotid artery disease
- to follow asymptomatic carotid bruits over time
- to determine origin of carotid bruit (below clavicle or within carotid tree)
- to assess the extent of stenosis
- to determine most appropriate therapy for disease (conservative follow-up, angiography, surgery)

Patient Teaching

Patients should be informed of the following regarding noninvasive carotid artery studies:

- The procedure requires thirty to sixty minutes for completion.
- Patient must cooperate during studies.
- The procedure can be done on an outpatient basis.

Nursing Implications

No specific preprocedure or postprocedure care is required.

Table 3-1 Noninvasive Carotid Artery Studies

Direct	Indirect
Phonoangiography	Oculoplethysmography (OPG)
Carotid Dopplers	Periorbital Doppler
Ultrasound	Electroencephalogram (EEG) with carotid compression
B-mode imaging	

TRANSCRANIAL DOPPLER SONOGRAPHY

Description

Ultrasound pulsation is applied to the thin areas of the temporal or occipital bones to obtain Doppler information about the basal cerebral circulation. The procedure allows direct access to blood velocity data from the circle of Willis.

Indications

Transcranial Doppler sonography may be used in any of the following situations:

- to supplement noninvasive carotid artery studies in the evaluation of cerebrovascular disease
- to diagnose and monitor cerebrovasospasm
- to assess hemodynamic implications of intracranial stenosis on collateral blood flow from the circle of Willis

Patient Teaching

Patients should be aware of the following regarding transcranial Doppler sonography:

- The procedure is noninvasive.
- The procedure requires about one hour to complete.

Nursing Implications

No specific preprocedure or postprocedure care is required.

ELECTROENCEPHALOGRAM (EEG)

Description

An EEG measures the brain's electrical activity under particular circumstances: rest, photostimulation, hyperventilation, sleep. Numerous electrode leads are placed on specified areas of the scalp, and EEG recordings are taken at rest and as the stimuli are applied.

A variety of EEG monitoring techniques are used in diagnosing and treating seizure disorders in addition to the conventional hard wires. Some of the techniques include nasopharyngeal electrode placement, sphenoidal and epidural-subdural electrodes, sleep-deprived EEG, video monitoring, and ambulatory telemetry. Advances in computerization have facilitated the ability to enhance EEG recordings by topographically mapping EEG frequency shifts and regional patterns. This technique of brain mapping, like the newer imaging techniques, presents great potential in the area of neuroscience.

Indications

EEG may be used in any of the following situations:

- to diagnose seizure disorders, particularly subclinical seizures
- to evaluate electrical activity of the brain during interventive procedures
- to evaluate for electrical silence of the brain, used as corroborating data in diagnosing brain death

Patient Teaching

Patients should be aware of the following regarding EEG:

- Avoid consumption of stimulants (caffeine, tobacco, medications) if possible.
- Remove wigs, hairpieces, pins, clips.
- Electrode paste should be washed from head as soon as possible after the procedure.

Nursing Implications

Nurses should be aware of the following regarding EEG:

- When used as corroborative data for brain death: hypothermia and drug intoxications can produce isoelectric EEGs.
- No specific postprocedure care, other than to assist in cleansing scalp of paste, is required.

ELECTROMYOGRAPHY

Description

Electromyography (EMG) involves insertion of needle electrodes into the muscles to be assessed to evaluate electrical activity of the muscle at rest and with movement. This procedure aids in differentiating neuromuscular dysfunction as being from neural or muscular origin.

Indications

EMG may be used in any of the following situations:

- to aid in the diagnosis of neuromuscular dysfunctions such as neuropathy, myopathy, myasthenia gravis, muscular dystrophy

Patient Teaching

Patients should be aware of the following regarding EMG:

- The patient will experience some discomfort as the needle is inserted into the muscle.
- The patient will be asked to move the muscle being tested at various times.

Nursing Implications

No preprocedure or postprocedure care is required.

NERVE-CONDUCTION VELOCITY STUDIES

Description

Nerve-conduction velocity studies measure the conduction time and velocity at which a nerve transmits an impulse to a muscle. One electrode is placed over the muscle to be innervated; the other is placed over the nerve to be stimulated.

Indications

Nerve-conduction velocity studies may be used in any of the following situations:

- to aid in the diagnosis of peripheral neuropathies
- to determine extent of trauma or compression to nerves

Patient Teaching

Patients should be informed of the following regarding nerve-conduction velocity studies:

- The patient will experience a tingling sensation as the nerve is stimulated with a minute amount of electrical current.

Nursing Implications

No preprocedure or postprocedure care is required.

EVOKED RESPONSES (EVOKED POTENTIALS)

Description

Evoked responses measure electrical response to stimuli applied to different sensory systems. The procedure consists of three types of tests: brain stem auditory-evoked responses (BAERs), visual-evoked responses (VERs), and somatosensory-evoked responses (SSERs). Any one or all three of these tests may be requested. Each involves the input of some form of sensory stimulus (sound, visual patterns, skin stimuli) and the subsequent recording of the electrical energy.

Indications

Evoked responses may be used in any of the following situations:

- to demonstrate abnormal sensory-system function
- to demonstrate presence of subclinical lesions (demyelination seen with multiple sclerosis)

- to assist in defining the distribution of a disease process
- to monitor pathway integrity that cannot be evaluated clinically (VIII cranial nerve pathway during acoustic neuroma surgery, extent of spinal cord injury and brain stem injury)

Patient Teaching

The patient should be informed of the following regarding evoked responses:

- Procedure may require thirty minutes to four hours, depending on number of tests done.

Nursing Implications

No preprocedure or postprocedure care is required.

SUGGESTED READINGS

American Association of Neuroscience Nurses. *Core Curriculum for Neuroscience Nursing.* Edited by Marilyn M. Ricci. Park Ridge, IL: American Association of Neuroscience Nurses, 1984.

Grolimund, P., R.W. Seiler, R. Aaslid, P. Huber, and H. Zurbruegg. "Evaluation of Cerebrovascular Disease by Combined Extracranial and Transcranial Doppler Sonography." *Stroke* 18(1987): 1018–1024.

Hickey, Joanne. *The Clinical Practice of Neurological and Neurosurgical Nursing.* Philadelphia: J.B. Lippincott, 1981.

Hunt, Ann Hankins. "Digital Subtraction Angiography: Patient Preparation and Care." *Journal of Neuroscience Nursing* 19(1987):222–225.

Kastrup, Erwin K., ed. *Drug Facts and Comparisons.* Philadelphia: J.B. Lippincott, 1987.

Nurse's Reference Library, Nursing86 Books. *Diagnostics.* 2nd ed. Springhouse, PA: Springhouse Corporation, 1986.

Plum, Fred, and Jerome B. Posner. *The Diagnosis of Stupor and Coma.* 3rd ed. Philadelphia: F.A. Davis, 1983.

Raimond, Jeanne, and Joyce Waterman Taylor. *Neurological Emergencies: Effective Nursing Care.* Rockville, MD: Aspen Publishers, 1986.

Regan, Patricia A., ed. *Teaching Guides for Patients with Neurologic Disorders.* Reston, VA: Reston Publishing Company, 1984.

Rothrock, J.F., P.D. Lyden, J.R. Hesselink, J.J. Brown, and M.E. Healy. "Brain Magnetic Resonance Imaging in the Evaluation of Lacunar Stroke." *Stroke* 18(1987):781–786.

Sullivan, H.G., J.D. Allison, T.B. Kingsbury, and J.J. Goode. "Analysis of Inhalation rCBF Data." *Stroke* 18(1987):495–502.

4
Increased Intracranial Pressure

Paramount to caring for a patient with cerebral injury is the understanding of the concepts involving increased intracranial pressure (ICP). Critical care nurses will often encounter patients who have developed or who are at high risk for developing increased ICP.

MUNRO-KELLIE HYPOTHESIS

The modified hypothesis states that once fully ossified, the skull is a rigid sphere that contains almost constant volumes of brain (80%), blood (10%), and cerebrospinal fluid (CSF) (10%). If any of these three components of the cranial cavity increases in volume, there must be a corresponding decrease in the other two, or ICP will rise. Normal ICP is 4 to 15 mm Hg or 80 to 180 cm H_2O.[1]

BLOOD-BRAIN BARRIER

The exact anatomical location of the blood-brain barrier (BBB) remains controversial. It is a physiological barrier that functions to maintain homeostasis for the brain. Contributing to its creation are tight endothelial junctions of the cerebral capillaries and an external membrane at the feet of the astrocyte cells.[2] It is easily permeated by oxygen, carbon dioxide, lipid-soluble substances, and water, as well as by such toxic substances as ethanol and chloroform.

Glucose and amino acids diffuse through the blood-brain barrier relatively easily, but larger proteins and other substances exogenous to the brain environment are excluded. The exclusivity of the blood-brain barrier in allowing access to the brain environment is a major factor in the use of drugs for neurological disorders.

VOLUME-PRESSURE RELATIONSHIPS

As the volume of the intracranial contents increases, compensatory mechanisms are initiated to decrease volume.

- CSF is displaced into the spinal canal.
- CSF absorption is increased.
- Blood is shunted to the venous sinuses.
- Brain tissue is compressed.

When these compensatory mechanisms have been exhausted, intracranial pressure begins to rise exponentially with volume increases.

Compliance and Elastance

The concepts of compliance and elastance are important in understanding volume-pressure relationships in the brain and in explaining structural shifts that occur with space-occupying lesions.

The ability of the brain to adjust to volume increases is termed compliance. A brain in a state of compliance can adjust to relatively large increases in volume without affecting major changes in pressure. Decreased compliance is indicated by high increases in pressure with relatively little increase in volume.

Elastance is the converse of compliance and reflects the resiliency of the brain. High elastance is indicated by high increases in pressure with relatively little increase in volume. Thus a brain in a decreased state of compliance is in a high state of elastance (Figure 4-1).

Brain compliance can be determined by performing a volume-pressure response test (VPR), which yields an approximation of the time necessary for CSF to displace from the intracranial contents. A minute amount (0.5 to 1.0 mL) of preservative-free, normal saline is injected into a ventricular catheter or subarachnoid screw or bolt and the patient's ICP response is monitored. The response is determined by the amount in millimeters of mercury the ICP rises after instillation of the saline (1 mm Hg/1 mL saline). A VPR greater than 2 reflects a brain with decreased compliance or high elastance.[3]

The initial increase in ICP in patients with compliant brains will drop to normal within one to two minutes. A patient with significant intracranial pressure and decreased compliance will maintain an increased ICP for longer intervals. It should be noted that VPRs done frequently on patients with known decreased compliance may contribute to increased ICP.

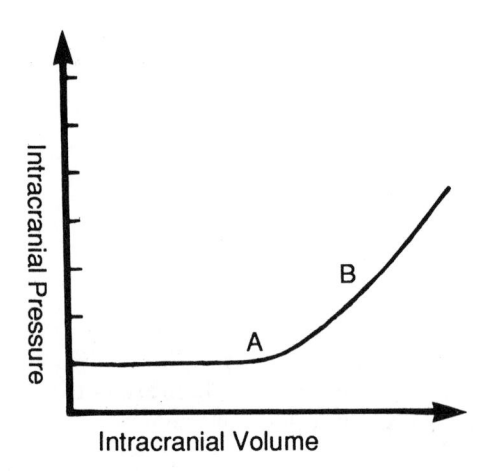

Figure 4-1 Volume-Pressure Curve. High compliance and low elastance are present in adjusting to volume increases at point A; by point B compliance decreases and elastance increases in response to volume added.

CEREBRAL BLOOD FLOW AND PERFUSION

Cerebral blood flow (CBF) is normally maintained at a steady state by a pressure autoregulatory mechanism present in the arterioles. Cerebral autoregulation provides for adequate cerebral perfusion despite variations in the mean systemic blood pressure between 50 and 150 mm Hg. Cerebral vascular resistance (CVR), determined by the arteriolar diameter, is also dependent on autoregulation. This autoregulatory mechanism can become impaired when there is local injury to brain tissue or when the ICP reaches 30 to 35 mm Hg.[3] At this point, CBF and CVR then become dependent on systemic arterial pressure.

Other Factors Affecting Autoregulation

Certain metabolic factors also influence cerebral autoregulation.

- vasodilating factors
  - carbon dioxide
  - hypoxia
  - hypercapnia
  - lactoacidosis
- vasoconstricting factors
  - hypocapnia
  - hyperoxia

Cerebral Perfusion Pressure

Cerebral perfusion pressure (CPP) is obtained by subtracting the mean ICP (MICP) from the mean systemic arterial pressure (MSAP): CPP = MSAP − MICP. Alterations in the SAP or ICP will affect the CPP. Normal CPP is 80 to 100 mm Hg; levels of at least 50 mm Hg must be maintained to ensure adequate cerebral blood supply (Table 4-1).[4] To measure clinically volume-pressure responses and cerebral perfusion pressures, the patient must have an ICP monitoring device in place.

CEREBRAL EDEMA

Cerebral edema may be localized or generalized and results from injury to the brain tissue. It may contribute to increased ICP if compensatory mechanisms are unable to manage the increased volume. Three types of edema have been defined: vasogenic, cytotoxic, and interstitial. Nursing care relative to managing cerebral edema is presented later in this chapter.

Vasogenic Edema

The following factors are descriptive of vasogenic edema:

- most common
- caused by disrupted blood-brain barrier producing increased vascular permeability and leakage of plasma proteins
- begins locally but may become generalized
- accumulation of fluid usually in white matter
- associated with ischemia, trauma, hemorrhage, neoplasms, surgical procedures

Table 4-1 Cerebral Perfusion Values

Normal CBF*	600–900 mL/min
Normal CPP*	80–100 mm Hg
CPP less than 50 mm Hg*	Ischemia begins
CPP less than 30 mm Hg*	Irreversible ischemia
CPP greater than 150 mm Hg*	Disrupts blood-brain barrier

*CBF is decreased by 25% when CPP is less than 40 mm Hg.
Abbreviations: CBF, Cerebral blood flow; CPP, Cerebral perfusion pressure.

- treatment focuses on treating the cause of the edema and symptomatic management of any increases in ICP

Cytotoxic Edema

The following factors are descriptive of cytotoxic edema:

- caused by influx of fluids into brain cells; may be referred to as cellular edema
- tends to be generalized; believed to be due to some toxic element affecting brain cells, such as hypoxia or hypercapnia; can occur with hyponatremia, syndrome of inappropriate secretion of antidiuretic hormone (SIADH), and following a cardiac arrest
- occurs most frequently in the gray matter
- associated with ischemic and anoxic events, hyponatremia
- focus of treatment on identifying the underlying cause, correcting any abnormalities in gas exchange, and maintaining fluid and electrolyte balance

Interstitial Edema

The following factors are descriptive of interstitial edema:

- also called extracellular or hydrostatic edema; occurs as a result of CSF or blood leaking into interstitial spaces under hydrostatic pressure
- associated with hydrocephalus, altered CSF absorption by arachnoid villi, and elevated blood pressures
- treatment focuses on reducing CSF and blood pressures

BRAIN SWELLING

Brain swelling is vascular engorgement of brain tissue occurring in the presence of an intact blood-brain barrier. Cerebral edema is a result of disruption of the blood-brain barrier, causing fluid shifts within the intracranial components. Attributed to disruption of autoregulation, it occurs rapidly and may occur concurrently with brain swelling. Treatment of brain swelling varies from that of brain edema in that mannitol would not be given, as it would increase intravascular volume and contribute to increased ICP. Hyperventilation is effective in constricting the cerebral vasculature and decreasing ICP.

ENTITIES ASSOCIATED WITH INCREASED ICP

Increases in the volume of brain tissue, blood, or CSF may produce increased ICP. Therefore any pathological processes affecting the intracranial contents may cause increased ICP (Table 4-2).

HERNIATION SYNDROMES

Brain tissue can be compromised by pressures within the cranial cavity, with or without intervening measures, to cause the tissue to be displaced through (1) supratentorial or (2) infratentorial herniation. The types of herniation syndromes and their clinical presentation are presented below.

Supratentorial Herniation

Cingulate Herniation

Definition. The cingulate gyrus, located above the corpus callosum, is forced under the falx cerebri by an expanding mass lesion in one hemisphere (Figure 4-2). Local tissues and blood vessels, particularly the anterior cerebral artery and internal cerebral vein, are compressed, leading to edema and ischemia.

Clinical Presentation. The individual will demonstrate altered consciousness and, perhaps, motor weakness of the upper body as the anterior cerebral arteries are compromised.

Table 4-2 Conditions Contributing to Increased ICP

Brain Volume	Blood Volume	CSF Volume
Neoplasms	Swelling	Hydrocephalus
Abscesses	Hypercapnia	Production
Hematomas	Hypoxemia	Absorption
Edema	Vasodilation	
Hemorrhages	Disrupted autoregulation	
	Increased intra-abdominal or intrathoracic pressure	
	Obstructed venous drainage	

Abbreviation: CSF, Cerebrospinal fluid.

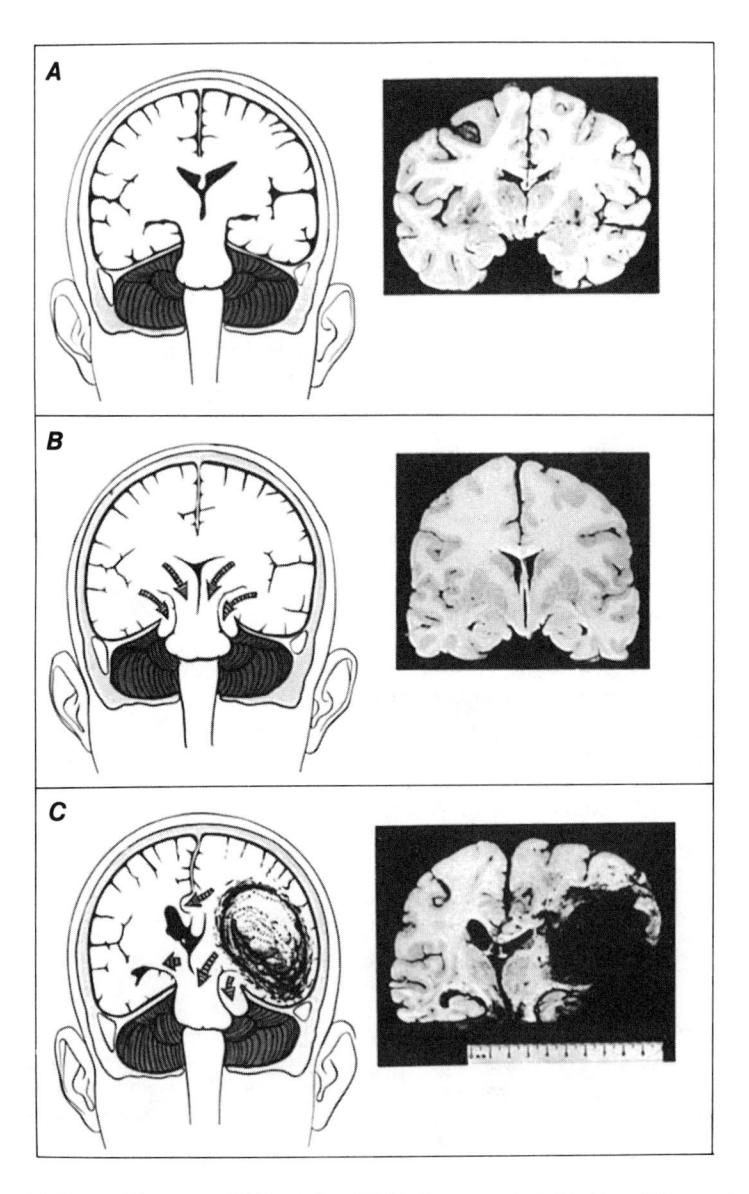

Figure 4-2 Types of Supratentorial Herniation. (A) Depicts normal relationships within supratentorial and infratentorial compartments; (B) Central herniation as the diencephalon is compressed from supratentorial swelling; (C) Cingulate and uncal herniation: The cingulate gyrus is forced under the falx cerebri, and the uncal portion of the temporal lobe is forced over the tentorium. *Source:* Reprinted from *The Diagnosis of Stupor and Coma*, 3rd ed., by F. Plum and J.B. Posner, p. 92, with permission of F.A. Davis Company, © 1983.

Central or Transtentorial Herniation

Definition. This situation results from downward displacement of the cerebral hemispheres and basal ganglia onto the diencephalon and midbrain through the tentorial notch (see Figure 4-2). It is associated with trauma, lesions of the supratentorial region, and other situations producing a mass effect.

Clinical Presentation. Clinical evidence of central herniation can be followed as the pressures in the supratentorial regions compress deeper cortical and brain stem structures.[5] Table 4-3 illustrates clinical symptoms.

Uncal Herniation

Definition. Lesions expanding in lateral portions of the temporal lobe may project its most medial point, the uncus, toward the midline and over the tentorial notch (see Figure 4-2). Among the crucial structures compressed with this event are the oculomotor nerve, the brain stem, and the posterior cerebral artery. It is associated with trauma, lesions in the temporal lobe, or lateral lesions in the middle fossa.

Table 4-3 Clinical Signs of Central Herniation

Initial Stage
- Decreased alertness progressing to drowsiness
- Deep sighing or yawning with respirations
- Small and reactive pupils
- Conjugate and roving eye movements
- Appropriate response to noxious stimuli, but with generalized, increased motor tone

Intermediate Stage
- Stuporous state progressing to coma
- Cheyne-Stokes respirations that progress to neurogenic hyperventilation
- Pupils become nonreactive at midposition and may be unequal in size
- Dysconjugate eye movements
- Response to noxious stimuli produces decorticate posturing that deteriorates to decerebrate posturing as the brain stem is compressed

Final Stage
- Coma
- Ataxic breathing with periods of apnea
- Pupils remain nonreactive, may begin to dilate from hypoxia
- Absent oculocephalic reflexes
- Flaccid extremities may show flexor response to stimuli

Clinical Presentation. Clinical symptoms can be divided into stages, with the final one similar to that of central herniation.[5] Lesions in this area exert pressure from one side of the brain, as opposed to from the top, so that the person demonstrates lateralizing signs of compression. Table 4-4 illustrates clinical symptoms.

Infratentorial Herniation

Definition

Expanding lesions in the posterior fossa may cause upward herniation through the transtentorium or downward herniation of the cerebellar tonsils through the foramen magnum (Figure 4-3). Infratentorial herniation occurs less frequently than supratentorial herniation.

Clinical Presentation

Upward herniations may produce focal signs of brain stem compression, including coma, hyperventilation, pinpoint, fixed and unequal pupils, upward-gaze paralysis, vomiting, and decerebration.

Table 4-4 Clinical Signs of Uncal Herniation

Initial Stage
- Level of consciousness may vary from restlessness and confusion to stupor and coma
- Eupneic respirations
- Moderate dilation and sluggish reaction to light of pupil ipsilateral to the lesion (early and major diagnostic sign)
- Gaze may be dysconjugate
- Noxious stimuli may produce a localized reaction; there may also be a contralateral Babinski's sign

Intermediate Stage
- Stupor progressing to coma
- Respirations will be neurogenic hyperventilation; rarely see Cheyne-Stokes respirations
- Ipsilateral pupil becomes fully dilated and nonreactive to light
- Paralysis of extraocular muscles
- Decorticate or decerebrate posturing

Final Stage
- Similar to that of central herniation
- May be unable to discern clinically between the two types of herniation at this point

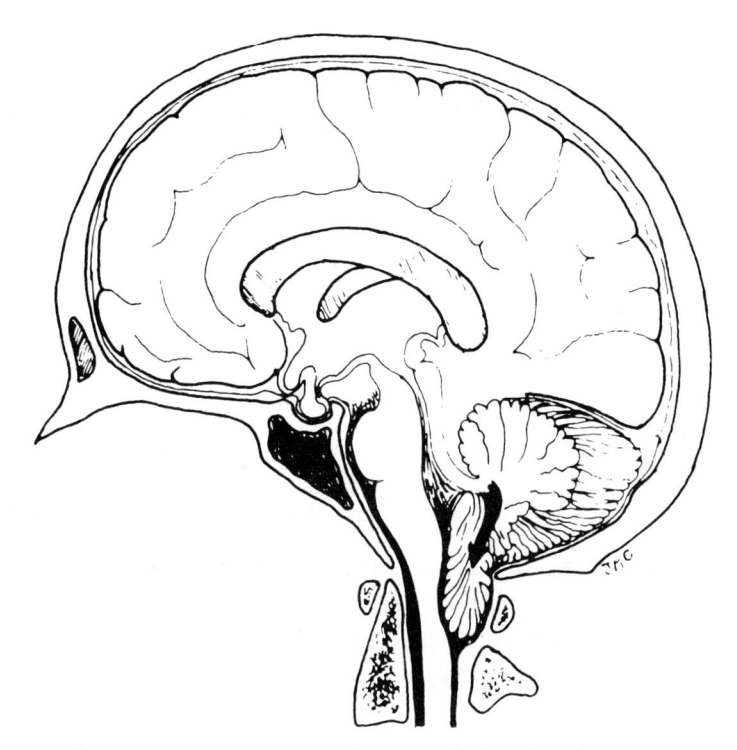

Figure 4-3 Infratentorial herniation of the cerebellar tonsils through the foramen magnum. *Source:* Reprinted from *Essentials of Neurosurgery* by R.R. Smith, p. 103, with permission of J.B. Lippincott Company, © 1980.

Downward cerebellar herniation may not be clear clinically, but the patient will display signs of brain stem dysfunction such as lower cranial nerve signs, abnormal respiratory patterns, fluctuating blood pressure, and cardiac dysrhythmias.[5] In both events death occurs following cardiac and/or respiratory arrest.

SIGNS AND SYMPTOMS OF INCREASED ICP

Pressure Levels

Increased ICP exists with pressure levels greater than 15 mm Hg. Physiological compensatory mechanisms are unable to buffer the cranial contents, and interventions are instituted to minimize irreversible neuronal cell death, which results from their subsequent compression. The Glasgow Coma Scale (GCS; refer to Chapter 2) should be used in documenting neurological status in addition to further elaboration within the medical record. ICP levels can be generalized under three categories (see Table 4-5). Aggressive interventions are usually initiated to treat ICP elevations once they are in the range of 20–25 mm Hg.

Altered Level of Consciousness

Level of consciousness is an extremely sensitive index of neurological status. The following signs and symptoms of altered level of consciousness may indicate increased ICP: restlessness, confusion, difficulty following simple commands, lethargy, or coma.

Pupillary Size and Reaction to Light

The following pupillary signs and symptoms may indicate increased ICP:

- Unequal pupils (unequal size or anisocoria may be baseline)
- Sluggish reaction to light—indicates oculomotor nerve compromise
- Pinpoint, fixed pupils—indicates pontine compression
- Midpoint, fixed pupils—indicates midbrain compression
- Dilated, fixed pupils—indicates oculomotor nerve compression bilaterally
- Dilated, fixed pupil—represents compression from space-occupying lesion on the same side

Other Eye Signs

Other eye signs that may indicate increased ICP are as follows:

- diplopia
- decreased visual acuity
- photophobia

Table 4-5 ICP Categories

Pressure Reading	Categorization
0–15 mm Hg	Normal
20–40 mm Hg	Moderately elevated
40 mm Hg and higher	Severely elevated

These categorizations may differ slightly among institutions.

- nystagmus
- papilledema, from optic nerve compression

Altered Motor and Sensory Function

The following signs and symptoms of altered motor and sensory function may indicate increased ICP:

- hemiparesis/hemiplegia on the side opposite the lesion
- decreased reflex responses, pathological reflexes (grasp/snout/Babinski's sign)
- decortication and/or decerebration when diencephalic and brain stem regions compressed
- decreased or loss of ability to interpret sensory information

Altered Respiratory Function

The following signs and symptoms of altered respiratory function may indicate increased ICP:

- Rate and quality deteriorate as ICP increases further compromise the brain stem. The type of respiratory alterations varies depending upon the portion of the central nervous system (CNS) compromised. Table 4-6 describes the types of respiratory patterns associated with CNS compressions. Illustrations of the respiratory patterns are found in Chapter 2. In general, respirations become irregular and slower.

Cardiovascular Alterations

The following signs and symptoms of cardiovascular alterations may indicate increased ICP. Note that these signs occur late in the course of increasing ICP, as the brain stem becomes compressed.

Table 4-6 Respiratory Patterns in Increased ICP

Area Compressed	Type of Respirations
Hemispheres/diencephalon	Cheyne-Stokes
Midbrain/pons	Central hyperventilation
Pons	Apneustic
Medulla	Ataxic

- Systolic blood pressure rises, pulse pressure widens; hypotension is seen in terminal stages of increased ICP
- Bradycardia; pulse slow and bounding
- Electrocardiogram (ECG) changes:
  1. Q waves with ST segment depression
  2. Large upright T waves; may have long QT intervals
  3. Variety of dysrhythmias, such as supraventricular tachycardia (SVT), atrioventricular (AV) block, premature ventricular contractions (PVCs)

Temperature Alterations

Very high fever due to pressure on the hypothalamic regions may indicate increased ICP.

Headache

The following factors regarding headache are relevant to increased ICP:

- may not be a complaint
- when present, usually worse in morning due to recumbent position and carbon dioxide retention during sleep

Vomiting

The following factors regarding vomiting are relevant to increased ICP:

- associated with space-occupying lesions of the cerebellum and brain stem
- may occur more frequently in the morning and may be projectile

MANAGEMENT OF THE PATIENT WITH INCREASED ICP

Identification of Cause

The following should be considered in identifying the cause of increased ICP:

- history
- diagnostic procedures
- treatment of underlying problem
- surgery not always indicated

Continuous Monitoring of Neurological Status

Continuous monitoring of neurological status in the patient with increased ICP is as follows:

- continuous neurological assessment using GCS
- continuous monitoring of vital signs
- possible insertion of ICP monitoring device
- possible sedation to quiet patient and to decrease metabolic demands of brain
- possible insertion of ventricular drainage device to decrease ICP through drainage of CSF

Respiratory Support

Respiratory support for the patient with increased ICP should be provided as follows:

- Controlled mechanical ventilation is necessary to prevent hypercapnia and hypoxia.
  - hyperventilation (25 to 30 mm Hg carbon dioxide) produces vasoconstriction, which reduces cerebral blood volume, contributing to decreased ICP
- Monitor arterial blood gases.
  - Arterial partial pressure of carbon dioxide ($Paco_2$) increases from 40 to 80 mm Hg double CBF, and levels below 20 mm Hg cause CBF to drop by half.[6] CO_2 is an extremely potent stimulus for cerebral vasodilatation.
  - Arterial partial pressure of oxygen (Pao_2) levels less than 50 mm Hg produce distinct increases in CBF; levels below 30 mm Hg increase CBF by half.[6]
- Frequent pulmonary hygiene is necessary to facilitate drainage of pulmonary secretions and to maintain airway patency.
- Breath sounds should be auscultated for signs of atelectasis and pneumonia.
- Positive end-expiratory pressure (PEEP) should be avoided or used at low physiological levels, as it elevates ICP by raising intrathoracic pressure.
- Physiological levels of continuous positive airway pressure (CPAP) might be initiated to prevent atelectasis in the intubated patient with spontaneous respiratory effort.
- Suctioning for prolonged intervals (greater than fifteen seconds) should be avoided, as it can raise ICP by inducing hypoxia.
- Hyperoxygenation and hyperventilation should be performed prior to suctioning.

Drug Therapy

Osmotic Diuretics

The following information is relevant to the use of osmotic diuretics to treat patients with increased ICP:

- Mannitol (Osmitrol) 20% in 500 mL dextrose (100 g) or 25% in 50 mL dextrose (50 g) given intravenous (IV) bolus at 0.5 to 1 g/kg body weight produces rapid diuresis within fifteen to twenty minutes of administration.
  1. Indwelling catheter should be in place to monitor urinary output.
  2. Use of mannitol is only recommended for short intervals because of the rebound effect it has in causing fluid retention.
- Monitor serum osmolality to maintain patient in state of near dehydration (serum osmolality 300 to 320 mOsm/kg serum water) to minimize cerebral edema; fluid is restricted to 1 to 2 L per 24-hour period.
- Monitor patient for signs of volume overload and congestive heart failure due to increase in circulating blood volume.
- Mannitol is not indicated for brain swelling.

Loop Diuretics

Furosemide (Lasix) contributes to decreasing cerebral edema by promoting systemic diuresis.

Corticosteroid Therapy

The following information is relevant to the use of corticosteroids to treat patients with increased ICP:

- Corticosteroids are most effective in treating local rather than diffuse areas of edema.
- Drugs often used are dexamethasone (Decadron) and methylprednisolone (Solu-Medrol) in four divided daily doses.
- High doses are given initially; then the drug is tapered down.
- Equivalency doses for corticosteroids are summarized in Table 4-7.

Anticonvulsant Therapy

The following information is relevant to the use of anticonvulsant therapy to control seizure activity:

Table 4-7 Steroid Equivalency Doses

Drug	Equivalent Doses
Methylprednisolone	5 mg
Dexamethasone	0.75 mg

- Phenytoin (Dilantin) is given in doses of 300 to 400 mg/day after a loading dose of 1 g (10 to 15 mg/kg) to control seizure activity. Therapeutic serum level is 10 to 20 μg/mL.
- Phenobarbital may be given in dosages of 100 to 400 mg/day instead of or in addition to phenytoin to control seizures. Therapeutic serum level is 10 to 30 μg/mL.
- Diazepam (Valium) may be used in the short-term control of seizure activity. Refer to Chapter 10 for more information relative to anticonvulsant drugs.

Laxatives

Constipation should be avoided in patients with increased ICP.

- Straining to produce a bowel movement may precipitate a Valsalva's maneuver, causing a rise in ICP.
- Docusate sodium (Colace), 100 mg given two to three times/day, will prevent straining.
- Milk of magnesia, 30 mL given at bedtime, will relieve constipation.
- Use of suppositories and manual disimpaction will require individual consideration because both methods cause vagal stimulation, which can increase ICP.

Histamine Receptor Antagonists/Antacids

The following information is relevant to the use of histamine receptor antagonists/antacids in patients with increased ICP:

- Cimetidine (Tagamet), 300 mg given three to four times/day, or ranitidine (Zantac), 150 mg twice daily, will decrease gastric secretions to minimize gastric ulcer formation.
- Antacids may be ordered to neutralize stomach acids in patients on corticosteroid therapy.

Barbiturate Coma

Barbiturate coma may be indicated in certain situations (head trauma, acute vascular insult) in which the ICP remains above 20 mm Hg despite conventional treatment options.

- Effects of barbiturates supporting the use of this therapy include
  1. decreased ICP through cerebral vasoconstriction and reduced hydrostatic pressure
  2. decreased metabolic needs of the brain
  3. shunting of blood from healthy brain areas to ischemic areas through increased cerebrovascular resistance in undamaged areas
  4. suppression of seizure activity
  5. immobilization of the patient[7]
- In addition to mechanical ventilation, expect that the patient will have continuous cardiac monitoring, an arterial line, and perhaps central venous pressure (CVP) monitoring. Two major side effects of barbiturate coma include cardiac dysrhythmias and hypotension.
- Depression of the CNS by the barbiturates mandates that an ICP monitoring device be in place to monitor neurological status through ICP levels.
- Continuous electroencephalographic (EEG) monitoring may be desired during barbiturate coma to monitor for prolonged EEG suppression, reflecting efficacy of the therapy in reducing the resting cerebral metabolic rate of oxygen ($CMRO_2$) and consequently CBF.[7]
- Pentobarbital sodium (Nembutal Sodium) is most often used in a continuous IV infusion of 1 to 3 mg/kg body weight after an initial loading dose of 3 to 5 mg/kg. ICP should drop 10 mm Hg within ten to fifteen minutes of the loading dose; a second loading dose can be given within two to three hours if the initial response was inadequate. Barbiturate therapy should be terminated if there is no response to a second loading dose. Serum barbiturate levels of 2 to 4 mg/dL are necessary to maintain the coma.

Positioning

The following information regarding positioning is relevant in managing the patient with increased ICP:

- Maintain head of bed elevation at 30 degrees to optimize cerebral venous drainage and to promote adequate respiratory exchange.
- Avoid positions known to cause ICP increases: hip flexion, lateral or anterior flexion of head or neck.

- If patient is conscious and able to follow commands, teach avoidance of isometric exercises: pushing self up in bed with feet and hands, pushing against a footboard.
- If patient is conscious and able to follow commands, teach avoidance of Valsalva's maneuver.

Temperature Control

The following information regarding temperature control is relevant in managing the patient with increased ICP:

- Monitor body temperature frequently.
- Treat fevers aggressively
  1. Culture possible sources.
  2. Use antipyretics.
  3. Give tepid baths.
  4. Use hypothermia blanket.
- Note that some patients may continue to spike fevers with no identifiable source of infection. Hypothalamic control over body temperature regulation may be impaired due to the nature of the injury. The diagnosis of "CNS" fevers is made on the basis of excluding infectious etiologies.

CSF Fluid Drainage

When using CSF fluid drainage to treat increased ICP, the following considerations are important:

- Of the three components of the cranial cavity, CSF is most amenable to reduction attempts. While a lumbar puncture provides easy access to CSF for its removal, this procedure is contraindicated in the presence of increased ICP, as it can precipitate herniation. Insertions of a device (ventricular catheter or reservoir system) into the lateral ventricle that can be externally drained allows CSF to be removed. It is hoped that CSF can be drained in amounts significant enough to relieve the compromised cranial cavity.
- The device, often a ventricular catheter, is inserted through a twist drill hole in the nondominant hemisphere and is guided to the lateral ventricle. To minimize the risk of infection, the device may be tunneled subcutaneously before it exits the skin through a stab wound.

- External drainage of the CSF is managed through gravity control, with the degree of resistance determined by the physician, predicated upon the individual patient and the collection system used.
- Nursing care of these devices is described under the next section.

INTRACRANIAL PRESSURE MONITORING

Measurement of ICP can be accomplished by insertion of a monitoring device through a twist drill hole or burr hole in the skull. Direct measurements can be obtained from any of the following devices:

- placement of a hollow screw or bolt into the subarachnoid space
- insertion of a catheter into one of the lateral ventricles
- insertion of a subdural cup catheter into the subdural space
- insertion of a fiberoptic transducer-tipped sensor device into the subarachnoid or subdural space or intraparenchymally

To minimize disruption to vital brain structures, intraventricular catheters are usually inserted into the nondominant hemisphere of the patient. The device is then connected to a fluid-filled tubing system via a stopcock or T-piece. The distal end of the nondistensible tubing is connected to the transducer, which is "zeroed" at the level of the foramen of Munro (tragus of the ear). The transducer is then connected to the monitoring port to allow conversion of the mechanical pressure into an electrical impulse that is displayed on an oscilloscope in numerical and waveform readouts.

Irrigation of the device with normal saline or lactated Ringer's solution is often necessary to maintain patency (particularly bolts, screws, and subdural cup catheters). It is important to note that pressure bags or heparinized solutions should never be used to irrigate ICP monitoring devices. The prophylactic instillation of an antibiotic such as gentamicin sulfate is controversial as to its efficacy in preventing infection.

Intraparenchymal, or brain tissue, ICP monitoring involves the insertion of a fiberoptic transducer-tipped sensor into the brain tissue just below the subarachnoid space via a bolt device.[8] Indirect measurement of increased ICP can be accomplished through insertion of a fiberoptic transducer-tipped sensor or a pneumatic flow sensor into the epidural space. The fiberoptic probe is then connected via its fiberoptic cable to a bedside monitor. The pneumatic flow sensor is connected to an external monitoring module.[9]

ICP monitoring is indicated in a variety of neurological conditions in which the patient is susceptible to or clinically displays increased ICP. The advantages and disadvantages of each of the monitoring devices are outlined in Table 4-8.

Increased Intracranial Pressure 99

Table 4-8 Comparison of ICP Monitoring Devices

Type of Device	Advantages	Disadvantages
Fiberoptic Transducer-tipped sensor or catheter	Easily placed Low infection rate Neither dura nor brain parenchyma is disrupted when placed epidurally	Breakage of fiberoptic cable may occur Cannot be recalibrated Cannot drain CSF Sensor may incur damage
Subarachnoid bolt or screw	Brain parenchyma not disrupted Can recalibrate easily Can drain CSF but may occlude device lumen; can be left in place five to seven days	Lumen may easily become occluded, requiring irrigation Potential for infection due to invasiveness System can be inadvertently disconnected
Subdural cup catheter	Less risk of infection due to tunneling process in insertion	Must be irrigated frequently to maintain patency; CSF leakage may occur
Ventricular catheter	Highly accurate for VPR monitoring; less dampening of waveforms than screw or bolt; can easily drain CSF intermittently or continuously; can recalibrate easily	Risk for infection increased with insertion times greater than five to seven days; can suddenly decompress ventricles if not managed properly; CSF leakage may occur if system inadvertently disconnected; complications associated with fluid-filled tubing

Abbreviations: CSF, Cerebrospinal fluid; VPR, Volume pressure response.

Observation of the insertion site for signs of infection, regardless of the device used, should be done with an occlusive dressing change every twenty-four hours. In some instances the physician may elect to change the dressing to maintain device stability.

Interpretation of ICP Pressure Waves

An ICP tracing from a patient with a subarachnoid bolt in place is demonstrated in Figure 4-4. The significance of ICP waves is summarized in Table 4-9. The interpretation of ICP waves must include the patient's clinical status to determine the accuracy of the pressure readings. Low pressure readings (0 to 10 mm Hg) may be attributed to

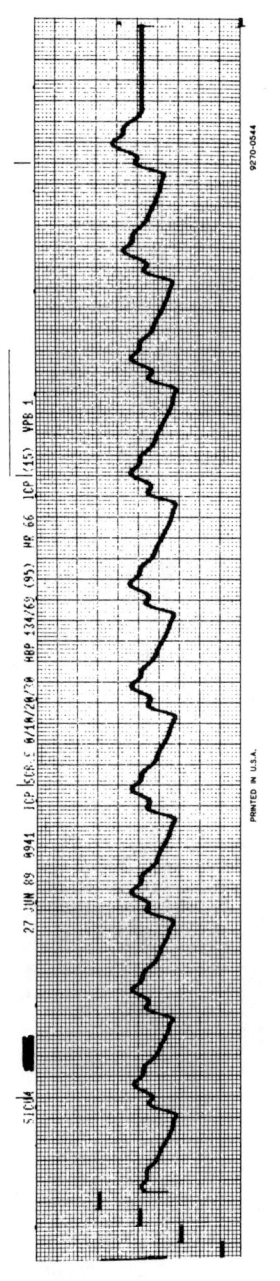

Figure 4-4 ICP Tracing from a Subarachnoid Bolt.

Table 4-9 Intracranial Pressure (ICP) Waves

A Waves (also known as plateau waves)
- Associated with ICP of 50 to 100 mm Hg; may be due to coughing or straining and occur transiently
- May be five to twenty minutes in duration
- If sustained, they reflect decompensating neurological function, which will be displayed clinically
- Persistence reflects poor prognostic outcome

B Waves
- Transient, sharp increases in ICP of up to 50 mm Hg for short periods (one to two minutes)
- May precede A waves in the compromised brain
- Often associated with changes in ventilation or blood pressure
- Clinical significance is not known

C Waves
- Rhythmic oscillation of ICP over 20 mm Hg occurring every four to eight minutes
- Associated with changes in blood pressure or respirations
- Clinical significance not known

- normal ICP for the patient
- too high a zero level
- excessive drainage of CSF
- dampened line
- hyperventilation[10]

Unusually high pressure readings can be caused by a zero level that is too low. Other causes of high ICP readings have been presented throughout this chapter. Research has documented the effect of nursing care activities on ICP, and the reader is referred to the Suggested Readings for further detail.

NOTES

1. J. Hickey, *The Clinical Practice of Neurological and Neurosurgical Nursing* (Philadelphia: J.B. Lippincott, 1981), 143.
2. L. Jimm-Zegeer, "Brain Edema: Concepts and Nursing Care," in *Acute Neuroscience Nursing: Concepts and Care*, ed. Jane Lundgren (Boston: Jones and Bartlett Publishers, 1986), 16.
3. B. Habermann-Little, "Increased Intracranial Pressure and Herniation Syndromes," in *Acute Neuroscience Nursing: Concepts and Care*, ed. Jane Lundgren (Boston: Jones and Bartlett Publishers, 1986), 3.

4. C.L. Pollack-Latham, "Intracranial Pressure Monitoring: Part I. Physiologic Principles." *Critical Care Nurse* 7(1987):47.

5. F. Plum, and J.B. Posner. *The Diagnosis of Stupor and Coma.* 3rd ed. (Philadelphia: F.A. Davis, 1982), 97–111.

6. B. Jennett, and G. Teasdale. *Management of Head Injuries* (Philadelphia: F.A. Davis, 1981), 52–53.

7. J.H. Piatt, and S.J. Schiff. "High Dose Barbiturate Therapy in Neurosurgery and Intensive Care." *Neurosurgery* 15(1984):427–444.

8. C.L. Pollack-Latham, "Intracranial Pressure Monitoring: Part II. Patient Care." *Critical Care Nurse* 7(1987):70.

9. S.F. Marcotty, and A.B. Levin. "A New Approach in Epidural Intracranial Pressure Monitoring." *Journal of Neuroscience Nursing* 16(1984):54–59.

10. Beverly A. Means, and Lynn Craven Taplett. *Quick Reference to Critical Care Nursing* (Rockville, MD: Aspen Publishers, 1986).

SUGGESTED READINGS

American Association of Neuroscience Nurses. *Core Curriculum for Neuroscience Nursing.* Edited by Marilyn M. Ricci. Park Ridge, IL: American Association of Neuroscience Nurses, 1984.

Franges, Ellie Z., and Mary Ellen Beideman. "Infections Related to Intracranial Pressure Monitoring." *Journal of Neuroscience Nursing* 20(1988):94–103.

Germon, Karin. "Interpretation of ICP Pulse Waves to Determine Intracerebral Compliance." *Journal of Neuroscience Nursing* 20(1988):344–349.

Hickey, Joanne. *The Clinical Practice of Neurological and Neurosurgical Nursing.* Philadelphia: J.B. Lippincott, 1981.

Kastrup, Erwin K., ed. *Drug Facts and Comparisons.* Philadelphia: J.B. Lippincott, 1987.

Means, Beverly A., and Lynn Craven Taplett. *Quick Reference to Critical Care Nursing.* Rockville, MD: Aspen Publishers, 1986.

Mitchell, Pamela. "Intracranial Hypertension: Influence of Nursing Care Activities." *Nursing Clinics of North America* 21(1986): 563–576.

Muwaswes, Marylou. "Increased Intracranial Pressure and Its Systemic Effects." *Journal of Neuroscience Nursing* 17(1985):238–243.

Plum, Fred, and Jerome B. Posner. *The Diagnosis of Stupor and Coma.* Philadelphia: F.A. Davis, 1983.

Pollack-Latham, Christine L. "Intracranial Pressure Monitoring: Part I. Physiologic Principles." *Critical Care Nurse* 7(1987):40–51.

Pollack-Latham, Christine L. "Intracranial Pressure Monitoring: Part II. Patient Care." *Critical Care Nurse* 7(1987):53–73.

Raimond, Jeanne, and Joyce Waterman Taylor. *Neurological Emergencies: Effective Nursing Care.* Rockville, MD: Aspen Publishers, 1986.

Robinet, Karen. "Increased Intracranial Pressure: Management with an Intraventricular Catheter." *Journal of Neuroscience Nursing* 17(1985):95–104.

Rudy, Ellen B., Mara Baun, Kathleen Stone, and Barbara Turner. "The Relationship Between Endotracheal Suctioning and Changes in Intracranial Pressure: A Review of the Literature." *Heart & Lung* 15(1986):488–494.

Snyder, Mariah, ed. *A Guide to Neurological and Neurosurgical Nursing.* New York: Wiley, 1983.

5
Brain Death

Advances in medical and scientific technology during this century have enabled many individuals to recover from pathological states that otherwise would have been fatal. Hand in hand with these advances have arisen moral, ethical, and legal issues relative to the quality of life, right to die, organ donation, and the allocation of scarce resources. Lengthy discussion of all of the issues is beyond the scope of this chapter, and the reader is referred to the Suggested Readings for additional reading.

Nurses at the bedside are more often than not the first to recognize that an individual has lost neurological functions. It is the nurse's interface with the patient's family that assists the family in coping with the devastation of having a loved one seriously injured. When brain death is declared, it is the nurse who continues to care for the brain-dead person until mechanical supports are withdrawn and who provides empathy and compassion for the family. The focus of this chapter is to present the definition and diagnosis of brain death and to discuss issues relevant to managing organ donors.

DEFINITION

Brain death as a concept was addressed by an ad hoc committee of Harvard Medical School in 1968.[1] This committee described several features characterizing brain-dead individuals.

- unreceptivity and unresponsiveness
- absence of all movements and reflexes
- apnea
- isoelectric (flat) electroencephalogram (EEG)

This initial report served as the basis for further research and investigation. Currently the accepted criteria for brain death are as follows:

- absent cerebral function and cerebral perfusion
- absent brain stem reflexes
- apnea
- permanency of the above[2]

Prerequisite criteria that must be met prior to invoking the clinical criteria for brain death include

- irreversibility of the condition
- exclusion of shock, hypothermia, and drug and metabolic toxicity as causes of the coma

Irreversibility of the condition implies that all technological interventions have been instituted to facilitate reversal of the comatose state. The presence of shock, hypothermia, and drug and metabolic toxicity precludes a diagnosis of brain death because of the depressant effects these conditions place on the central nervous system (CNS). Hypotension and hypothermia are not uncommon in individuals with absent or near-absent brain function. Presence of these states may require treatment with fluid-volume replacement, vasopressors, and warming blankets to normalize their conditions. Additional constraint in invoking the criteria is placed when children are involved, as their brains demonstrate increased resistance to injury and may recover function.

APPLICATION OF THE CRITERIA

The diagnosis of brain death is a clinical one made by a physician and made before any life-support machinery is discontinued. While the documentation of brain-death criteria and the findings of specific corroborating diagnostic tests may vary from one institution to another, the basic concepts are similar. The length of time the criteria must exist in an individual before brain death can be declared varies. The minimal duration may range from six to twenty-four hours.

Cerebral Unresponsiveness

Clinical examination of the patient is done by a physician, ideally a neurologist or neurosurgeon. There must not be any responsiveness to noxious stimuli, including posturing of the extremities. Spinal reflexes may be present and do not preclude diagnosis of brain death, as they are mediated at the level of the spinal cord rather than at the brain stem or cerebral cortex.

Absent Brain Stem Reflexes

Corneal, oculocephalic, and, in some instances, oculovestibular reflexes may be assessed to determine the absence of brain stem function. There must not be any response of these reflexes. Refer to Chapter 2 for discussion of the assessment techniques for these reflexes mediated by the brain stem.

Apnea

Essentially, apnea testing consists of removing the patient from the ventilator for a specified period of time (up to ten minutes or longer) or until a predetermined arterial partial pressure of carbon dioxide ($Paco_2$) level is obtained to determine whether there are any spontaneous respiratory efforts. Brain stem respiratory centers should trigger spontaneous respiratory effort at $Paco_2$ levels of 55 to 60 mm Hg. The procedure for apnea testing may vary from institution to institution: Some may preoxygenate with 100% oxygen; others may provide continuous passive oxygenation during the test.

Corroborative Diagnostic Procedures

The number and type of diagnostic procedures required to corroborate the clinical diagnosis of brain death is determined by individual institutions. One or more of several tests may be employed.

Isoelectric EEG

Flat EEGs, while demonstrating absence of cortical activity, are not without drawbacks in their use as confirmation of brain death. Drug toxicity and hypothermia may induce cortical silence. Artifact data may be difficult to differentiate from cortical activity on the EEG.

Brain Stem Auditory-Evoked Responses

Since brain stem auditory-evoked responses (BAERs) evaluate conduction pathways through the brain stem, they may be employed to confirm brain death. The pre-existence of auditory pathology (deafness) must be determined prior to accepting it as valid. Another concern in using this procedure is that injury to the auditory pathways may have occurred during the trauma. Absence of responses in such an individual may not mean that brain-stem function is absent.

Cerebral Angiography

Performance of a four-vessel angiography study can confirm absence of blood flow to the brain. Major concerns in the use of angiography as a confirmatory test are its expensiveness, invasiveness, and need to transport an unstable patient from the intensive care unit (ICU).

Cerebral Blood Flow Studies

Tracing for presence of an inhaled or injected radioisotope in brain circulation can determine absence of blood flow to the brain.

DECLARATION OF BRAIN DEATH

Individual institutions may have specific policies regarding the declaration of brain death. Responsible nursing practice mandates that nurses be familiar with the policies governing their institutions. Brain death is a legally acceptable determination of death. Physicians and nurses must address their own moral, ethical, and religious beliefs regarding brain death to deliver the highest quality of care to the individual and the involved family.

Once brain death is declared, it should be immediately documented in the medical record, along with any corroborative testing. Some institutions may require that do-not-resuscitate orders be written, while others may accept written documentation of brain death as adequate medical orders not to resuscitate. Removal of life-support equipment should not occur until such documentation and determination of organ donor candidacy.

Support for Family and Staff

The family may or may not have had time to become acclimated to the full meaning of their loved one's injury. It may be that the family can accept the diagnosis and advance from there. Often, however, conveyance of the diagnosis, attempts at removal of life-support equipment from the individual, or queries regarding organ donation may be met with disbelief by grief-stricken families. All available support systems should be called upon to assist the family during this trial. The institution's social worker and chaplain may prove to be of paramount assistance in helping the family deal with the psychological and religious turmoil brought about by the situation. Neuroscience clinical nurse specialists, psychiatric clinical nurse specialists, and staff psychiatrists can be of tremendous help in assisting nursing and medical staff to cope with grief reactions that they themselves are experiencing.

ORGAN DONATION

Critical care nurses in emergency departments, ICUs, and recovery rooms are in prime positions to identify potential organ donors. The demand for organ transplants far exceeds the supply, and early recognition of a potential donor may mean extended life for another person.

The Uniform Anatomical Gift Act is legislation enacted in 1968 and is in effect in some form in all 50 states.[3] It provides for the donation of organs for transplant by any individual aged eighteen years or over as stated on a donor card, in a will, or, in some areas, on a driver's license. The family of the brain-dead individual may also donate the person's organs by signing consent. In some states the written wishes of the individual donor may be usurped by family disagreement with organ donation.

Organ-Donor Criteria

In general, the best organ donor is one who is young, in good health, and who has suffered a traumatic event. Brain-dead individuals whose cause of death is due to primary neurological dysfunction are the ideal organ donors because all other body systems should be in optimal health. Each area of the United States has its own organ donor bank, and the reader is referred to his or her specific area to obtain the policies and procedures that govern that region. The criteria for donation of specific organs is described in Table 5-1.

Evaluation of the Organ Donor

Each potential donor is individually evaluated for multiple-organ donation by the donor-bank coordinator. The laboratory data wanted as baseline and as ongoing assessment will be recommended to the staff physician by the donor bank.

Donor Management

In many instances the knowledge of brain death or impending brain death may be known several hours or days prior to the actual onset. Families should be approached as soon as feasible about the possibility of organ donation, once the prognosis of the individual is explained by the physician. The local organ-donor bank should be notified of the possibility of a donor as soon as possible to facilitate donor evaluation and management.

Table 5-1 Criteria for Organ Donation

Organ	Age	General Criteria
Kidney	Newborn–65 years	History of diabetes mellitus or hypertension will be individually evaluated.
		Gastrointestinal (GI) surgery with contamination of abdominal cavity by intestinal contents will be individually evaluated.
		There is no history of malignant neoplasms (except primary intracranial neoplasms) or certain skin cancers.
		There is no history of pyelonephritis or other chronic renal disease.
		There is no current systemic infection.
		There is no history of intravenous (IV) drug abuse.

Criteria for the following organ donations are similar to those described for kidney donation, the exception being age requirements.

Liver	Newborn–50 years	There is no history of pre-existing organ disease.
Pancreas	Newborn–50 years	There is no history of pre-existing organ disease.
Heart	Males: Newborn–40 years Females: Newborn–45 years	There is no history of pre-existing organ disease.
Heart-lung	2–3 years	There is no history of pre-existing organ disease.
Lung	10–50 years	There is no history of pre-existing organ disease.

Source: Adapted from *Organ and Tissue Donation for Transplantation* by R.M. Ippolito (Ed.), p. 3, with permission of New England Organ Bank, Inc., © 1986.

Families may need to discuss at length their decision to permit organ donation. Fears of disfigurement need to be allayed as well as any concerns about not burying the deceased as a "whole person." Families can and do find much comfort in knowing that their deceased loved one has contributed to the ongoing life of another individual. Critical care nurses are instrumental in assisting families with the decision to donate organs. They are also instrumental in supporting the natural grief reaction that families experience.

There are specific management protocols identified by donor banks to help ensure that the organs remain viable. Nursing care of the organ-donor patient is aimed at supporting physiological function of remaining body systems.

Volume and Blood Pressure Support

To maintain kidneys for transplant, it is important to adjust fluid volume to ensure adequate renal perfusion. Fluid administration is aimed at producing an hourly urine output of 30 to 50 mL/hour. Diabetes insipidus can be expected due to absent diencephalic function and should be treated with aqueous pitressin subcutaneously or via IV titration. (See Chapter 6 for further information on diabetes insipidus.)

Hypotension is not uncommon; vasopressors may be necessary to facilitate organ perfusion. Intropin (dopamine) is the vasopressor of choice because it can be used effectively, except at high doses (greater than 20 µg/kg/min), without decreasing renal perfusion. While other vasopressor agents decrease renal blood flow and are to be avoided if at all possible, some donor banks will accept donors who have received other drugs. The transplant team may have an ordered preference for the type of vasopressor used if Intropin is ineffective. Such preference might be administration of isoproterenol (Isuprel) and levarterenol bitartrate (Levophed) in the presented order.[4]

Diuretics may be administered if volume infusion and vasopressors are insufficient in maintaining perfusion. Mannitol, 12.5 to 25 g IV, may be given every four to six hours as necessary to promote diuresis. Furosemide (Lasix) may be necessary if mannitol is ineffective. Electrolytes and renal function values must be monitored and treated.

General Considerations

Any unnecessary arterial or IV lines should be discontinued to minimize the likelihood of infection. Treatment of local infectious processes should continue unless otherwise designated by the organ-bank physician. Regarding eye donors, particular attention should be paid to maintaining corneal integrity, such as frequent saline washes and taping of the lids if they do not completely close.

NOTES

1. Ad Hoc Committee of Harvard Medical School, "A Definition of Irreversible Coma." *Journal of the American Medical Association* 205(August 5, 1968):337–340.

2. Carol Millman, "Brain Death: Determination, Decision, and Donation," in *Acute Neuroscience Nursing: Concepts and Care*, ed. Jane Lundgren (Boston: Jones and Bartlett Publishers, 1986), 207.

3. Nancy J. Brent, "Uniform Determination of Death Act Implications for Nursing Practice." *Journal of Neurosurgical Nursing* 15(October 1983):265–267.

4. Rosann M. Ippolito, ed. *Organ and Tissue Donation for Transplantation*. (Boston: New England Organ Bank, 1986), 4.

SUGGESTED READINGS

Bartucci, Marilyn Rossman. "Organ Donation: A Study of the Donor Family Perspective." *Journal of Neuroscience Nursing* 19(1987):305–309.

Cox, Julia. "Organ Donation: The Challenge for Emergency Nursing." *Journal of Emergency Nursing* 12(1986):199–204.

Davis, Karen M., and Denise Miller Lemke. "Brain Death: Nursing Roles and Responsibilities." *Journal of Neuroscience Nursing* 19(1987):36–39.

Henneman, Elizabeth A. "Brain Resuscitation." *Heart & Lung* 15(1986):3–12.

Means, Beverly A., and Lynn Craven Taplett. *Quick Reference to Critical Care Nursing*. Rockville, MD: Aspen Publishers, 1986.

Millman, Carol, and Charlotte Hill. "Brain Death: Determination, Decision, and Donation; Guidelines for Requesting Donations." In *Acute Neuroscience Nursing: Concepts and Care*. Edited by Jane Lundgren. Boston: Jones and Bartlett Publishers, 1986, 205–224.

Safar, Peter. "Cerebral Resuscitation after Cardiac Arrest: A Review." *Circulation* 74(1986):Supplement IV, 138–153.

6

Head Trauma

The words head trauma can reflect a multitude of conditions in which injury of varying severity to the skull and/or brain occurs. The etiology of the injury may arise from motor vehicle accidents, falls, assaults, occupational injuries, and sporting accidents. Critical care nurses will encounter moderately and severely head-injured individuals who frequently sustain other general trauma injuries as well. This chapter presents the types of skull and brain injuries that can occur and the management concerns.

TYPES OF HEAD INJURIES

Several terms exist to describe the type of trauma incurred by the brain during a head injury.

Penetrating (Open) Head Injury

Penetrating injuries are direct-impact injuries that occur when an object pierces the cranium and gains access to the environment of the brain. Two examples of such injuries are gunshot and stab wounds. Bullet wounds to the head create tissue injury predicated upon

- caliber
- velocity
- trajectory
- proximity when fired
- whether the bullet was hollow or solid

The severity of stab wounds depends upon the location and degree to which the intracranial environment has been disrupted. Figure 6-1 illustrates the destruction caused by a bullet wound to the head.

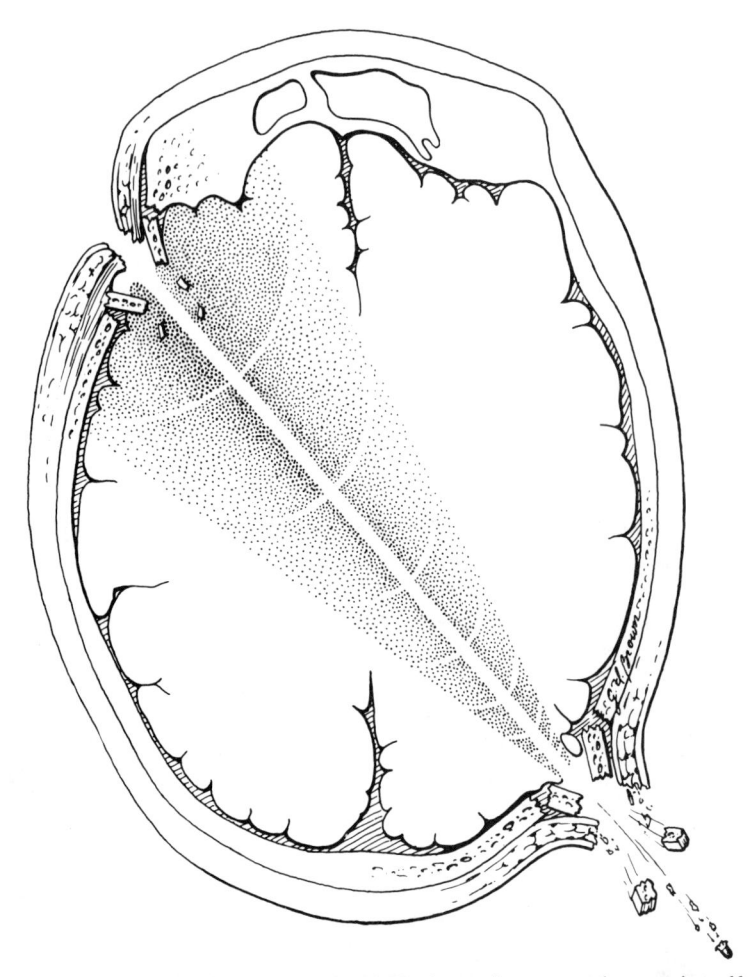

Figure 6-1 Disruptive Forces of a Gunshot Wound. The damage is greatest at the entry site and lessens as the bullet's energy is dissipated through the brain tissue, although the exit site is larger than the entry site. Guns fired with the muzzle next to the head allow the entry of expanding gases, which travel through the brain tissue. *Source:* Reprinted by permission of the authors from *Neuropathology: A Summary for Students* by R.W. Leech and R.M. Shuman, p. 104, J.B. Lippincott Company, © 1982.

Nonpenetrating (Closed) Head Injury

Nonpenetrating, or closed, head injuries occur as a result of an indirect or direct impact injury in which the integrity of the skull has not been disrupted. Indirect injuries to the brain may result after a fall during which the brunt of the trauma was absorbed by the lower extremities or trunk but a jarring effect occurred to the brain. Direct impact injuries may also be described as blunt trauma injuries, which may produce neurological disruption of varying degrees.

Coup and Contrecoup Injuries

Coup injuries are those that occur directly below the site of trauma impact, while contrecoup injuries are those that occur to the brain tissue opposite the site of impact. Contrecoup injuries result from the rebounding of brain tissue within the cranium.

Mechanisms of Injury

There are several forces at play that contribute to the pathology of head injury. Acceleration-deceleration and rotational forces come into operation in disrupting the intracranial environment during head injuries. The contents of the cranial cavity (blood, brain, cerebrospinal fluid [CSF]) have varying molecular weights that contribute to the extent and severity of the head injury by exerting tension and creating shearing forces during rotational injuries (Figure 6-2).

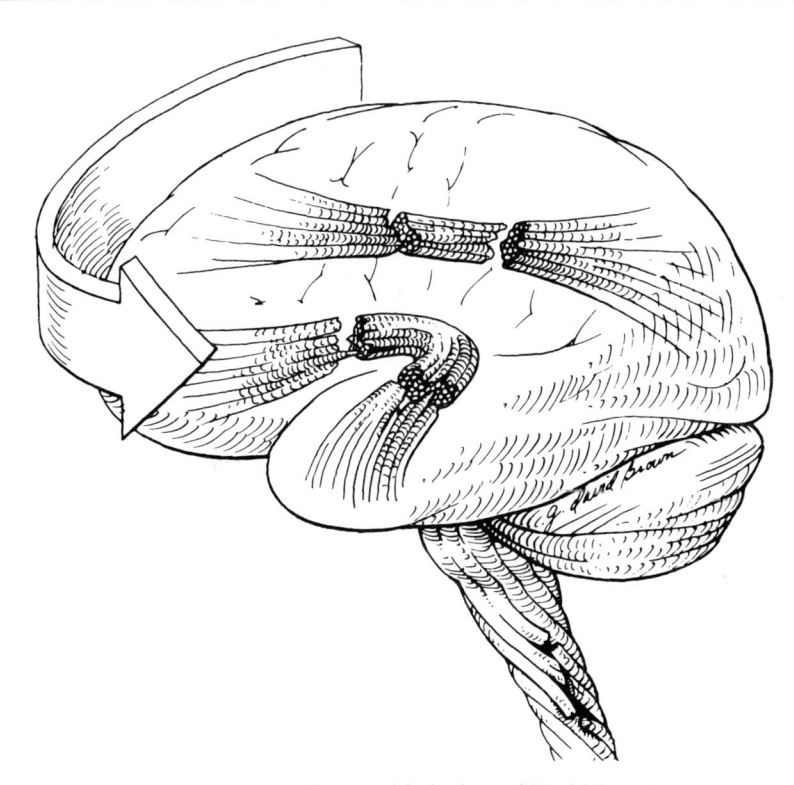

Figure 6-2 Rotational and Shearing Forces as Mechanisms of Head Injury. *Source:* Reprinted by permission of the authors from *Neuropathology: A Summary for Students* by R.W. Leech and R.M. Shuman, p. 99, J.B. Lippincott Company, © 1982.

When a stationary head is placed into motion (eg, with a blow from a baseball bat) or a moving head is stopped by an object (a dashboard), the intracranial contents are set into motion within the confines of the rigid skull. The contents of the cranium accelerate as they glide over the inner surface of the skull, rotate on the brain stem, and then decelerate as the momentum is dissipated. These forces, coupled with the different speeds of movement of the intracranial contents, cause distortion of the brain tissue and can result in shearing of the tissues.

SKULL FRACTURES

While skull fractures may occur in the process of a head injury, they are not always clinically significant. Their presence does represent that significant pressure has been brought to bear on the head. Visual inspection and palpation of the cranium can reveal skull fractures prior to radiographs in some instances. Skull films are frequently obtained, even in minor head injuries, to rule out fractures. While skull fractures in and of themselves may not be life threatening, the disruption they can potentially produce on brain tissue, blood vessels, and meninges can be. Figure 6-3 illustrates the following fractures.

Linear Fracture

Linear fractures, the simplest and most common type of skull fracture, appear as thin cracks or lines on a skull film. The bone plate is disrupted but not displaced, and the intracranial contents are not disrupted. The neurological deficit sustained depends upon the degree to which the underlying tissues were traumatized.

Comminuted Fracture

Fragmentation of the skull bone into numerous pieces occurs in a comminuted fracture. Multiple small cracks may occur in the bone, which radiate from the impact site. As with linear fractures, the extent to which the brain was traumatized determines the neurological deficit.

Depressed Fracture

With this skull fracture, bone fragments are depressed inward toward the brain. There may or may not be laceration of the brain associated with them.

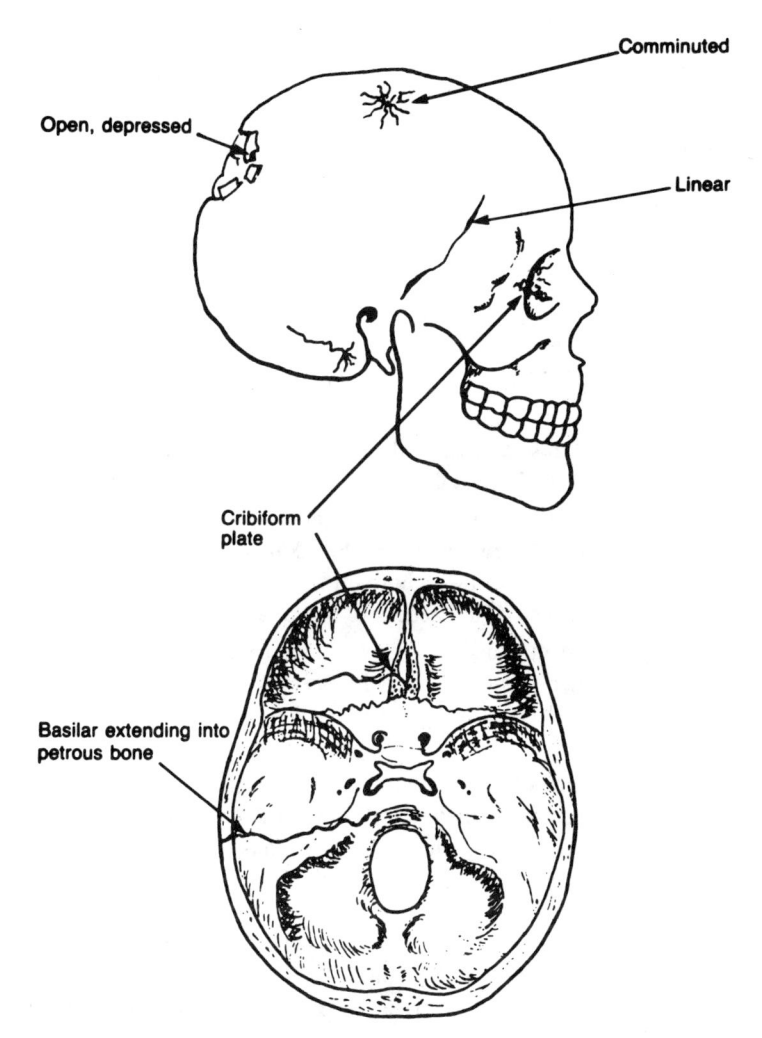

Figure 6-3 Types of Skull Fractures. *Source:* Reprinted from *Neurological Emergencies: Effective Nursing Care* by J. Raimond and J.W. Taylor, p. 195, Aspen Publishers Inc., © 1986.

Compound or Open Fracture

A depressed fracture in the presence of a scalp laceration constitutes an open-skull fracture. These conditions together allow communication from the external environment into the intracranial cavity. There may be extensive neurological trauma from the penetrating injury.

Basilar Fracture

A basilar fracture refers to fracture of bones at the base of the skull, which are often difficult to visualize on radiographs. They may be an extension of a linear fracture but may also be comminuted, depressed, or compound fractures. The anterior and middle fossae are the more common sites, although the posterior fossa may incur a basilar fracture through upward thrust of the cervical vertebrae against the base of the skull.

Complications of Basilar Fractures

The following complications may occur with basilar fractures:

- Basilar skull fractures can extend the frontal bone into the paranasal sinuses, tear the dura, and produce leakage of CSF, referred to as rhinorrhea.
- Extension of basilar skull fractures into the petrous portion of the temporal bone can also tear the dura, and the CSF leakage produced through the ear is termed otorrhea. A concern with both rhinorrhea and otorrhea is the potential for meningitis because of the access of bacteria to the intracranial cavity.
- Basilar fractures occurring near the entrance to the cranium of the carotid artery may produce hemorrhage if the vessel is lacerated or may create a communication between the carotid artery and the cavernous sinus, producing a carotid-cavernous fistula.
- Cranial nerve injuries of the oculomotor (III), trochlear (IV), and abducens (VI) nerves may occur as they pass through the cavernous sinus. This may produce paralysis of the eye movements (ophthalmoplegia) controlled by those cranial nerves. Blindness can result from orbital plate fractures that injure the optic nerve. The olfactory nerves may be injured with basilar skull fractures that affect the cribriform plate, part of the ethmoid bone through which these nerves pass. The resultant loss of the sense of smell may be transient, or, if the olfactory nerves were sheared, it may be permanent.

MANAGEMENT OF SKULL FRACTURES

Skull fractures, especially linear fractures, may require no treatment. In treating other types of fractures, the degree to which the cerebral environment has been disrupted and the clinical presentation of the individual will determine treatment.

Basilar skull fractures may not be immediately evident following head trauma. Basilar fractures may not be readily apparent and may appear several hours or later after an injury. Indicators of a basilar fracture include

- raccoon's eyes (periorbital ecchymoses)
- Battle's sign (ecchymoses of the mastoid process behind the ear)
- the presence of rhinorrhea and otorrhea
- hematotympanum (bleeding into the middle ear)

A major concern with rhinorrhea and otorrhea is the possibility of meningitis developing as bacteria from the external environment penetrate the intracranial cavity. CSF drainage frequently produces a halo sign on the pillow case, which is a dark area surrounded by a lighter (halo) area.

Differential diagnosis of whether or not a particular drainage is CSF can be obtained by collecting some of the drainage for chloride evaluation.

- CSF chloride levels (118 to 132 mEq/L) are higher than serum levels (95 to 105 mEq/L).
- Using Dextrostix to assess for glucose can also be used as a differential (CSF contains glucose, mucus does not). Concomitant superficial lacerations to the nasal mucosa may, however, make assessment for glucose content a less reliable method.

SCALP LACERATIONS

The scalp is very vascular and has relatively poor vasoconstrictive properties, which accounts for the profuse bleeding seen with these lacerations. Scalp lacerations may occur without presenting further compromise to the nervous system. A skull series will determine the presence of fracture.

INJURIES TO THE BRAIN

Traumatic brain injuries may be focal or diffuse in nature. Focal injuries may be as devastating as diffuse brain trauma, depending upon the anatomical areas affected.

Focal Brain Injuries

Focal injuries are those in which there is a local laceration or space-occupying lesion that causes mass effect. An individual with focal injuries will demonstrate neurological deficits specific to the area of the brain injured.

Contusions

Contusions are bruises that result from tearing and shearing of superficial cortical vessels. They are the most common type of head-injury lesion. Contusions are associated with coup and contrecoup injuries and are frequently found beneath depressed skull fractures. The frontal and temporal poles and their basal areas are the most common sites for cerebral contusions. As the brain glides within the rigid skull after an impact, the frontal and temporal poles are stopped by the frontal and sphenoid bones. The basal portions of these lobes are at risk because they are adjacent to the jagged, uneven, bony foundation of the skull base.

Clinically the patient with a contusion will manifest focal neurological deficits. Skull films may reveal a depressed fracture, and a computed tomographic (CT) scan will demonstrate the contused brain areas. Contusions may extend to secondary events, such as increased intracranial pressure (ICP), subarachnoid hemorrhage, or an intracerebral hematoma.

Lacerations

Brain lacerations may be caused by shearing forces within the skull with blunt trauma, by depressed skull fractures, and/or by penetrating injuries. Due to the nature of the injury, they are frequently associated with contusions and hemorrhage (Figure 6-4). Localized response to the laceration results in edema and tissue necrosis, which may become more generalized depending upon the extent of the trauma. When the laceration is caused by a penetrating missile injury, such as a bullet or stab wound, there is the added risk of meningitis and brain abscesses from the contaminated missile. Lacerations are a severe brain injury. The recovery potential of the individual is dependent upon the extent of the laceration and its location. Deficits may be more severe than with contusions, owing to the actual separation of brain tissue that occurs with lacerations.

Epidural (Extradural) Hematomas

Epidural hematomas result from bleeding into the potential space between the skull and the dura. The causative extracerebral vessel is usually an artery (the middle meningeal artery most commonly), although it may be a vein. The middle meningeal artery is often involved due to its location. This vessel transverses the external dura mater vertically, beneath the temporal bone, which is relatively thin. Direct impact injuries to this region can produce depressed skull fractures, the bony fragments of which can then lacerate vessels and brain tissue.

The morbidity and mortality once associated with epidural hematomas have decreased in part due to increased recognition skills of providers and more sophisticated scanning techniques. Diagnosis can be made by CT scan or arteriography. On CT scans epidural hematomas appear as elliptical shapes with convex inner

Head Trauma   119

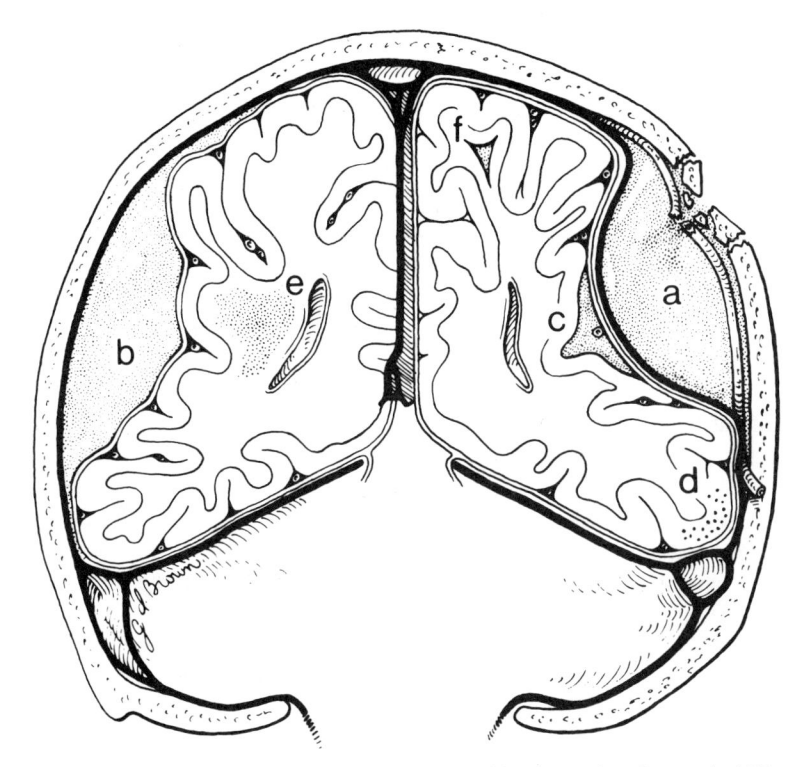

Figure 6-4 Types of Intracranial Hemorrhages. (a) Epidural hematoma from lacerated middle meningeal artery. (b) Subdural hematoma. (c) Subarachnoid hemorrhage. (d) Cortical petechiae. (e) Intracerebral hemorrhage. (f) Shear hemorrhage in subcortical white matter. *Source:* Reprinted by permission of the authors from *Neuropathology: A Summary for Students* by R.W. Leech and R.M. Shuman, p. 100, J.B. Lippincott Company, © 1982.

---

margins; the bleeding separates the dura mater from the inner skull table and compresses the brain medially.

The classical clinical picture of a person sustaining an epidural hematoma is dramatic, but it is important to recognize that it may not always occur. Typically there is history of head trauma with an immediate loss of consciousness. Consciousness is regained relatively quickly, and the person is lucid for several minutes to hours. As the hematoma expands and the brain can no longer maintain its tamponade effect, the individual deteriorates neurologically and presents with headache, drowsiness, and vomiting.

As the hematoma, which is essentially a mass lesion, compresses the brain medially, the person will demonstrate lateralizing neurological signs from the compression of anatomical structures (see Figure 6-4). One can expect contralateral (side opposite the lesion) hemiplegia and ipsilateral (same side as the lesion) pupillary changes, although in some instances decreased motor function can be seen on the ipsilateral side.

Without intervention, the hematoma will continue to expand and to compress anatomical structures; given the closed vault nature of the cranium, eventual herniation of the cranial contents through the foramen magnum will occur.

Surgical evacuation of the hematoma is necessary to reverse its compressive effects, along with ligation of the bleeding vessel. In emergent situations, twist drill holes may be done to afford partial removal of the clot and to provide transient stabilization of the patient.

Subdural Hematomas

Subdural hematomas are arterial or venous bleeds from the cerebral vessels. The majority of subdural hematomas are venous in nature because, as you will recall from Chapter 1, the dura contains a number of large venous sinuses. Shearing and rotational forces can also cause tearing of smaller blood vessels that bridge the subdural space. Subdural hematomas occur between the inner layer of the dura mater and the outer layer of the arachnoid membrane of the meninges (see Figure 6-4).

The morbidity and mortality rates associated with subdural hematomas are greater than those for epidural hematomas. CT scans of subdural hematomas demonstrate a concave mass spreading over the hemisphere. Subdural hematomas are classified as one of three types based upon the time interval between injury and presentation of symptoms: acute, subacute, and chronic.

Acute Subdural Hematoma. Acute subdural hematomas occur within 48 hours of injury and often are associated with contusions and lacerations. Clinically the patient will complain of a headache and will display altered consciousness: drowsiness, lethargy, restlessness and/or irritability, and confusion. The expanding clot will compress cerebral structures, causing them to shift, and will contribute to further decrease in the level of consciousness. As structural shifts occur, the ipsilateral pupil will dilate and react sluggishly to light, eventually becoming fixed as the oculomotor nerve is compressed. Contralateral hemiparesis may become evident as the level of consciousness deteriorates.

Treatment of acute subdural hematomas depends on the size of the clot. Small hematomas causing no neurological deficits often resolve spontaneously. When the individual's neurological status is compromised, surgical evacuation of the clot is indicated.

Subacute Subdural Hematoma. Subacute subdural hematomas occur greater than forty-eight hours but less than two weeks following head injury. Individuals with this type of lesion appear to be improving, then suddenly begin to demonstrate deterioration in their neurological status. Clinical signs and symptoms are similar to what occurs with an acute subdural hematoma. Treatment is surgical excision.

Chronic Subdural Hematoma. Chronic subdural hematomas can develop months after such a minor head injury, that the incident is forgotten. Slow bleeding occurs from a torn vessel traversing the subdural space; within seven to ten days postinjury, a fibrous membrane envelops the clot. Over time the clot continues to enlarge, perhaps from continued bleeding or from osmotic changes. Because the clot mass expands slowly, the cranial contents adapt to its presence. Eventually, however, the clot becomes large enough to act as a space-occupying lesion.

While an acute subdural hematoma can be identified as an area of increased density on CT scan, chronic subdurals become isodense (similar to brain tissue) and are often not apparent on CT scans. Ventricular shifting can be an important clue in identifying these lesions.

Clinically chronic subdural hematomas may not present with localized signs and symptoms. The individual may complain vaguely of a headache and may demonstrate apathy, lethargy, and decreased attentiveness. Surgical excision of the clot and its enveloping membrane is required.

Two high-risk groups for development of subdural hematomas are the elderly and alcoholics. The elderly are at risk because the aging process causes some degree of cerebral atrophy, which increases the subdural space. This larger area between the dura and cerebral vessels creates more tension on the bridging blood vessels, making them more susceptible to even minor head trauma. The increased space available allows more room for subdurals to expand before they become symptomatic, and when they do, symptoms may be mistaken for dementing processes.

Cerebral atrophy also occurs in alcoholic persons, along with abnormal clotting processes from a diseased liver. The incoordination experienced by inebriated individuals makes them more prone to falls, which can cause subdural hematomas. Obtaining a history of head trauma from an alcoholic may be difficult due to impaired memory processes unless accompanied by a witness or obvious evidence of trauma.

Intracerebral Hematomas

Intracerebral hematomas refer to bleeding that has occurred directly into the brain parenchyma (see Figure 6-4). In head injury they are frequently associated with contusions and lacerations of the frontal and temporal lobes and may also occur in the deeper cortical matter secondary to shearing and rotational forces on feeder vessels. Bleeding can extend from the parenchyma into the ventricles and/or subarachnoid space. Their occurrence may be single or multiple in number.

Clinically the patient will demonstrate focal signs relative to the clot

- decreased level of consciousness
- contralateral hemiparesis/hemiplegia
- ipsilateral dilating pupil

Signs and symptoms of meningitis will also be demonstrated with extravasation of blood into the ventricles. Untreated, the individual is at risk of herniation from the concomitant cerebral edema and swelling. CT scanning and magnetic resonance imaging (MRI) will demonstrate location and extent of the clot.

Since the clot directly involves brain tissue, a craniotomy for surgical evacuation is not usually the definitive treatment, as the clot may not be easily accessible. Increased ICP management and ventricular drainage of CSF are used to control mass effect and to maximize brain-tissue viability.

Diffuse Brain Injuries

Diffuse injuries are those in which there has been global damage to the intracranial contents. It is caused by the shearing forces in blunt trauma. The term refers to a range of injuries from concussion to diffuse axonal injury. The types of neurological deficits demonstrated by the individual with diffuse brain trauma will be of greater complexity in that large amounts of brain tissue are involved.

Concussion

Concussions are diagnosed on the basis of a transient alteration in the level of consciousness following a head injury. The alteration in consciousness is attributed to temporary disruption of neuronal conduction caused by the stretching of axons during the injury. It is postulated that injury to the reticular formation, which contributes to consciousness, may play a role in concussion. CT scans do not reveal evidence of structural damage.

The individual may be unconscious for a brief time (less than five minutes), may be momentarily confused, or may be in a dazed state. Other clinical signs of a concussion include loss of reflexes, bradycardia with a fall in blood pressure, and respiratory arrest lasting a few seconds. The degree of symptoms will vary.

Recovery from the immediate effects of a concussion occurs in time over a few minutes to a few days. Vomiting may occur when the person regains consciousness, and disorientation for hours to days is not uncommon. The individual may experience memory loss for a period of time prior to the injury (retrograde amnesia) as well as for some time following the injury (post-traumatic amnesia).

Retrograde amnesia is defined as the memory loss related to the time before the injury, while post-traumatic amnesia reflects the time elapsed between the injury and return of a clear memory. The severity of the concussion is usually predicated upon the duration of unconsciousness and the degree of memory loss.

Postconcussion Syndrome. Postconcussion syndrome has been described as a series of dysfunctions that may be experienced for weeks to months following a head injury. Characteristics of this syndrome are listed in Exhibit 6-1.

Most often persons with a mild concussion whose loss of consciousness was five minutes or less will be discharged home after treatment. Teaching prior to discharge should include signs and symptoms that warrant immediate return to an emergency department (Exhibit 6-2) as well as information on postconcussion syndrome.

Exhibit 6-1 Characteristics of Postconcussion Syndrome

- Recent memory loss
- Impaired concentration
- Impaired abstract reasoning
- Impaired judgment
- Headache
- Emotional lability
- Fatigue
- Insomnia
- Photophobia

Exhibit 6-2 Instructions After a Head Injury

1. Return to the emergency department, or notify your private physician if any of the following occur.
    (a) Persistent, severe headache
    (b) Persistent vomiting
    (c) Stiff neck or fever
    (d) Pupils that are unequal in size
    (e) Convulsions or difficulty staying awake
    (f) Leakage of clear fluid from the nose or ear
    (g) Persistent confusion or other type of unusual behavior
2. The patient should be awakened every two to three hours during the first night to check for the above symptoms.
3. Avoid any medications other than aspirin or acetaminophen unless specifically directed by your physician.

While full recovery can be expected to occur following a concussion, repeated concussions may have a cumulative effect on the brain. The repetitive stretching and possible shearing of axons during a concussion contribute to cerebral atrophy and loss of neurons in both the cerebrum and cerebellum, thus rendering the damage permanent. "Punch-drunk encephalopathy" is a syndrome identified with repeated concussions. The most vivid example of this syndrome is seen with boxers. It is characterized by

- forgetfulness
- decreased intellectual capabilities
- dysarthria
- extrapyramidal signs (slow, shuffling gait)
- cerebellar signs (incoordination, ataxia)

Diffuse Injury

Diffuse injuries are caused by the same mechanisms that produce concussions; however, the degree of neurological impairment is greater. It is differentiated from a concussion by several features.

- The period of unconsciousness is greater than twenty-four hours and may last days or weeks.
- Typically the individual presents with a Glasgow Coma Scale (GCS) score of 8 or less.
- Withdrawal from painful stimuli is evident; purposeful movement may occur intermittently.
- The post-traumatic amnesia experienced is far more severe than with a concussion.
- The persistence of long-term cognitive, intellectual, and personality disorders beyond the rehabilitation phase is not uncommon.

Diffuse Axonal Injury

Diffuse axonal injury (DAI) has been identified as the most serious form of diffuse injury. Individuals surviving DAI have significant neurological deficits. Many remain in a persistent vegetative state; many victims die from the injuries incurred in the incident. The shearing and rotational forces that cause concussion occur to a more significant degree, disrupting ascending and descending axons throughout the cerebrum and brain stem.

DAI can be differentiated from diffuse injury by the following:

- depth and duration of unconsciousness
- presence of brain stem signs
- symptoms of autonomic involvement

CT scans may reveal many areas of small hemorrhaging within the deeper cortical areas, and MRI may demonstrate the same within brain stem regions. Brain stem auditory-evoked responses (BAERs) demonstrate delayed conduction through the brain stem.

Clinically the individual presents in deep coma, which may last for weeks. Brain stem involvement is demonstrated by cranial nerve deficits (impaired oculocephalic, corneal, and gag reflexes) and decerebrate posturing. Shearing injuries to the hypothalamic area produce autonomic nervous system dysfunction, as evidenced by hyperthermia and hypertension.

SECONDARY PROBLEMS

There are a number of physiological processes enacted following head trauma that create challenges in managing the victim.

Brain Swelling and Cerebral Edema

Brain swelling is caused by hyperemia generated from the physiological cerebral, vasodilating response to the injury. The resultant increased blood volume is a significant factor in increasing ICP. It is best managed by controlling arterial partial pressure of oxygen (Pa_{O_2}) and arterial partial pressure of carbon dioxide (Pa_{CO_2}) (see Chapter 4).

Cerebral edema is the major cause of increased ICP with head injuries. It can be expected to peak two to four days postinjury. Refer to Chapter 4 for management discussion.

Hemorrhages

Subarachnoid and intraventricular hemorrhages may occur as sequelae to contusions and lacerations incurred in head injury. Intraventricular hemorrhages may result from a subarachnoid hemorrhage or may extend from an intracerebral hemorrhage. Insertion of a ventricular drain to allow drainage of CSF assists in minimizing obstructive hydrocephalus, which results from these hemorrhages.

Hydrocephalus

Hydrocephalus is a common occurrence after a head injury; it may be communicating, noncommunicating, or normal pressure.

Communicating Hydrocephalus

Intraventricular and subarachnoid hemorrhages contribute to the development of communicating hydrocephalus in that the blood within the ventricular system impedes the absorption of CSF from the arachnoid villi. Accumulation of CSF within the ventricles leads to their dilation, compression of cerebral structures, and increased ICP. Treatment involves performing a ventriculostomy to allow external CSF drainage.

Noncommunicating (Obstructive) Hydrocephalus

Compression of cerebral structures may impinge upon the ventricular system, blocking the flow of CSF and creating obstructive hydrocephalus. Treatment focuses upon eliminating the cause of obstruction.

Normal Pressure Hydrocephalus

Degeneration and atrophy of white matter or scarring of cerebral tissue (gliosis) from trauma contributes to decreased cerebral mass and dilation of the ventricles. This condition is also seen as a part of the aging process and is referred to as normal-pressure hydrocephalus. Initial treatment may involve insertion of a ventriculostomy with a permanent shunting procedure at a future date.

Post-traumatic Seizures

Seizure development after head trauma is the most common delayed complication. Many individuals will develop seizure activity within the first six months postinjury; others may not have a seizure until close to two years after the incident; still others may never experience any seizure activity. Victims of penetrating head injuries are far more likely to develop seizure activity, but it does occur in cases of blunt trauma. Scarring of cerebral tissue often serves as the source of the seizure activity.

The critical care nurse needs to be aware that seizures may also develop immediately or soon after injury from mass effect and compression. Chapter 10 presents detailed information on seizure management and status epilepticus.

Vascular Injuries

Head trauma may create trauma to extracranial vessels in addition to intracranial vessels, as demonstrated by an epidural hematoma. Injuries to the carotid artery may produce carotid dissection, resulting in hemiplegia of the affected side. Treatment involves emergent ligation of the lacerated vessel.

A carotid-cavernous fistula can result from laceration of the carotid artery as it lies within the cavernous sinus. Since the ophthalmic veins communicate with the cavernous sinus, arterial pressures occur within this system, producing distention. Signs and symptoms of a carotid-cavernous fistula are related to the increased pressure and may include

- exophthalmos (protruding eye) or proptosis (downward displacement of the eye)
- ocular palsies
- complaints of a rushing sensation within the head

The resultant bruit can be auscultated with extracranial Dopplers. Depending upon the size of the fistula, the bruit may be auscultated with a stethoscope placed directly over the orbit. While some instances of carotid-cavernous fistulae may close spontaneously, others may require that closure be achieved through balloon occlusion.

Other vascular injuries may occur as a result of whiplash injuries to the neck, and the vertebral arteries can incur trauma through hyperextension injuries.

Subdural Hygromas

Subdural hygromas are a collection of CSF and blood in the subdural space. They result from a tear in the arachnoid membrane during a head injury, which then allows seepage of CSF into the subdural space. If fluid accumulation is sufficient enough to create surrounding cerebral edema, the hygroma will act as a space-occupying mass and present symptoms similar to a subdural hematoma. The treatment for subdural hygromas is surgical excision, at which time it is differentiated from a subdural hematoma.

Metabolic Disruptions

Head trauma can precipitate major metabolic sequelae. The extent of metabolic involvement depends on the severity of the head injury and, to a great degree, the duration of a comatose state.

Syndrome of Inappropriate Antidiuretic Hormone Secretion

Inappropriate secretion of antidiuretic hormone (ADH) with subsequent hyponatremia and water retention frequently occurs following trauma to the hypothalamic region. This condition is usually time limited and resolves within three to four days postinjury. Increased amounts of ADH within the body signal the kidneys to retain water, contributing to cerebral edema. Other contributing etiologies of the syndrome of inappropriate ADH secretion (SIADH) include the following:

- manipulation of the hypothalamic-pituitary area during surgery
- bronchogenic cancer
- endocrine abnormalities (Addison's disease, hypopituitarism)
- administration of vasopressin agents

The clinical symptoms of SIADH begin with that of water retention but progress to demonstrate water intoxication.

- anorexia
- diarrhea
- nausea and vomiting
- altered mental status: confusion

SIADH can be identified by certain laboratory data, which are outlined in Table 6-1.

Treatment of SIADH centers upon restricting fluids to less than 2000 mL/day, with severe cases restricted to 500 mL/day. The infusion of hypertonic saline as well as administration of diuretics may be considered when the serum sodium falls to less than 125 to 130 mEq/L. If these interventions are ineffective, demeclocycline, 150 mg every six hours, may be administered to inhibit vasopressin secretion.

Also contributing to water retention in this patient population is mechanical ventilation, as volume receptors in the left atrium and pulmonary arteries stimulate ADH secretion through the positive pressure exerted on them. The head-trauma individual is at risk for more severe increases in ICP due to the water retention and seizure activity from the low serum sodium.

Table 6-1 Laboratory Characteristics of SIADH and Diabetes Insipidus (DI)

	SIADH	DI
Serum sodium	Less than 134 mEq/L	Greater than normal
Urine sodium	Above 30 mEq/L	Low in relation to serum
Serum osmolality	Less than normal	Greater than normal
Urine osmolality	Greater than serum	Low in relation to serum
Urine specific gravity	Greater than 1.003	Less than 1.003

Hypernatremia

Hypothalamic injury may trigger pituitary secretion of adrenocorticotrophic hormone (ACTH) and aldosterone with subsequent sodium retention. This is usually self-limiting, resolving within seventy-two hours, and followed by diuresis.

Diabetes Insipidus

Trauma to the hypothalamus or posterior pituitary may alter ADH secretion such that diabetes insipidus (DI) develops. In this condition insufficient amounts of the hormone ADH are secreted, resulting in subsequent excess urinary excretion of body water. Other etiologies contributing to the development of DI include

- manipulation of the hypothalamic-pituitary area during surgery
- destruction of the posterior pituitary gland or its neuronal connections with the hypothalamus from a space-occupying lesion
- abnormalities of the renal tubules, which produces nephrogenic DI

An individual with DI can excrete tremendous amounts of fluid each day, and without adequate replacement, the body is vulnerable to dehydration and hypovolemic shock. DI is usually a transient state in head injury unless there has been irreversible damage to the posterior pituitary and/or hypothalamic innervating area.

Clinically one will observe high hourly urine outputs, poor skin turgor, polyuria, and polydipsia. Laboratory data indicating DI are summarized in Table 6-1. The polyuria and polydipsia associated with DI are extremely uncomfortable to the individual. While an alert individual can notify care providers of their polydipsia, the majority of hospitalized head trauma patients are not capable of doing so. Treatment consists of providing fluid replacement equal to urinary volume excretion and vasopressin administration. The types of ADH supplements are listed in Exhibit 6-3.

Exhibit 6-3 Forms of ADH Replacement

Short Acting

Aqueous vasopressin—Five to ten units may be given subcutaneously (SC) or intramuscularly (IM); duration of action is four to six hours. It may also be administered intravenously (IV) and titrated hourly. It is the best choice in treating transient DI.

Lypressin (Diapid) intranasal spray—one to two sprays to each nostril; duration of action four to six hours.

Intermediate Acting

Deamino-D-Arginine Vasopressin (DDAVP)—0.05 to 0.4 mL instilled intranasally; duration of action twelve to twenty-four hours

Long Acting

Vasopressin tannate in oil—5 units IM; duration of action twenty-four to seventy-two hours; oil is peanut extract; avoid in persons with known peanut allergies; must be warmed and thoroughly mixed to ensure vasopressin dissolved in solution. Because of its long duration of action, this is not the drug of choice in alleviating symptoms of transient DI.

Hyperglycemia

The body's physiological release of catecholamines and cortisol in response to the head injury may precipitate hyperglycemia. Catecholamines promote gluconeogenesis and glycogenolysis while suppressing insulin secretion. Cortisol also promotes gluconeogenesis. Individuals with diabetes mellitus and those with borderline glucose tolerance are particularly vulnerable. The use of mannitol and corticosteroids to treat cerebral edema may further contribute to hyperglycemia. Treatment is aimed at achieving and maintaining normal glucose levels through administration of insulin.

Negative Nitrogen Balance

Trauma and stress increase the body's metabolic rate and energy use; thus its need for calories is also increased. If insufficient calories are available for anabolic needs, catabolic processes break down skeletal muscle protein to provide the necessary energy stores. Negative nitrogen balance will result from the catabolism, and the individual will be placed in a further state of compromised recovery.

To maintain adequate nutritional intake, enteral and/or parenteral nutrition is a necessary treatment. It is important to note that head-trauma victims who are awake, not intubated, and have no swallowing impairments may still have cognitive impairments that preclude adequate nutritional intake.

Increased Gastric Acid Secretion

Physiological feedback to the diencephalon triggers increased gastric acid secretion during times of stress. Gastric ulcer formation can occur to severely traumatized individuals as a result. The use of steroids to minimize the effects of cerebral edema can contribute to ulcer formation. Prophylactic administration of antacids can facilitate neutralization of highly acidic gastric contents. Histamine H_2-receptor antagonists such as ranitidine (Zantac) help to reduce gastric acid production and to minimize ulcer formation in patients on steroids.

MANAGEMENT

Initial Management

Initial treatment of the head-injured victim begins at the scene. Until disproved, all head-trauma victims should be managed as though they also had a spinal injury; therefore the spine should be immobilized as soon as possible. Goals at this point are to stabilize the victim and to transport him or her for emergency care. Upon arrival in an emergency department, the GCS (see Chapter 2) or trauma scale scores as well as a description of the trauma incident serve as excellent triage indicators. Goals at this point include the following:

- Establish a patent airway; intubate if necessary.
- Assess and monitor vital signs, including neurological assessments; initiate necessary resuscitative measures.
- Assess extent of head wound, and evaluate existence of other trauma.
- Stabilize for diagnostic procedures (skull and spine radiographs, CT scan, operative intervention).

Acute Management

A prime focus in the acute management of the head-injured patient is to maximize therapies to reduce or to prevent shifting of anatomical structures from increased ICP or mass lesions. It is more frequent than not that a head-trauma victim also has varying degrees of injury to other body systems. The interventions outlined below are limited to head trauma, with the recognition that the nurse is most likely also assessing and intervening for other injuries.

Frequent Neurological Assessment

Frequent neurological assessment provides data as to extension or resolution of neurological deficits.

Airway Maintenance

Ensuring an unobstructed airway is necessary to prevent aspiration as well as hypoxemia. Unconscious victims unable to protect their airways will be electively intubated. Mechanical ventilation also provides adequate oxygenation and the ability to hyperventilate the individual.

Management of Increased ICP

Aggressive management of increased ICP is necessary to maintain cerebral perfusion pressure at optimal levels and to minimize structural damage to neurons. Positioning is of paramount concern in helping to manage increased ICP (see Chapter 4).

Care of Head Wound

Scalp lacerations and penetration injuries place the individual at risk for localized infection and meningitis. Insertion of ICP monitoring and CSF drainage devices warrants aseptic management to prevent nosocomial infection.

Immobilization and Sedation

Agitated and combative behavior is not uncommon in head-injured individuals and may lead to disconnection of IV and arterial lines as well as other monitoring equipment. Minimizing environmental stimuli can reduce some of the agitated behavior. Sedation with barbiturates or diazepam (Valium) may be required in some individuals. Note that the CNS will be depressed due to sedation when assessing neurological function.

It may be necessary to administer IV bolus or continuous infusion of a short-acting neuromuscular blocking agent to induce skeletal muscle paralysis. Use of neuromuscular blockers mandates that the patient be intubated and mechanically ventilated. Two such agents are listed below.

1. pancuronium bromide (Pavulon)—0.04 to 0.1 mg/kg, with increments of 0.01 mg/kg to maintain skeletal muscle paralysis
2. vecuronium bromide (Norcuron)—0.08 to 0.15 mg/kg. This drug is more potent than pancuronium bromide yet has a shorter duration at initially equipotent doses and has a recovery index that is more rapid than pancuronium bromide.

Temperature Control

Maintenance of normothermia is optimal, as any fever will increase basal metabolic requirements. Hyperthermia should be aggressively investigated and treated, although the patient should not be allowed to shiver, as this will increase intracranial pressure.

Seizure Control

Seizure activity will further compromise the cerebral environment. The decision to place a patient on prophylactic anticonvulsants may depend greatly on the severity and the nature of the injury. Seizures, when they occur, require prompt and aggressive management. Seizure management is discussed in detail in Chapter 10.

Fluid and Electrolyte Balance

Fluid intake, urinary excretion, and electrolytes require close monitoring to assess for adequate fluid volume, renal function, and electrolyte balance.

Caloric Intake

Adequate nutrition is paramount in preventing catabolic processes. Nutritional support needs to be instituted as soon as paralytic ileus, if it has occurred, is resolved.

Bowel Function

Prevention of constipation and impaction will minimize straining and the likelihood of manual disimpaction, both of which can trigger a Valsalva's maneuver, which can cause increased ICP. Administration of a stool softener should begin once nutritional support is instituted.

Hazards of Immobility

In addition to orthopedic and skin injuries that may have occurred during the trauma, the patient is prone to the general effects of prolonged bedrest. Compromised nutritional status places the patient at further risk for tissue breakdown. Placement of the patient in a bed (CircoElectric, kinetic bed) designed to promote pressure relief and postural drainage is an option. Diligent attention to the skin integrity is crucial.

Venous stasis may precipitate deep-vein thrombosis in the lower extremities, leaving the patient susceptible to pulmonary emboli. Use of sequential compression devices on the legs might be considered.

Family Coping

The family and significant others of the patient are themselves in a period of crisis regarding the trauma to their loved one; the presence of legal issues regarding the trauma often further complicates family dynamics and coping. Maintaining frequent contact and brief descriptions of the implications of the trauma facilitates coping mechanisms on the part of the family. The consultative services of the institution's chaplaincy program, psychiatry service, and neuroscience and psychiatric clinical nurse specialists should be used as needed. Should the trauma pose a fatal outcome for the patient, nursing is in a prime position to approach the family regarding organ donation (see Chapter 5).

Factors Affecting Outcome

Poor prognostic indicators for recovery from comas caused by head injury include the following:

- age of 50 years or older
- absence of pupillary or oculocephalic responses
- decorticate or decerebrate posturing or flaccid extremities to noxious stimuli
- duration of coma[1]

Glasgow Outcome Scale

Life-style quality status post-head injury has tremendous societal and economic implications for those who survive the injury. Bond[2] and Jennett and Teasdale[3] devised the Glasgow Outcome Scale predicated upon the social abilities and physical dependency of head-injury survivors. Patients are assessed at specified intervals postinjury. Four categories of survival states have been described as follows:

1. Vegetative state
   (a) This state is often the result of diffuse axonal injury (DAI) or the secondary effects of hypoxia, necrosis, or increased ICP.
   (b) Patient's eyes are open, but there is no recognition of the environment; cognition is absent.
   (c) Patient is totally dependent upon others for survival.
2. Severe disability
   (a) Patient is conscious of environment, but dependent upon others for care.

(b) Disability may be motor, speech, cognitive, or any combination of the three.
(c) Institutional care may be necessary.
3. Moderate disability
   (a) Patient has some form of disability but is independent.
   (b) Depending upon the occupation, some patients may be capable of returning to work.
   (c) Disabilities may include hemiparesis, dysphasia, cranial nerve deficits, ataxia, post-traumatic seizures, memory difficulties, behavioral disorders, or cognitive impairments.
4. Good recovery
   (a) Patient resumes social life and returns to work.
   (b) Memory difficulties, behavioral disorders, and post-traumatic seizures may persist.

NOTES

1. Fred Plum and Jerome B. Posner. *The Diagnosis of Stupor and Coma*. 3rd ed (Philadelphia: F.A. Davis Company, 1983), 330–334.
2. Michael R. Bond, "Assessment of Outcome after Severe Brain Damage," *Lancet* 1(1975):489.
3. Bryan Jennett and Graham Teasdale. *Management of Head Injuries* (Philadelphia: F.A. Davis Company, 1981), 304–305.

SUGGESTED READINGS

Alves, Wayne M., Austin R.T. Colohan, Thomas J. O'Leary, Rebecca W. Rimel, and John A. Jane. "Understanding Posttraumatic Symptoms after Minor Head Injury." *The Journal of Head Trauma Rehabilitation* 1(1986):1–12.

Auerbach, Sanford H. "Neuroanatomical Correlates of Attention and Memory Disorders in Traumatic Brain Injury: An Application of Neurobehavioral Subtypes." *The Journal of Head Trauma Rehabilitation* 1(1986):1–12.

Baggerly, Joanne. "Rehabilitation of the Adult with Head Trauma." *The Nursing Clinics of North America* 21(1986):577–588.

Bourdon, Susan E. "Psychological Impact of Neurotrauma in the Acute Care Setting." *The Nursing Clinics of North America* 21(1986):629–640.

Colohan, Austin R.T., Ralph G. Dacey, Wayne M. Alves, Rebecca W. Rimel, and John A. Jane. "Neurologic and Neurosurgical Implications of Minor Head Injury." *The Journal of Head Trauma Rehabilitation* 1(1986):13–22.

Franges, Eleanor Z. "Assessment and Management of Carotid Artery Trauma Associated with Mild Head Injury." *Journal of Neuroscience Nursing* 18(1986):272–274.

Gardner, Doreen. "Acute Management of the Head-Injured Adult." *The Nursing Clinics of North America* 21(1986):555–562.

Gennarelli, Thomas A. "Mechanisms and Pathophysiology of Cerebral Concussion." *The Journal of Head Trauma Rehabilitation* 1(1986):23–30.

Hanscom, David A. "Acute Management of the Multiply Injured Head Trauma Patient." *The Journal of Head Trauma Rehabilitation* 2(1987):1–12.

Hickey, Joanne. *The Clinical Practice of Neurological and Neurosurgical Nursing.* Philadelphia: J.B. Lippincott, 1981.

Hinkle, Janice. "Nursing Care of Patients with Minor Head Injury." *Journal of Neuroscience Nursing* 20(1988):8–16.

Hoyt, David B., and Peggy Hollingsworth-Fridlund, eds. *Trauma Quarterly: Head Injuries* 2(1985):1–93.

Jennett, Bryan, and Graham Teasdale. *Management of Head Injuries.* Philadelphia: F.A. Davis, 1981.

Johndrow, Peggy Dean, and Shari Thornton. "Syndrome of Inappropriate Antidiuretic Hormone: A Growing Concern." *Focus on Critical Care* 12(1985):29–34.

Kastrup, Erwin K., ed. *Drug Facts and Comparisons.* Philadelphia: J.B. Lippincott, 1987.

Leech, Richard W., and Robert M. Shuman. *Neuropathology: A Summary for Students.* Philadelphia: Harper & Row, 1982.

Lundgren, Jane, ed. *Acute Neuroscience Nursing: Concepts and Care.* Monterey, CA: Jones and Bartlett Publishers, 1986.

Means, Beverly A., and Lynn Craven Taplett. *Quick Reference to Critical Care Nursing.* Rockville, MD: Aspen Publishers, 1986.

Nikas, Diana L., ed. "Head Trauma, Part 1: The Spectrum of Critical Care." *Critical Care Nursing Quarterly* 10(1987):1–84.

Nikas, Diana L., ed. "Head Trauma, Part 2: Nursing Issues and Controversies." *Critical Care Nursing Quarterly* 10(1987):1–91.

Palmer, Moya, and M. Anne Wyness. "Positioning and Handling: Important Considerations in the Care of the Severely Head-injured Patient." *Journal of Neuroscience Nursing* 20(1988):42–49.

Plum, Fred, and Jerome B. Posner. *The Diagnosis of Stupor and Coma.* 3rd ed. Philadelphia: F.A. Davis Company, 1983.

Raimond, Jeanne, and Joyce Waterman Taylor. *Neurological Emergencies: Effective Nursing Care.* Rockville, MD: Aspen Publishers, 1986.

Ropper, Allan H., Sean Kennedy, and Nicholas T. Zervas. *Neurological and Neurosurgical Intensive Care.* Rockville, MD: Aspen Publishers, 1983.

Rudy, Ellen B. *Advanced Neurological and Neurosurgical Nursing.* St. Louis: Mosby, 1984.

Spielman, Gerri. "Metabolic Complications Associated with Severe Diffuse Brain Injury." *Journal of Neurosurgical Nursing* 17(1985):83–88.

Taylor, Joyce Waterman, and Sally Ballenger. *Neurological Dysfunctions and Nursing Intervention.* New York: McGraw-Hill, 1980.

7

Spinal Cord Injuries

Spinal cord injuries occurring from motor vehicle accidents, falls, and sports injuries number about 10,000 new injuries per year. About half of these injuries occur to persons under the age of 25 years and more commonly to men.[1] Injuries to the spinal cord may also come about as the result of metastatic disease, vascular disorders, and musculoskeletal abnormalities of the vertebral column. A large majority of these injuries require the expertise of intensive care units (ICUs) and critical care nurses.

MECHANISMS OF INJURY

Acceleration and deceleration forces that cause head injury are also involved in producing spinal cord injuries. These forces cause the head to hyperextend and/or hyperflex on the neck during the event. The degree to which the hyperextension or hyperflexion occurs can significantly impact the integrity of the spinal cord without necessarily causing vertebral fracture or dislocation. The ligaments that maintain vertebral alignment and help to protect the spinal cord can incur significant stretching and shearing forces. Rotation of the neck during the injury can displace and distort the vertebrae and cause subsequent injury to the spinal cord itself.

Compression forces that impact either the rostral (head) or caudal (tailbone) ends of the vertebral column can result in fractures and dislocations of the vertebral bodies. Injury to the vertebral column can potentially result in spinal cord injury from

- concussion
- contusion
- compression
- disruption of the spinal cord blood supply

VERTEBRAL FRACTURES

Fractures can occur at each level of the vertebral column, although they are more common in the cervical and lumbar regions than in the thoracic.

Simple Fracture

Simple fractures usually occur to the spinous or transverse processes, do not disrupt vertebral alignment, and do not cause spinal cord injury. The fractured bone is surgically repaired by fusion.

Compression Fracture

Flexion injuries to the vertebral column can compress the anterior portion of the vertebral body, causing a wedge or teardrop fracture (Figure 7-1). Compression forces may also cause a linear fracture. Surgical intervention is usually required because of the propensity for vertebral dislocation and displacement of the intervertebral disc.

Comminuted Fracture

Vertical forces brought upon the vertebral column can produce burst or blow-out fractures at any level. The bony portions of the vertebrae are shattered or fragmented, and pieces may be driven into the spinal cord.

Cervical Fractures

Several distinct types of fractures may occur in the cervical vertebrae predicated upon their anatomical characteristics. While not all cervical fractures require surgical intervention for stabilization, the large majority do. The extent to which the cervical spine is unstable contributes to the decision of whether an anterior or posterior surgical approach for fusion is required.

Jefferson's Fracture

This burst fracture occurs to the ring of the first cervical vertebra (the atlas). It often results from a fall in which the individual lands on the head. There may not be any neurological sequelae (Figure 7-2).

Spinal Cord Injuries 139

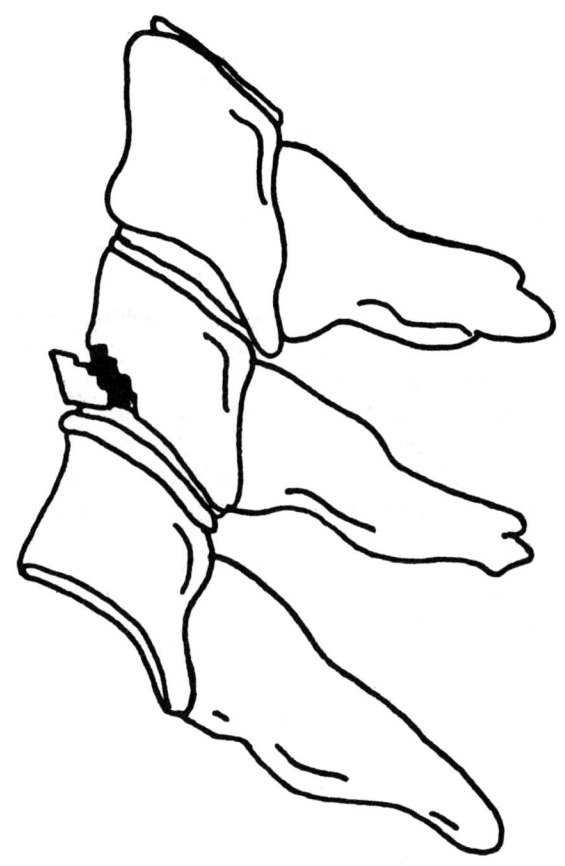

Figure 7-1 Teardrop or Wedge-Shaped Compression Fracture. *Source:* Reprinted from *Neurological Emergencies: Effective Nursing Care* by J. Raimond and J.W. Taylor, p. 218, Aspen Publishers, Inc., © 1986.

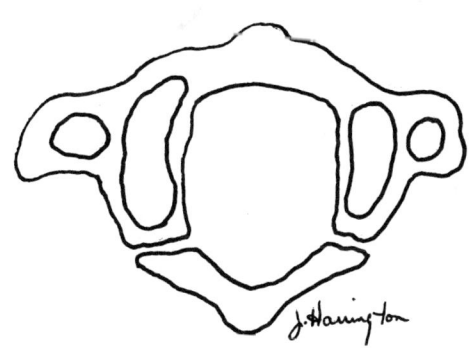

Figure 7-2 Jefferson Fracture of C1.

Hangman's Fracture

In a hangman's fracture the body of the second cervical vertebra (the axis) is separated from its posterior components (Figure 7-3). It is caused by severe hyperextension of the neck, which may result in subluxation onto the third cervical vertebra. This fracture can compress the spinal cord significantly enough to cause death almost immediately.

Odontoid Fracture

Trauma commonly results in fracture of the odontoid process of C2 (Figure 7-4). There may be transient or significant neurological deficits as a result. The relatively wide space at the top of the cervical canal often allows enough room for displacement of the fracture without impinging upon the cord. Severe displacement of the fractured bone can impinge upon the spinal cord and cause immediate death. Because of the location of the odontoid process at the base of the skull, fractures of this area may be missed unless open-mouth anteroposterior (AP) skull radiographs are taken.

Sacral and Coccygeal Fractures

Falls in which the victim lands on the buttocks can inflict trauma to the sacral and coccygeal vertebrae severe enough to cause compression fractures. The spinal

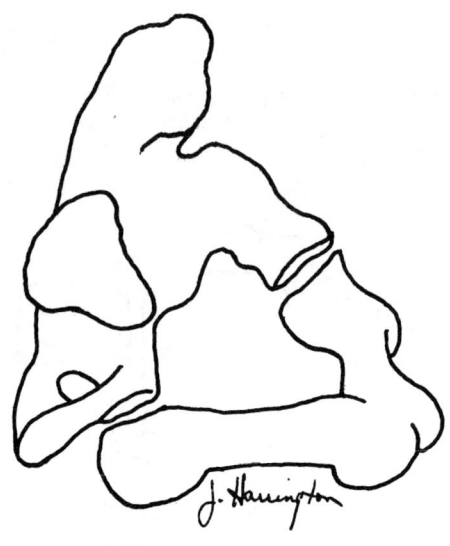

Figure 7-3 Hangman's Fracture of C2.

Figure 7-4 Fracture of Odontoid of C2.

cord itself is above this area and safe from direct injury, but it may receive indirect trauma. The sacral nerve roots, however, may incur injury. Bowel, bladder, and sexual function may be impaired due to injury of these nerves.

Dislocations

Dislocations of the articulating facets between the vertebrae can occur when there is injury to the supporting ligaments, causing the vertebral bodies to sublux on one another. Hyperextension injuries frequently involve the anterior longitudinal ligament, while hyperflexion injuries involve the posterior longitudinal ligament.

TYPES OF SPINAL CORD INJURY

The etiology of the injury and the degree of spinal cord impingement obviously contribute to the permanency and extent of any neurological deficits incurred. Sensory and motor system assessment is an important contribution in identifying the level of injury. Spine radiographs can reveal vertebral fractures. Flexion and extension views and fluoroscopy can reveal disrupted ligaments. Computed tomography (CT) scan, magnetic resonance imaging (MRI), and angiographic and myelographic procedures may all be necessary to determine the extent of spinal tissue trauma.

Spinal cord injuries may be classified according to whether upper or lower motor neurons are involved or according to extent of spinal cord compression.

Upper Motor Neuron Lesions

As discussed in Chapter 1, an upper motor neuron (UMN) lesion is one that affects the neuron at any point from the motor cortex of the frontal lobe down through the point at which it synapses with the lower motor neuron in the anterior horn of the specific spinal cord level. Upper motor neuron injuries are characterized by

- hypertonia (spasticity)
- hyperactive deep tendon reflexes (DTRs) (see Chapter 2)
- presence of Babinski's sign

Initially, UMN lesions present with flaccid paralysis secondary to spinal shock, which will become spastic over time.

Lower Motor Neuron Lesions

Lower motor neuron (LMN) lesions are those that occur to the neuron from its originating point in the anterior gray matter of the cord out through the point at which it synapses with the appropriate muscle fibers. LMN lesions are characterized by

- atonia (flaccidity) or hypotonia
- areflexia or hyporeflexia
- atrophy of muscles

When these lesions occur in the lumbar and sacral regions of the cord, bowel and bladder control may be permanently lost, and sexual function may be impaired.

Complete Spinal Cord Compression

Complete compression, sometimes referred to as transection, produces a functional disconnection between ascending and descending pathways in the spinal cord at the level of the injury. Three distinct features occur with complete transection: motor loss, sensory loss, and spinal shock. While each of these may occur with any injury to the cord, all three appear with complete compression.

1. Motor loss—Flaccid paralysis occurs at the level of injury and below it, secondary to spinal shock. Lesions in the cervical area result in varying degrees of tetraplegia, while injuries to the thoracic and lumbar areas result in some degree of paraplegia. Functional loss attributed to specific spinal cord segments is summarized in Table 7-1. The flaccid paralysis is eventually replaced by spastic paralysis as the LMNs below the level of injury become hyperactive from the loss of inhibition from UMNs. Hyperactivity in LMNs innervating visceral organs also occurs.
2. Sensory loss—All sensory modalities below the level of the injury that require communication with areas above the level of the injury are lost. The level of sensation perceived by the patient is a parameter to be assessed in the initial stages of the injury, as there is the potential for unstable injuries to ascend to higher levels of the spinal cord.
3. Spinal shock—This is a transient state that occurs when the cord is insulted or injured, with the subsequent loss of innervation to motor, sensory, and autonomic pathways below the level of the injury. Its onset is within an hour of injury, and its duration may be several days to one month. Resolving spinal shock is heralded by the onset of reflex activity below the level of the lesion, such as peristalsis, spasticity, or return of anal sphincter tone. Injuries above the level of T6 interrupt sympathetic nervous system outflow and can produce
    (a) hypotension from absent vasomotor tone
    (b) bradycardia
    (c) loss of body temperature control below the injury level
    (d) loss of normal perspiration below the level of the injury
    (e) initial retention of bladder and bowel contents
    (f) priapism (prolonged penile erection) in males

Incomplete Spinal Cord Compression

There are several syndromes that may occur when the functional disruption to the spinal cord is partial, or incomplete. The patient may present with some motor or sensory functions intact below the level of the injury, or the clinical presentation may be of complete flaccidity resulting from spinal shock. The presence of rectal sphincter tone and a bulbocavernosus reflex indicates that there is sacral sparing, or preservation of the more peripheral spinal cord tracts. Sacral sparing reflects partial compression of the spinal cord.

Anterior Cord Syndrome

Hyperflexion injuries, acutely herniated discs, or disruption of blood supply from the anterior spinal artery may produce anterior cord syndrome. The motor

Table 7-1 Functional Loss from Spinal Cord Injury

Segmental Level of Injury	Functional Loss	Rehabilitative Potential
Above C-3	Quadriplegia and total loss of respiratory function Risk of hypotension, hypothermia, ileus, and atonic bladder Sensory loss from neck down	Will be ventilator dependent unless phrenic nerve stimulator used Probably unable to survive with less than skilled nursing care
C-3 to C-4	Quadriplegia and may have loss of respiratory function due to edema involving phrenic nerves; may resolve with return of diaphragmatic breathing Risk of hypotension, hypothermia, ileus, and atonic bladder Sensory loss below clavicles	Can live in community with attendant; operate electric wheelchair with tongue switch; use adaptive tools held in mouth; may require intermittent ventilator; return of bowel and bladder reflexes can "trigger" bladder emptying
C-5 to C-6	Quadriplegia with partial function of shoulders and forearms Phrenic nerves intact, but not intercostals; will have diaphragmatic breathing Risk of hypotension, hypothermia, ileus, and atonic bladder Sensory loss below clavicles, but some arm sensation	Can operate electric wheelchair; needs assistance to transfer; return of bowel and bladder reflexes
C-6 to C-7	Quadriplegia (incomplete) with intact biceps but not triceps, partial wrist function Diaphragmatic breathing Risk of hypotension, hypothermia, ileus, and atonic bladder Sensory loss below clavicles and parts of arms	May be able to propel wheelchair; can drive car with quad controls; return of bowel and bladder reflexes
C-7 to C-8	Quadriplegia (incomplete) with biceps and triceps intact; limited function of hands Diaphragmatic breathing Risk of hypotension, hypothermia, ileus, and atonic bladder Sensory loss upper chest down and part of hands	Independent in transfers; can propel wheelchair; can drive car with quad controls; return of bowel and bladder reflexes
T-1 to L-2	Paraplegia with various amounts of intercostal and abdominal muscle function Risk of hypotension, hypothermia, ileus, and atonic bladder if injury above T-6 level	Completely independent in wheelchair; return of bladder and bowel reflexes; limited, difficult ambulation, with long leg braces, corset, and underarm crutches

Table 7-1 continued

Segmental Level of Injury	Functional Loss	Rehabilitative Potential
	Sensory loss depends on level: T-4 supplies nipple line; T-10 supplies umbilicus; T-12 supplies groin area; L-2 supplies upper thighs	
Below L-2	Paraplegia (incomplete) Various bowel and bladder dysfunctions Sensory loss depends on level: Lumbar: loss of sensation to upper legs, part of lower legs, feet, and ankles Sacral: loss of sensation from lower legs, feet, and perineum	Completely independent in wheelchair; varying ability to walk with braces; bladder remains areflexive if sacral segments involved

Source: Reprinted from *Neurological Emergencies: Effective Nursing Care* by J. Raimond and J.W. Taylor, pp. 223–224, Aspen Publishers, Inc., © 1986.

---

fibers are affected, producing paralysis below the injury level, as is the lateral spinothalamic tract (the sensory pathways for pain and temperature), which will also be lost below the level of injury. Functional improvement may occur with aggressive management of edema or prompt surgical decompression of a herniated disc.

Central Cord Syndrome

Hemorrhage, edema, or decreased blood flow impacting the central gray matter of the cervical spinal cord can produce central cord syndrome. The motor fibers most vulnerable are those of the corticospinal tract to the upper extremities. The patient will present with

- paresis or paralysis of the upper extremities of greater severity than the lower extremities
- varying sensory deficits
- varying degrees of bowel and bladder dysfunction

Aggressive management of the etiology of the injury may result in various degrees of function return.

Brown-Séquard Syndrome

Penetrating trauma injuries or invasive tumors can cause a transection of one half of the spinal cord, producing a Brown-Séquard syndrome. Clinical presentation demonstrates involvement of the corticospinal tract, the lateral spinothalamic tract, and the posterior columns, producing

- ipsilateral motor paralysis below the injury
- ipsilateral loss of proprioception below the injury
- contralateral loss of pain and temperature below the injury (This tract crosses soon after it enters the cord, so that fibers ascending on one side are carrying sensory input from the contralateral body.)

This syndrome is not frequently seen in its pure form; patients may display signs of Brown-Séquard mixed with signs of central cord syndrome. Aggressive treatment may allow some return of function.

Horner's Syndrome

Horner's syndrome deserves discussion because it may be seen in incomplete spinal cord transections that affect the chain of sympathetic neurons in the cervical area. Horner's syndrome is characterized by

- ipsilateral pupil smaller than contralateral one
- ipsilateral eyeball recession into its orbit
- ptosis of the ipsilateral eyelid
- ipsilateral loss of facial perspiration

MANAGEMENT OF SPINAL CORD INJURIES

Initial Management

Individuals suspected of having sustained a spinal cord injury should not be moved until the spine has been immobilized on a backboard by skilled personnel. Improper management of an unstable spine can precipitate or extend spinal cord injuries. Trauma patients are assumed to have a possible spinal cord injury until proved otherwise by diagnostic examination. Goals initially are to

- initiate resuscitation procedures if necessary (Jaw thrust maneuver should be used to open the airway of a victim suspected of having a cervical spine injury.)

- ensure an adequate airway
- assess and monitor vital signs, including neurological assessment of motor and sensory function
- assess and evaluate extent of other trauma
- stabilize and transport for diagnostic procedures, emergent surgical procedures

Acute Management

Patients with spinal cord injuries may have other major trauma as well, including head injury. Care of the patient with a spine injury revolves around maintaining an immobilized spine until the injury is stabilized or disproved and maintaining other body systems.

Monitoring the Level of Injury

Assessment of neurological status and level of injury is an ongoing process that includes use of the Glasgow Coma Scale (GCS) and evaluation of the neuromuscular function (see Chapter 2). The highest sensory level should be assessed frequently in the initial phase, and any upward progression should warrant immediate investigation for ascending injury. Examples of motor function and sensory innervation levels according to spinal cord segments are listed in Table 7-2.

Respiratory Management

The ability of the patient to breathe effectively will be determined in part by the level of the injury to the spinal cord. The presence of thoracic trauma will also be a contributing factor. Persons with lesions above C4 may suffer respiratory arrest

Table 7-2 Segmental Levels of Motor and Sensory Control

Level	Motor Function	Level	Sensory Innervation
C4-5	Shoulder shrug	C5	Clavicle
C5-6	Elbow flexion	C6	Thumb
C7-8	Elbow extension	C8	Fourth and fifth digits
T1-7	Intercostal muscles	T4	Nipple line
T6-12	Abdominal muscles contract	T10	Umbilicus
L1-3	Hip flexion	L1-4	Inner and anterior thigh surfaces
L2-4	Knee extension	L4-5	Great toe
S1-2	Foot extension	L5-S2	Outer and posterior thigh surfaces
S3-5	Anal sphincter	S3-5	Perineal sensation

and will need nasotracheal intubation or emergency tracheostomy to maintain respiratory function. The neck must remain in a neutral and fixed position during intubation to avoid extension of the injury.

Diaphragmatic motor innervation by the phrenic nerve is intact in lesions at C4 and below; intercostal muscles are innervated by levels T1-7; patients with injuries in these regions may need varied respiratory support. Lesions in the regions of T7-12 affect the abdominal musculature, which is necessary to produce effective coughing.

Mechanical ventilation is frequently required in the initial stages of management. Patients with injuries at C4 and below are more easily weaned than patients with lesions above that level. Breathing exercises in the form of incentive spirometry should begin immediately to facilitate diaphragm and rib-cage excursions.

Routine pulmonary hygiene for patients with lesions above T6 should be an ongoing intervention. Frequently it is necessary to employ the help of a second person in providing postural drainage and chest percussion and vibration to these patients. The assisted cough technique (Heimlich maneuver) can facilitate movement of secretions from the lower lung bases. This technique can be performed by exerting positive pressure at the level of the diaphragm as the patient attempts to cough.

Immobilization

After radiographic confirmation, unstable injuries from the C1 through T1 region are placed in cervical traction to provide stability to the vertebral column. The type of cervical tongs used with the traction apparatus often depends on physician preference. Types of cervical tongs available include Gardner-Wells, Barton, Crutchfield, and Trippi-Wells. Regardless of the particular type of tongs applied, the pin sites must be cleaned daily and assessed for signs of infection.

As a general rule, 5 lb of traction weight is applied for each level involved. Flexion and extension radiographs of the cervical area may be obtained after traction application and as follow-up several weeks postinjury.

It may be the preference of a particular institution to place a patient in cervical tongs in a specialized bed to help minimize complications of prolonged bed rest. Such beds include a Stryker frame, and CircOelectric, Roto-rest, low air loss, as well as kinetic beds. Patients in cervical traction can be safely cared for in a conventional hospital bed with properly applied traction.

Fractures of the thoracic and lumbar spine are managed with strict bed rest. Two persons should assist the patient to log roll from side to side every two hours to prevent pulmonary complications and pressure ulcer development. Patients in cervical traction should not be turned or moved by less than three people: one to move and to maintain the traction, one at the shoulders, and one at the hips.

Surgical intervention may be indicated to

- debride penetrating injuries
- decompress the spinal cord
- place Harrington rods or other stabilizing hardware
- fuse the involved areas, if indicated

A halo apparatus may be necessary following surgical fusion, and it may need to remain in place for several weeks to months to maximize bone healing. The halo frame is anchored with pins to the skull table and is stabilized by vertical and horizontal metal posts that attach to a hard plastic vest, which is lined with sheepskin. This apparatus prevents flexion, extension, and rotational movements of the neck while allowing the patient mobility. It is important to note that the patient should not be turned or mobilized by using the halo frame, metal stabilizing bars, or vest, as doing so may disrupt the pin alignment. The patient and halo apparatus should be moved together.

Patients with cervical spine injuries whose operative approach was anteriorly should be monitored closely postoperatively for respiratory compromise due to surgical manipulation of neck structures and swelling.

General Considerations

The following general considerations should be kept in mind when caring for patients with spinal cord injuries:

- Spinal cord edema—The use of high-dose corticosteroids to control spinal cord edema is controversial. More information on steroids can be found in Chapter 6. Mannitol may also be administered to facilitate extracellular diuresis but should be avoided in the presence of hypovolemic shock.
- Fluid replacement and electrolyte balance—The patient with a spinal cord injury may need volume replacement and electrolyte management due to shock. Adequate volume replacement is also necessary to promote sputum production and bladder and bowel function. Care must be taken not to overhydrate, which can lead to pulmonary edema. It is not unusual for patients with a cervical injury to have baseline blood pressures of 100/70 mm Hg. The tetraplegic patient without parenteral fluids may need particular attention to fluid intake. Antibiotic therapy may be indicated if penetrating injuries occurred to any body system.
- Gastrointestinal (GI) motility—A paralytic ileus can be expected due to the onset of spinal shock. Insertion of a nasogastric tube to suction is indicated to minimize gastric distention and vomiting, as well as to prevent decreases in diaphragmatic excursion.

- Bladder function—Urinary retention will occur as the bladder is rendered flaccid from the spinal shock. An indwelling catheter should be inserted as soon as possible to prevent bladder distention and subsequent stretching of receptors within the bladder wall. Continued bladder wall stretching will interfere with future rehabilitative interventions for bladder training.
- Traction care—The entry sites to the skull for the cervical traction and halo brace apparatus should be assessed daily for signs of infection and cleansed with saline or half-strength hydrogen peroxide. The halo vest apparatus is equipped with buckles just below the clavicular and suprascapular areas, and on either side. Release of the buckles provides access to the chest and back for skin cleansing and inspection.

Trimming of the hard plastic vest at areas where it presses into the skin and/or extra padding placed at the edges of the vest are measures which can prevent skin breakdown. It is recommended that patients in a halo device have a wrench attached to the jacket to release the vertical stabilizing bars in the event chest access is necessary (cardiopulmonary resuscitation [CPR]).

SECONDARY PROBLEMS

The physiological response of the body to spinal cord injuries produces changes in all body systems. Some of the changes may not be apparent for weeks postinjury and thus may not be considered in the ICU setting. Anticipating the changes that occur can help prevent them from becoming major management concerns at a future date.

Altered Respiratory Function

Loss of or decreased intercostal and abdominal muscle function places the patient at increased risk for atelectasis and pneumonia due to decreased lung expansion and ineffective cough. Scheduled pulmonary hygiene protocols individualized to patient needs requires prompt initiation. Regular monitoring of tidal volumes, vital capacities, and blood gases may be indicated.

Cardiovascular Alterations

Spinal shock induces loss of vasomotor control in injuries above T6 and subsequent hypotension, which usually responds to volume. Again, caution must be used when administering volume because of the potential for overhydrating the patient and producing pulmonary edema. Vasopressor drugs may be necessary initially to maintain blood pressure. Orthostatic hypotension may continue to occur when the patient is placed in a sitting from a recumbent position and tends to be most severe in patients who have been recumbent for long time periods and who have incurred cervical cord injuries.

Gradual increases in the head of the bed level, once the spinal injury is stabilized, will facilitate adjustment to decreased or absent vasomotor tone. The use of elastic wraps to the legs, special-order stockings, and abdominal binders will facilitate venous return in patients prone to hypotension. Orthostatic blood pressures should be monitored when mobilizing these patients.

The same interruption in sympathetic outflow that causes hypotension also causes bradycardia. Impaired gas exchange and low body temperatures may potentiate the bradycardia and require intervention with atropine.

Immobility, decreased venous return, and loss of muscle tone place the spinal cord-injured patient at high risk for developing deep vein thromboses (DVT) and possibly pulmonary emboli. Calf assessment for swelling and redness should be part of the patient's daily routine. Low-dose heparin subcutaneously (SC) is used as prophylactic therapy in some institutions as well as antiembolic stockings and external vascular compression therapy to the legs.

Bladder and Bowel Alterations

Bladder dysfunction due to injuries of the nervous system are referred to as neurogenic bladders. Injuries above the sacral level produce a hypertonic or spastic UMN bladder; the spinal reflexes modulating bladder function are left intact but no longer have higher cortical control. The onset of spinal shock in complete cord transections will initially produce atonic bladders in these injuries. Sacral lesions affecting the LMNs innervating the bladder produce atonic bladders. Variations of both UMN and LMN bladders may be seen due to trauma to the UMN and LMN units or pre-existing disease states.

Intermittent catheterization of the spinal cord-injured patient should begin as soon as medical stability is established and there is no longer a need for large volumes of intravenous (IV) fluids; it need not wait until spinal shock has resolved. The increased incidence of urinary infections with indwelling catheters is an added problem this patient population does not need.

Patients with atonic bladders are usually well managed on intermittent catheterization programs. Depending upon the level of the injury, self-catheterization may be appropriate.

Patients with LMN cord lesions who have some bladder function intact may learn to empty their bladder by the Credé method, in which pressure is applied to the external bladder wall and a Valsalva's maneuver is performed to stimulate bladder emptying. The administration of bethanechol chloride (Urecholine) to potentiate bladder contraction and sphincter relaxation is often used in this population. Catheterization for postvoid residuals should accompany the initial phase of bladder management to ensure adequate bladder emptying.

Patients with spastic bladders have intact spinal reflex arcs to initiate bladder emptying but lack voluntary control when the bladder empties. Stimuli to the bladder wall often cause bladder emptying before it reaches normal capacity. The administration of propantheline bromide (Pro-Banthine) may help to decrease the frequency of this reflex and to facilitate development of an appropriate bladder-voiding regimen. Patients soon become aware of common physiological signs of a full bladder (sweating, distended abdomen) and can use physical stimuli to trigger bladder emptying, such as

- stroking the inner thigh, lower abdomen, or genital areas
- pulling pubic hair
- digital stimulation of the anus

Urodynamic studies prior to initiation of a bladder program will identify bladder dynamics present to establish an appropriate bladder program. Close attention to fluid intake and urine output is necessary to assist the patient in developing a bladder program that will meet individualized needs. If more than 500 mL of urine is drained at any time, the frequency of intermittent catheterization should be increased or fluid intake decreased. Large volumes of urine will contribute to stretching of volume receptors in the bladder, requiring larger volumes to trigger emptying and setting the stage for infections from urinary stasis.

Gastric motility is usually hypoactive initially, and a paralytic ileus should always be suspected. Once the ileus is resolved, bowel motility will return. It may be a week or so before normal bowel activity resumes. Patients with sacral sparing will be continent of feces. Patients with complete cord lesions or lesions of the conus medullaris will not be continent. Bowel programs involving high fiber, adequate fluid intake, exercise, stool softeners, scheduled suppository instillation, and digital stimulation are very effective in establishing a predictable pattern of bowel elimination.

Autonomic Dysreflexia

Also known as autonomic hyper-reflexia, or mass reflex, autonomic dysreflexia can occur in patients with lesions above the level of T6 after resolution of spinal shock and constitutes a medical emergency. Spinal shock begins within the hour following injury and usually persists for several days but may persist for several weeks. Noxious sensory stimulation of receptor sites below the level of the injury causes reflex stimulation of the autonomic nervous system: the sympathetic nervous system elicits a mass discharge of reflex activity, and the parasympathetic inhibition is lost due to the level of the injury.

The mass sympathetic reflex causes vasoconstriction below the level of the injury, resulting in hypertension. The increased blood pressure produces a pounding headache; vasodilation above the injury level produces facial and truncal flushing, vascular engorgement of head and neck vessels, and nasal congestion. Vagal stimulation initiates bradycardia, and sweating occurs above the level of the injury. Left untreated, the consequences of autonomic dysreflexia include seizures, stroke, myocardial infarction, and death. Potentiators of autonomic dysreflexia include

- distended bladder or urinary tract infection
- fecal impaction
- skin irritations (pressure sores, wrinkled clothing, ingrown toenails, localized infections)
- uterine contractions during labor

If experiencing autonomic dysreflexia, the patient should not be left alone, and interventions should be instituted immediately. Common interventions for this situation are as follows:

- Place the patient in bed in an upright sitting position.
- Monitor blood pressure.
- Assess for a distended bladder and catheterize; lubrication of the catheter with a topical anesthetic such as lidocaine is recommended to prevent further sympathetic stimulation. If an indwelling catheter is in place, assess for patency. Gentle instillation of 30 to 50 mL of saline should clear the catheter if it is clogged. No more than 500 mL of urine should be drained at one time to prevent additional sympathetic stimulation. Some institutions advocate instillation of tetracaine into the bladder after it has drained and the blood pressure is down to prevent the bladder from going into contractions and reinitiating the dysreflexia.
- If the bladder is not the cause, next suspect the bowel. A topical anesthetic agent should be inserted prior to rectal disimpaction to prevent sympathetic stimulation caused by the digital stimulation.
- When bladder and bowel fullness are ruled out as causes, the next suspicious area should be the skin.

Drug therapy will be instituted if symptoms do not subside with the above interventions, and some institutions possess standing protocols for drugs to be administered. Among the pharmacological agents used are the following:

- Hydralazine (Apresoline)—10–20 mg IV push
- Ganglionic blocking agents—may be given orally on a scheduled routine to patients predisposed to frequent episodes of autonomic dysreflexia; such agents are phenoxybenzamine (Dibenzyline), mecamylamine (Inversine), and guanethidine sulfate (Ismelin).

Care must be taken not to overmedicate the patient; should the cause be relieved with antihypertensive agents on board, the patient is at risk for profound hypotension. Patients at risk for autonomic dysreflexia should be taught early about the signs and symptoms signaling an episode. Family and/or other care providers need to learn management interventions because of the possible sequelae if left untreated.

Alteration in Body Temperature Control

Interruption of the sympathetic pathways results in the loss of appropriate sweating and vasodilation below the level of the injury. Subsequent to this, the body is unable to regulate body temperature below the level of the injury. The body temperature approaches that of the surrounding environment, potentially exposing the patient to hypothermia. Interventions include

- providing adequate warmth while hospitalized, and teaching the patient to do the same when discharged
- avoiding becoming overheated

Alteration in Tissue Integrity

Perhaps the most important information the spinal cord-injured patient will learn during recovery and rehabilitation will be that of skin care. Development of pressure sores puts added stress on the patient and is extremely time consuming and costly to treat. Loss of innervation to tissue causes them to break down more easily and to heal much more slowly than innervated tissues.

Position changes every one to two hours, or more often as the patient desires, are a major preventive factor in preventing pressure ulcer formation. Other preventive measures that can be instituted to minimize the likelihood of pressure sores include

- protective foot and elbow coverings
- foam, water, low air-loss or air-fluidized bed therapies
- maintenance of clean and dry skin surfaces
- use of a minimal number of wrinkle-free linens on the bed

- avoiding use of incontinence pads directly beneath the skin
- adequate nutrition
- application of products to the skin that enhance skin toughening as opposed to skin softening
- early involvement of the patient in directing care
- use of specialized pressure-relief cushions in wheelchairs
- teaching patient to inspect skin daily with a hand mirror or to direct another to do it if unable
- teaching patient to change own position frequently whether in bed or in wheelchair

Musculoskeletal Alterations

A physical therapy consult should be initiated during the acute phase to identify a physiotherapy program specific to the neurological level of the individual; the program is advanced as the patient advances from the acute stage. The physical therapy program will include evaluation of the muscle power of which the patient is capable as well as muscle strengthening and stretching exercises and breathing exercises. Predicated upon the level of injury, the therapist can make recommendations for devices such as wheelchairs, pressure-relief cushions, foot splints, and braces that will serve to optimize the functional capabilities of the patient.

Occupational therapy should also be consulted during the acute phase of the injury. The focus of the occupational therapist is to devise an individualized occupational therapy program to help the patient become as independent as possible in the activities of self-care: toileting, hygiene, dressing, homemaking, and eating. The work of the occupational therapist will also help prepare the individual to function within the community and to pursue personal, educational, and vocational goals.

Sexuality

As a general rule the patient with a spinal cord injury is ready to discuss the impact of the injury on sexual functioning when he or she begins to ask relevant questions. Being alert to leading queries posed by the patient and providing honest answers is definitely the best policy. Referral to skilled counselors whose expertise is rehabilitation or sexual counseling is appropriate once the patient displays interest.

Sacral spinal levels control sexual function. Males with UMN lesions are capable of reflex penile erections, although they may not all accomplish coitus. Males with LMN lesions to the sacral area are not capable of reflex erections but may have psychogenic erections. Ejaculation is variable with both reflexogenic and psychogenic erections. Fertility in males with spinal cord injuries is generally impaired. Males and females with complete spinal cord injuries lack perineal sensation regardless of the lesion location.

Females with UMN spinal cord injuries will experience reflex clitoral engorgement and vaginal lubrication with genital stimulation. LMN injuries in women will require the use of alternative lubricants during coitus. Since the female reproductive system is not affected by the injury, these women can become pregnant and can deliver children.

NOTE

1. Therese S. Richmond. "The Patient with a Cervical Spinal Cord Injury." *Focus on Critical Care* 12 (April 1985), 23–33.

SUGGESTED READINGS

Bell, JoAnn, and Kathleen Hannon. "Pathophysiology Involved in Autonomic Dysreflexia." *Journal of Neuroscience Nursing* 18(1986):86–89.

Blazier, Carol J., Mark N. Hadley, and Robert F. Spetzler. "The Transoral Surgical Approach to Craniovertebral Pathology." *Journal of Neuroscience Nursing* 18(1986):57–62.

Browner, Carol M., Mark N. Hadley, Volker K.H. Sonntag, and L. George Mattingly. "Halo Immobilization Brace Care: An Innovative Approach." *Journal of Neuroscience Nursing* 19(1987): 24–29.

Buchanon, Lorraine E, and Deborah A. Nawoczenski, eds. *Spinal Cord Injury: Concepts and Management*. Baltimore: Williams and Wilkins, 1987.

Goddard, Leslie R. "Sexuality and Spinal Cord Injury." *Journal of Neuroscience Nursing* 20(1988): 240–244.

Hickey, Joanne. *The Clinical Practice of Neurological and Neurosurgical Nursing*. Philadelphia: J.B. Lippincott, 1981.

Kastrup, Erwin K., ed. *Drug Facts and Comparisons*. Philadelphia: J.B. Lippincott, 1987.

Pettibone, Kristine A. "Management of Spasticity in Spinal Cord Injury: Nursing Concerns." *Journal of Neuroscience Nursing* 20(1988):217–222.

Raimond, Jeanne, and Joyce Waterman Taylor. *Neurological Emergencies: Effective Nursing Care*. Rockville, MD: Aspen Publishers, 1986.

Richmond, Therese S., and Judith Metcalf. "Psychosocial Responses to Spinal Cord Injury." *Journal of Neuroscience Nursing* 18(1986):183–187.

Ropper, Allan H., Sean Kennedy, and Nicholas T. Zervas. *Neurological and Neurosurgical Intensive Care*. Rockville, MD: Aspen Publishers, 1983.

Rudy, Ellen B. *Advanced Neurological and Neurosurgical Nursing*. St. Louis: Mosby, 1984.

Taylor, Joyce Waterman, and Sally Ballenger. *Neurological Dysfunction and Nursing Intervention*. New York: McGraw-Hill, 1980.

Zejdlik, Cynthia M. *Management of Spinal Cord Injuries*. Belmont, CA: Wadsworth, Inc, 1983.

8
Central Nervous System Neoplasms

The Association for Brain Tumor Research estimates that 25,000 to 30,000 new cases of brain tumors are diagnosed each year in the United States.[1] These figures represent both primary tumors and metastases to the central nervous system (CNS). Primary CNS tumors rarely metastasize outside the CNS, but "seeding" of tumor cells throughout the CNS occurs through blood and cerebrospinal fluid (CSF) circulation; metastasis to the CNS from other primary sites is not uncommon.

Accurate statistics for the frequency of CNS tumors are unavailable, but rough estimations are included. The prognosis for survival depends on the type of tumor, its cellular differentiation, its responsiveness to radiation therapy and effective chemotherapeutic agents, as well as to its location within the CNS.

Critical care nurses are apt to encounter these patients postoperatively, when mass effect from the tumor growth produces neurological deterioration or when obstructive processes caused by the tumor give rise to increased intracranial pressure (ICP).

CLASSIFICATION OF CNS TUMORS

There exists a number of different reference systems for tumors of the CNS. The least confusing is reference to tumors predicated upon the anatomical or cellular origin.

- Intracerebral versus extracerebral—differentiating tumors based on whether they occur within the cerebral parenchyma or outside it
- Primary versus secondary—differentiating tumors based on whether the primary site is within the CNS or a metastasis from another body site
- Childhood versus adult onset—Some tumor types occur more frequently in children than adults (eg, medulloblastoma) and vice versa.

- Histology—the use of the terms "malignant" and "benign" to describe the biological characteristics of the tumor. In CNS tumors, even neoplasms considered histologically benign may become malignant by virtue of their location.
- Supratentorial versus infratentorial—refers to whether the tumor is located above or below the tentorium. Infratentorial tumors are also referred to as posterior fossa tumors.
- Extradural versus intradural—refers to spinal tumors and their location outside or inside of the dural layer of the meninges
- Cellular or anatomical origin—probably the most descriptive definition of CNS tumors. The cellular or anatomical basis for the neoplasm is used to describe the particular tumor growth. The ensuing description of CNS tumors is predicated on this reference methodology.

CLINICAL PRESENTATION

The focal symptoms demonstrated by patients with CNS tumors is predicated upon the location of the tumor. The degree to which the patient is symptomatic depends upon the site of the neoplasm, the presence of concomitant problems, and the extent of mass effect (the amount of compression and structural shifting caused by the tumor bulk).

Supratentorial Tumor Symptoms

The majority of tumors seen in adults occurs in the supratentorial region. This incorporates the anterior and middle fossae contents: both cerebral hemispheres and deep cortical structures.

Headache

Headache described as being of moderate severity and usually in the frontal area is experienced by some. Tumor headaches are not relieved by aspirin or acetaminophen. They tend to be more severe upon arising due to pressure on the dura from being in a recumbent position.

Papilledema

Often associated with visual field defects, diplopia, and decreased visual acuity, papilledema is seen in about three fourths of patients with supratentorial tumors.

Seizures

Seizure activity may be the initial symptom, in some patients, of a brain tumor. Compression of cortical areas by the growing mass acts as an epileptogenic foci.

Changes in Mentation or Personality

Lesions of the frontal lobe may produce changes in intellectual function and personality characteristics that produce a profound impact on the patient's activities of daily living. The patient frequently does not recognize or will not admit to the changes; physician referral is often made at the insistence of a family member.

Motor and Sensory Dysfunction

Lesions affecting the frontal lobe or other components of the motor system are displayed by weakness or paralysis of motor function. Sensory alterations can be caused by lesions in the parietal and temporal lobes and by the involvement of cranial nerves.

Endocrine Abnormalities

Tumors of the pituitary gland or affecting the hypothalamic-pituitary axis may create myriad endocrine abnormalities. Some of these might include

- acromegaly
- Cushing's syndrome
- amenorrhea
- loss of libido
- impotence
- diabetes insipidus
- glycosuria
- the visual field defect of bitemporal hemianopsia

Infratentorial Tumor Symptoms

Infratentorial tumors are those that occur in the region beneath the tentorium cerebelli, which constitutes the posterior fossa. The focal signs and symptoms displayed reflect the anatomical structures in this area: the brain stem and cerebellum.

Ataxia

Difficulty walking and making coordinated movements can be produced by lesions in or compressing the cerebellum.

Cranial Nerve Dysfunction

Deficits with cranial nerves coming off the brain stem may be caused by compression of the peripheral portion of the nerve or by compression or infiltration of its corresponding nucleus in the brain stem. Some of the deficits that might be demonstrated include

- paresis or paralysis of extraocular movements (EOMs)
- impaired facial sensation
- facial muscle weakness
- hearing deficits
- dysphagia
- hoarseness

Nausea and Vomiting

Compression of the reflex center in the medulla may cause vomiting. It frequently occurs in the morning, is totally unrelated to food intake, may be projectile, and may or may not be accompanied by nausea.

Altered Level of Consciousness

Compression of the fibers that constitute the reticular activating system (RAS) can disrupt the ability of this system to maintain a conscious state, causing the patient to present as lethargic or even obtunded.

Symptoms Based on Mass Effect

Tumor mass, hydrocephalus from obstructed CSF flow, cerebral edema, and hemorrhage of the neoplasm all can contribute to increased ICP.

IDENTIFIED RISK FACTORS

As with other types of malignancies, certain agents have been identified as possible risk factors in the development of brain tumors.

- chemical carcinogens
- familial predisposition

- drugs and immunosuppression
- infectious agents
- radiation

Diagnosis

Diagnosis of a CNS tumor is predicated upon the following (plus other diagnostic studies may be indicated):

- history
- neurological examination
- diagnostic studies
  1. computed tomography (CT) scan
  2. lumbar puncture
  3. magnetic resonance imaging (MRI)
  4. myelogram
  5. angiogram
  6. electroencephalogram (EEG)
  7. endocrine studies
  8. ophthalmology and audiology studies
  9. biopsy

INTRACRANIAL TUMORS

Discussion of all CNS tumors that occur is beyond the scope of this text; discussion will focus on the more commonly found tumors within the cranial cavity and spinal canal.

Glial Cell Tumors

Glial cell tumors refer to aberrant growth of the tissues that provide structure and nourishment for the neurons. Glial tumors in general tend to be destructive tumors that infiltrate (except for ependymomas) the brain parenchyma; they represent about 50% of all CNS neoplasms. The infiltrating nature of glial tumors contributes to their being regarded as malignant.

A grading system widely accepted for identifying glial tumors was developed in 1949 by Kernohan and associates.[2] This system classifies glial tumors according to growth rate and the ability to differentiate them from normal cells. Grades I and

II tend to be slow growing tumors that are considered mildly malignant, although they have the propensity to convert to a more malignant form within three to five years after presentation.[3] Grades III and IV are considered highly malignant tumors with rapid growth rates. Each tumor may contain several different cell types. The various types of glial tumors are described below.

- Astrocytomas
  1. Arise from the astrocyte cells
  2. Graded on a scale of I to IV, with grades I and II being fair to good cellular differentiation. Grades III to IV are poorly differentiated cells; tumors of this type are referred to as glioblastoma multiforme, an extremely malignant tumor.
  3. Clinical presentation depends upon the location of the tumor.
  4. Tend to be found in the frontal, parietal, and temporal lobes of adults
  5. Grades I and II are treated with partial surgical resection, which may be necessary to repeat at a future date.
     (a) Complete resection is usually not possible due to the infiltrating characteristics of the tumor.
     (b) Radiation therapy may not be advised unless there is obvious tumor residual, as the risks of radiation necrosis may outweigh any benefit of the radiation at this point.
     (c) The life span after treatment averages seven years or longer.
  6. Glioblastoma multiforme is a rapidly growing malignancy with an average prognosis of twelve to eighteen months.
  7. Glioblastoma multiforme tumors are very vascular due to the collateral blood flow they develop for nourishment, and hemorrhaging with necrosis of the tumor bed is common.
  8. Partial surgical excision with decompression of necrotic areas is often indicated to relieve the structural compression they produce.
  9. Radiation therapy and chemotherapy are indicated to suppress neoplastic growth.
- Oligodendrogliomas
  1. Arise from oligodendrocytes near the basal ganglia and extend along the myelinated fibers.
  2. Also graded on a I to IV system.
  3. Tend to be slow growing and well demarcated.
  4. Found throughout the cerebrum.
  5. Clinical presentation depends on the location of the tumor.
  6. Treatment involves surgical resection with radiation therapy if the resection was partial. Oligodendrogliomas tend to be very responsive to radiation.
  7. The life span after treatment may surpass five to seven years.

- Ependymomas
  1. Develop from the ependymal cell layer that gives rise to the ventricular system.
  2. Found more frequently in children and young adults and can be graded as being I to IV on a cellular differentiation basis.
  3. Growth of these tumors can rapidly obstruct the CSF circulation, producing increased ICP through obstructive hydrocephalus. Insertion of a ventriculoperitoneal or ventriculoatrial shunt is often necessary to decrease increased ICP prior to treating the tumor.
  4. May be inaccessible surgically due to their location within the ventricular system
  5. Do not respond very well to radiation
  6. The average life span may be five or more years.
  A variety of other tumors may arise in the ventricular areas and include
  1. papillomas of the choroid plexus
  2. colloid cysts
  3. invasion from outside growths such as other gliomas or pineal tumors
- Mixed Gliomas
  1. Defined as involvement of more than one cell type.
  2. Clinical presentation depends upon the location of the neoplasm.
  3. Treatment aimed at the predominant cell type present. The presence of astrocytoma cells grades III to IV signals a poor prognostic outcome.
  4. Surgical resection and radiation therapy indicated.

Meningiomas

The following information is descriptive of the meningioma:

- These are benign tumors that arise from the meningeal layers of the CNS. They are extracerebral, do not invade brain tissues, but can compress anatomical structures.
- A meningioma is an encapsulated, slow-growing tumor, which accounts for it often becoming a sizable mass before the patient is symptomatic.
- Women after the age of 50 years appear to be more likely to present with a meningioma.
- The tumor may be found anywhere along the meninges. Frequent sites of occurrence are the convexities of the frontal and parietal lobes, the sphenoid wing, olfactory grooves, cerebellopontine angle, and the spinal canal.
- The presenting symptoms will localize the tumor site.
- The capsule in which the meningioma is enclosed facilitates complete resection during surgery. Location of the meningioma may preclude complete

resection because of the risk to surrounding structures and may necessitate repeat resection at a later date.
- The prognosis is usually excellent with these tumors.

Meningeal metastases may occur from other primary sites both within and outside the CNS. Examples of neoplasms that metastasize to the meninges include

- sarcomas
- melanomas
- lymphomas
- gliomas
- leukemias

Diagnosis is made through examination of CSF cells. Treatment may include surgery, radiation, and chemotherapy.

Pineal Tumors

The following information is descriptive of pineal tumors:

- These tumors may arise from the cells of the pineal gland itself (pinealomas), from embryonic tissue (germinomas, teratomas), or from glial cells (gliomas).
- The patient may present only with symptoms of increased ICP or may display the inability to move the eyes to look upward; patient may have pupils that react to accommodation but not light.
- This latter symptom is caused by the hydrocephalic pressures placed on the midbrain.
- Treatment consists of surgical biopsy or resection and radiation therapy.

Acoustic Neuroma

The following information is descriptive of the acoustic neuroma:

- Arises from Schwann's cell sheaths that encase cranial and spinal nerves. The tumor is more accurately described as a schwannoma.
- An encapsulated tumor, it can reach the size of a chestnut before the patient becomes symptomatic.

- Proximity of the eighth cranial nerve to others in the pontine area (trigeminal, facial, glossopharyngeal, and vagus) is such that dysfunctions of these cranial nerves may occur in addition to the acoustic nerve deficits.
- May compress the cerebellum.
- Treatment is surgical excision, either complete or partial. When less-than-complete excision occurs, the tumor will return.

Other tumors that may occur in this area, referred to as the cerebellopontine angle, include

- meningiomas
- gliomas
- neuromas associated with neurofibromatosis (von Recklinghausen's disease)

Medulloblastoma

The following information is descriptive of medulloblastomas:

- More common in young children, medulloblastomas are seen in adolescents and young adults.
- Arise from the anterior portion of the cerebellum and roof of the fourth ventricle. The exact cellular origin is not known, and it is included here as an embryonic tumor.
- Can rapidly obstruct the fourth ventricle and seed into other ventricles via CSF flow. As with ependymomas, a ventricular shunting procedure is usually indicated.
- Treatment is surgical resection with radiation and chemotherapy. These tumors tend to be fairly responsive to radiation.
- The average life span after treatment may surpass five to seven years.

Sella and Parasellar Tumors

Sella and parasellar tumors include meningiomas, gliomas, pituitary tumors, and craniopharyngiomas (the latter two of which are described below).

- Pituitary tumors
  1. Arise from the cellular tissue of the gland
  2. Usually a benign tumor

3. Clinically demonstrated by headache in the frontal/orbital area, visual disturbances, and endocrine dysfunction
4. Classified as secreting or nonsecreting tumors
5. Depending upon the tumor histology, the individual may present with symptoms of hypopituitarism, Cushing's syndrome, or acromegaly
6. Approached surgically through a transsphenoidal or subfrontal craniotomy approach
7. Patient may be a candidate for proton-beam therapy if the tumor is small and contained within the sella. This type of radiation therapy allows low doses of focused radiation to be delivered to specific target areas.
- Craniopharyngiomas
    1. Arise from squamous epithelial cells at the junction of the pituitary gland and the infundibular stalk, which connects the gland with the hypothalamus
    2. Tend to grow upward out of the sella turcica, impinging on the optic chiasm, the pituitary gland, and the third ventricle
    3. Treatment is surgical excision through a transsphenoidal or subfrontal craniotomy approach.
    4. The tumor cells are very responsive to radiation therapy.

SPINAL CANAL TUMORS

Tumors of the spinal canal occur much less frequently than intracranial tumors and are much more commonly seen in adults. Spinal tumors are referred to as extradural or intradural. If a spinal tumor is intradural, it is further categorized as being intramedullary or extramedullary

- Intramedullary—originating within the cord
- Extramedullary—originating outside the cord but within the dura

About three fourths of spinal canal tumors are primary tumors; the remaining fourth that occur are metastases or intraspinous extension from primary sites in other parts of the body.

Extradural Spinal Tumors

These epidural tumors originate between the periosteum and the dura, develop in the surrounding bone, and destroy it. Examples of tumors that occur in this region include

- meningiomas
- neurofibromas
- hemangiomas
- metastases from primary sites in the breast, lung, and prostate

Clinical indicators of spinal canal tumors include

- constant pain
- motor weakness or paralysis
- sensory alterations
- possible bladder and/or anal sphincter abnormalities

Surgical treatment is aimed at relieving spinal cord compression, stabilizing the vertebral column, and preserving as much function as possible. Radiation and chemotherapy may be indicated, depending upon the type of tumor.

Intradural Spinal Tumors

Intradural tumors originate from the inner surfaces of the dura mater or the spinal nerve roots. Gliomas, ependymomas, and lipomas are examples of intradural tumors. Clinical symptoms and treatment are the same as for extradural tumors.

MANAGEMENT CONCERNS

Deciding upon the most appropriate form of treatment for brain and spinal cord tumors is dependent, obviously, on the biopsy results. Postoperatively patients with brain tumors are not usually very ill, unless they demonstrate advanced progression of the neoplasm or have concomitant systemic disease. The major concern in the acute postoperative period is to manage increased intracranial pressure, if present (see Chapter 4). Patients with surgery of the posterior fossa are more prone to develop acute, increased ICP and respiratory difficulties due to the space limitations of the area.

Patients who have had decompressive surgery for spinal cord tumors may require immobilization postoperatively, depending upon the type and extent of the pathology. These patients may complain of severe pain and muscle spasm following surgery due to the manipulation of muscles during the intraoperative period.

The lengthy operative time many neurosurgical procedures require places the patient at risk for impaired tissue integrity over bony prominences. The patient should be assessed postoperatively for signs of pressure on prominent bony joints, and interventions should be instituted immediately.

Wound Management

Craniotomy sites need to be assessed daily for signs of infection. Cleansing with hydrogen peroxide and normal saline can facilitate the removal of bacteria at the incision site. The removal of hair for the surgery may be a source of body image disturbance for the patient. Roomy elastic stocking caps and large kerchiefs can be stylishly worn to minimize this discomfort.

Spinal surgical incisions also need to be monitored daily for signs of infection. The patient may have some type of drainage device (Jackson-Pratt, Hemovac) in place postoperatively to minimize the occurrence of a hematoma developing at the surgical site.

Drug Therapy

Anticonvulsants

Patients who have had supratentorial craniotomies for tumor biopsy and/or resection can be expected to be placed on an anticonvulsant postoperatively if not before. Surgical manipulation of the cortical tissue and compression by the tumor mass can serve as epileptogenic foci.

Corticosteroids

The administration of dexamethasone (Decadron) or prednisolone (Solu-Medrol) is common practice in alleviating the symptoms of focal edema presented by space-occupying lesions. High dosages can be expected preoperatively and postoperatively, with the dose being gradually tapered down to minimize the occurrence of adrenal crisis and steroid psychosis. Patients with brain tumors may require maintenance doses of the steroids to help control symptoms, which places them at risk for all the side effects of long-term steroid administration. Concomitant administration of histamine-blocking agents such as cimetidine (Tagamet) and antacids can be expected to decrease the formation of stress ulcers in these patients.

Analgesics

The headache that patients with brain tumors complain of postoperatively is most often due to incision discomfort rather than pain from the tumor itself. It is usually relieved by acetaminophen; more severe headache can be alleviated with codeine. Patients who have spinal canal surgery may have much discomfort related to muscle and bone manipulation in addition to the discomfort caused by the pathology involved.

Surgical Intervention

Definitive diagnosis of the type of tumor involved is made through biopsy. Stereotactic techniques now make it possible to gather tissue from different parts of the brain-tumor bed for analysis. Pathological identification of the cells involved greatly facilitates further medical management and provides a basis for predicting prognostic outcome.

As stated earlier, even histologically benign tumors may not be totally resected due to location and can pose a continual threat to optimal neurological function. Decompressive surgery to decrease tumor bulk and to alleviate increased ICP or spinal cord compression is often indicated with malignant tumors, although tumors infiltrating the brain stem or spinal cord may not be appropriate for decompression.

Radiation Therapy

Radiation therapy is indicated in many partially resected CNS tumors to destroy malignant cells and to retard further cell growth. The dosage or duration of a specific type of therapy is determined by the tumor type. While external-beam radiation therapy is instituted after the surgical incision is healed and the patient is beyond the critical care environment, patients may be readmitted to the intensive care unit (ICU) setting due to deteriorating neurological status. The deterioration may be caused by the edema precipitated by the localized effects of the radiation or by progression of the tumor itself. Radiation necrosis may occur months following completion of the radiation therapy and may present as a functional decline in the patient's mental and physical capabilities.

Chemotherapy

Advances in chemotherapeutic management of CNS tumors has not been as great as in other cancers, owing in part to the selective permeability of the blood-brain barrier. Tumor type, quality of life, and the presence of concomitant systemic disease are factors to be considered in deciding the appropriateness of a patient for chemotherapy. Oncological consultation will be sought to assist in deciding the most appropriate agent(s) for the tumor type. Some of the chemotherapeutic drugs used in treating brain tumors include

- methotrexate
- vincristine sulfate (Oncovin)
- carmustine (BCNU)
- lomustine (CCNU)

Interstitial Brachytherapy

This is a relatively new technique in the treatment of brain tumors by which radioactive iodine 125 seeds are directly implanted into the tumor bed. Brachytherapy offers the advantages of providing focal radiation exposure to the tumor cells while minimizing exposure to other areas of brain tissue. It is used in small (less than 5 cm), well-circumscribed, supratentorial gliomas that are not located near the midline.[4]

General Management Concerns

The management of neoplastic growths within the CNS requires a multimodality approach. Investigation of more effective techniques in treating CNS cancers remains an ongoing process. Major concerns for nursing management are the side effects associated with radiation and chemotherapy. These side effects may include nausea and vomiting, diarrhea, appetite suppression, alopecia, bone marrow suppression, renal compromise, stomatitis, neurological deterioration, impaired tissue integrity at the radiated site, and radiation necrosis.

Goals of patient management are listed below.

- frequent neurological assessment—Patient is at particular risk for increased ICP during first five to seven days postoperatively and during initial stages of radiation therapy
- management of concomitant systemic disease processes
- maintenance of adequate fluid and electrolyte balance and caloric intake
- identification of home and community services necessary for discharge

NOTES

1. Gail Segal. *A Primer of Brain Tumors* (Chicago, IL: Association for Brain Tumor Research, 1985), 7.

2. A. Butler, W. Brooks, and M. Netsky. "Classification and Biology of Brain Tumors." in *Neurological Surgery*. Vol 5. ed. J. Youmans (Philadelphia: W.B. Saunders, 1982), 2659–2701.
3. M. Salcman. "The Morbidity and Mortality of Brain Tumors: A Perspective on Recent Advances in Therapy." *Neurology Clinics* 3(1985):229–257.
4. P.H. Gutin, S.A. Leibel, W.M. Wara, A. Choucair, V.A. Levin, T.L. Philips, P. Silver, V. Da Silva, M.S.B. Edwards, R.L. Davis, K.A. Weaver, and S. Lamb. "Recurrent Malignant Gliomas: Survival Following Interstitial Brachytherapy with High-Activity Iodine-125 Sources." *Journal of Neurosurgery* 67(1987):864–873.

SUGGESTED READINGS

Daumas-Duport, Catherine, Bernd W. Scheithauer, and Patrick J. Kelly. "A Histologic and Cytologic Method for the Spatial Definition of Gliomas." *Mayo Clinic Proceedings* 62(1987):435–449.

Hickey, Joanne. *The Clinical Practice of Neurological and Neurosurgical Nursing*. Philadelphia: J.B. Lippincott, 1981.

Kastrup, Erwin K., ed. *Drug Facts and Comparisons*. Philadelphia: J.B. Lippincott, 1987.

Raimond, Jeanne, and Joyce Waterman Taylor. *Neurological Emergencies: Effective Nursing Care*. Rockville, MD: Aspen Publishers, 1986.

Randall, Tina M., Denise K. Drake, and Wilfred Sewchand. "Neuro-Oncology Update: Radiation Safety and Nursing Care During Interstitial Brachytherapy." *Journal of Neuroscience Nursing* 19(1987):315–320.

Resio, Maria J., and Hetty L. DeVroom. "Spiromustine and Intracarotid Artery Cisplatin in the Treatment of Glioblastoma Multiforme." *Journal of Neuroscience Nursing* 18(1986):13–22.

Ropper, Allan H., Sean Kennedy, and Nicholas T. Zervas. *Neurological and Neurosurgical Intensive Care*. Rockville, MD: Aspen Publishers, 1983.

Rudy, Ellen B. *Advanced Neurological and Neurosurgical Nursing*. St. Louis: Mosby, 1984.

Taylor, Joyce Waterman, and Sally Ballenger. *Neurological Dysfunction and Nursing Intervention*. New York: McGraw-Hill, 1980.

Welsh, Deborah M., and Connie B. Zumwalt. "Volumetric Interstitial Hyperthermia: Nursing Implications for Brain Tumor Treatment." *Journal of Neuroscience Nursing* 20(1988):229–235.

Willis, Dawn, Helen Rittenmeyer, and Patrick Hitchon. "Intracranial Interstitial Radiation." *Journal of Neuroscience Nursing* 18(1986):153–156.

9

Cerebrovascular Events

Cerebrovascular accidents (CVAs), or strokes, follow heart disease and cancer as the third leading cause of death per year in the United States.[1] The term stroke is used to describe any pathological process disrupting cerebral blood supply. It is not a disease process confined to the older population; it affects all age groups. Critical care nurses encounter patients who sustain cerebrovascular insults on a regular basis. This chapter will provide an overview of the etiology of strokes and will present current management concepts.

RISK FACTORS

Epidemiological studies have identified several factors which contribute to stroke, and attention to these factors is believed to have decreased the incidence of stroke during the past 20 years. Among the factors identified are

- atherosclerosis
- hypertension
- heart disease
- diabetes
- familial history
- smoking
- obesity
- oral contraceptives
- elevated hematocrit

Many of these factors can be controlled and thus the incidence of developing cerebrovascular disease further minimized.

CLASSIFICATION

Interruption of cerebral vascular supply can be categorized into two main classifications: ischemic stroke and hemorrhagic strokes. The etiological factors and treatment methodologies vary depending upon the classification, as does the prognostic outcome.

Ischemic Strokes

Ischemic processes represent the most commonly occurring stroke and result from a thrombotic or embolic event. Ischemic events lead to infarction and necrosis of the involved area. Cerebral edema accompanying the infarct can be significant enough to cause increased ICP.

Thrombosis

Thrombotic events, in which the arterial lumen is progressively occluded, are most common. Causes include

- plaque formation
- hypercoagulability conditions
- hypoperfusion

Patients may present with

- the stroke in evolution, in which the severity of neurological deficit increases over the course of hours or days until the compromised area becomes infarcted
- a completed stroke in which the infarction has already occurred and the patient presents with maximal neurological deficits
- transient ischemic attacks (TIAs), which last from a few minutes up to twenty-four hours; they produce neurological deficits reflecting the compromised blood flow and resolve when the attack ends

Embolus

Embolic events occur within minutes and result from the occlusion of a vessel from circulating particles within the blood flow. These patients present with a completed stroke. The middle cerebral artery (MCA) is the most frequent site of embolic events due to its immediate bifurcation from the internal carotid artery.

Patients with heart disease, specifically atrial fibrillation or flutter, are at high risk for embolizing a blood clot to the cerebral circulation. Other sources of emboli include

- carotid artery stenosis
- fat particles
- septic debris
- microparticulates from cardiac and vascular surgery

Hemorrhagic Stroke

Hemorrhagic events produce bleeding into the intracranial cavity or directly into the brain parenchyma. Uncontrolled hypertensive disease is a common predisposing factor. Constant high pressures on the arterial wall eventually disrupt the vessel's integrity, and bleeding occurs into the brain tissue or subarachnoid space. Subarachnoid hemorrhages from ruptured cerebral aneurysms or arteriovenous malformations may also precipitate a hemorrhagic event.

DIAGNOSIS OF CEREBROVASCULAR EVENTS

Specific diagnostic procedures, in addition to patient history and physical examination, can be expected in the diagnosis of stroke. Further detail on the diagnostic procedures can be obtained in Chapter 3. The following list represents some of the more frequently used diagnostic interventions and is not inclusive.

- lumbar puncture
- computed tomography (CT) scan
- magnetic resonance imaging (MRI)
- positron emission tomography (PET) or single photon emission computed tomography (SPECT) scan, where available
- angiography
- noninvasive carotid studies
- regional blood flow studies
- electrocardiogram (ECG)
- noninvasive cardiology studies

ISCHEMIC STROKE SYNDROMES

Depending upon the vessels involved, disruption of blood supply to brain regions will produce characteristic deficits. The systemic arterial supply to the brain may be disrupted from either its anterior (carotid arteries) or posterior (vertebral arteries) source.

Anterior Circulation Disruption

Middle Cerebral Artery Syndrome

The MCA as it bifurcates off the internal carotid artery is the most frequent site for infarctions of the anterior blood supply to the brain. This vessel is large, providing approximately 80% of the blood flow to the anterior cerebral hemispheres.

In addition to supplying the lateral surfaces of the cerebral hemispheres, it also provides blood flow to the deeper, subcortical areas of the basal ganglia and internal capsule. The symptomatology displayed depends on the extent of the infarcted area and the hemisphere affected. Right hemisphere lesions can be expected to produce

- contralateral hemiparesis/hemiplegia due to motor cortex involvement of the frontal lobe
- contralateral sensory alterations due to parietal lobe involvement
- homonymous hemianopsia of the left visual field due to involvement of the optic pathways as they traverse back toward the occipital lobe
- lack of impulse control and lack of insight into the demonstrated deficits
- spatial and perceptual deficits such as impaired position sense and balance, neglect of the left side of the body, and the inability to interpret objects through the senses (agnosias; see Chapter 2)
- possibly, evidence of apraxias (See Chapter 2 for more discussion of apraxias.)

Left hemisphere lesions generally affect communication, as this hemisphere is dominant for speech in the majority of the population. Specific communication dysfunction may be comprised of varying degrees of aphasia—nonfluent, fluent, or global—as well as alexia and agraphia (see Chapter 2). Other deficits to expect with left hemisphere lesions include

- contralateral hemiparesis/hemiplegia
- contralateral sensory alteration
- right homonymous hemianopsia
- right-to-left confusion
- disorganization and confusion when performing tasks

Internal Carotid Artery Syndrome

Lesions of the internal carotid artery (ICA) will often result in infarction of the MCA territory and produce symptomatology as above. Additionally the ICA provides blood supply to the optic nerve and retina. TIAs involving the ICA often present as transient episodes of blindness in the affected eye.

Anterior Cerebral Artery Syndrome

Lesions involving the anterior cerebral artery (ACA) are not as frequent as in other vessels due to its anatomical location. The ACA provides blood flow to the medial aspects of the frontal and parietal lobes. Interrupted blood supply to these territories will produce

- contralateral paresis/paralysis of the lower extremity, and the upper extremity may also be affected but not to the same extent as the lower
- gait apraxia
- lack of spontaneous affect
- cognitive impairments, including amnesia and perseveration
- urinary incontinence due to involvement of frontal lobe center for micturition
- pathological grasp and suck reflexes

Watershed Infarcts

Also referred to as border-zone infarcts, these strokes reflect ischemic changes at the outermost borders of the large cerebral vessels, which are the last areas to receive perfusion from a specific vessel (Figure 9-1). The cause is often prolonged hypotension, which does not allow adequate cerebral perfusion to all brain tissue. The patient typically demonstrates visual field defects, perhaps cortical blindness as well as other evidence of ischemia.

Lacunar Infarcts

Lacunar infarcts refer to multiple, small, petechial hemorrhages that occur in the penetrating cerebral branches of the major arteries. The size of the infarct is so small that clinical symptomatology of the infarct is not evident. As the infarcted

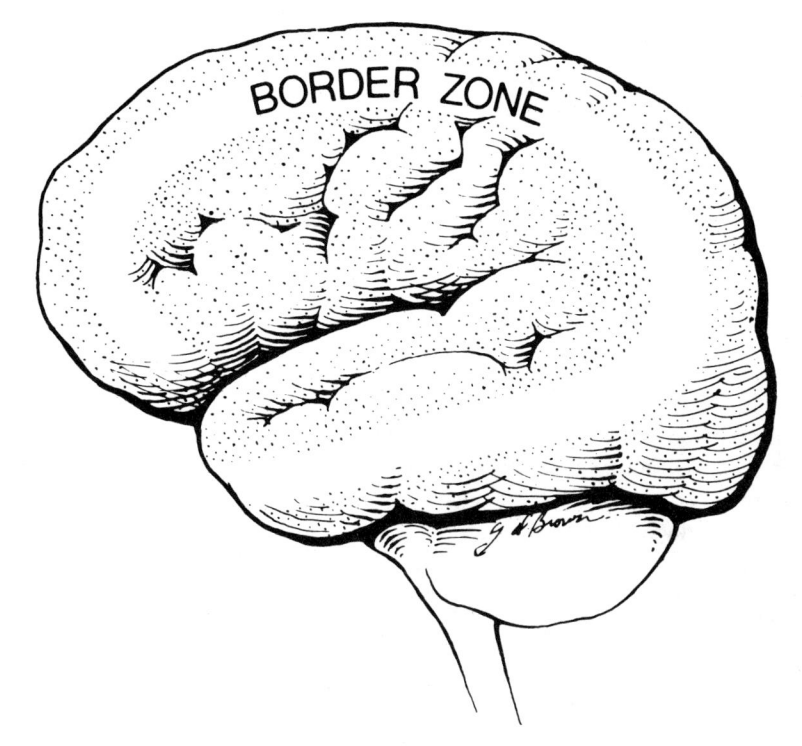

Figure 9-1 Diagram of Watershed or Border Zone Area. *Source:* Reprinted by permission of the authors from *Neuropathology: A Summary for Students* by R.W. Leech and R.M. Shuman, p. 37, J.B. Lippincott Company, © 1982.

---

tissue is phagocytized, small holes or lacunes are left in place of the neuronal tissue. Over time, with enough infarcted tissue, the patient may become symptomatic. Lacunar infarcts may occur in the deep cortical matter of the cerebrum or in the brain stem. The presence of lacunar infarcts has been correlated with hypertension and atherosclerotic disease.[2]

Posterior Circulation Disruption

The vertebral arteries (VAs) provide the remaining 20% of the cerebral blood flow as they arise from the subclavian arteries. They supply blood flow to portions of the brain stem and cerebellum. The VAs join to form the basilar artery over the upper brain stem region, which also provides blood flow to the brain stem and cerebellar areas.

The posterior cerebral arteries (PCAs) usually arise from the basilar artery, though they may arise from the carotid system. Among the major structures supplied by these vessels are the

- visual cortex of the occipital lobe
- medial parts of the occipital and temporal lobes
- midbrain and hypothalamic regions

Vascular events in the distributory territories of the vertebrobasilar system may produce varying neurological deficits.

Lateral Medullary Syndrome

Lateral medullary syndrome is caused by disruption of branches of the vertebral blood supply, resulting in deficits that are "crossed" in relation to the lesion due to involvement of pathways before and after decussation. Symptoms seen with this syndrome includes

- ipsilateral impaired facial sensation
- ipsilateral ataxia and leaning toward the affected side
- ipsilateral Horner's syndrome (see Chapter 6)
- ipsilateral truncal and extremity numbness
- nausea and vomiting, diplopia, and nystagmus
- deficits of cranial nerves IX and X
- contralateral decrease in pain and temperature sensation

Basilar Artery Syndromes

The basilar artery may incur occlusion to any of its branches or may be completely occluded. Branch occlusion of the basilar most commonly produces symptoms of

- ipsilateral ataxia
- slurred speech
- Horner's syndrome
- ipsilateral cranial nerve deficits
- contralateral hemiplegia

Complete occlusion of the basilar artery may produce

- tetraplegia and bilateral sensory deficits
- disturbances of extraocular movements, such as gaze paralysis or nystagmus

- a variety of visual field defects, including blindness
- coma

Posterior Cerebral Artery Syndrome

Since this vessel supplies the visual cortex, the most characteristic symptom associated with a lesion of the PCA is homonymous hemianopsia. Involvement of both arteries can produce cortical blindness, of which the patient may be unaware or may deny. Involvement of branches supplying the temporal areas may result in memory disturbances. Infarction of the thalamic portion of the PCA may produce "thalamic syndrome," which is characterized by

- the loss of contralateral sensory modalities
- spontaneous and intractable pain
- a myriad motor disabilities

MANAGEMENT OF ISCHEMIC EVENTS

The goals of managing an acute ischemic event focus on

- treating and alleviating the cause of the ischemia
- maintaining supportive care to the patient

While the consequences of neurological damage from completed ischemic events cannot be reversed, interventions can minimize future occurrences. Those patients in whom a cardiac origin is determined for their embolic events will have the underlying problem treated.

Patients who present with TIAs benefit most from prophylactic therapy, as their ischemic events have not caused permanent dysfunction. One can expect these patients to be placed on some form of anticoagulant or platelet antiaggregate, as a large majority of these patients have pathology significant enough to progress to infarction. The following medical and surgical interventions remain controversial but are used in the management of ischemic events.

- Platelet Antiaggregates
  1. Aspirin, 650 mg once or twice a day, has shown effectiveness in decreasing the incidence of stroke, although the recommended dosage varies.
  2. Dipyridamole (Persantine), shown to be effective in preventing cardiovascular disease, may be used in conjunction with aspirin, although it may not offer any additional benefits to the patient with cerebrovascular disease.

3. Low-dose dextran infusion may be employed during the initial acute phase to decrease platelet aggregation following infarction.
- Anticoagulation
  1. Intravenous (IV) heparin administration for patients with thrombi and stenotic vessels or for those in whom a cardiac embolic source is suspected is used to decrease further ischemia. The risk for hemorrhage is great, and the recommended dosage of heparin is titration to a partial thromboplastin time 2½ times the normal.
  2. Long-term therapy is accomplished with warfarin (Coumadin) or platelet antiaggregate therapy. The use of warfarin may be contraindicated depending upon concomitant pathological processes the patient may possess.
- Hemodilution
  1. The efficacy of treating acute stroke victims (within twenty-four hours) by hemodilution is currently being investigated. An inverse relationship has been demonstrated between cerebral blood flow (CBF) and hematocrit.[1]
  2. The aim is to increase CBF by lowering the hematocrit. The premise is that patients who have recently incurred a stroke may be volume depleted and that by administering volume expanders, CBF can be optimized.
  3. A major concern with this therapy is the risk it poses for increasing ICP and causing fluid volume overload.
- Calcium Channel Blockers
  1. Administration of dihydropyridines (nifedipine, nicardipine, and nimodipine) after stroke is undergoing multicenter investigation to determine the ability to prevent the cytotoxic effects of calcium influx after ischemia.[1]
  2. The potential for these drugs to cause hypotension requires careful IV titration of the drug and continual blood pressure assessment.
- Thrombolytic Therapy
  1. Clinical studies are currently in progress to examine the efficacy of thrombolytic agents in re-establishing cerebral perfusion after an ischemic stroke.[1]
  2. Streptokinase has demonstrated a high incidence of cerebral hemorrhage in pilot studies.
  3. A focus of current investigation is on the use of tissue plasminogen activator, an agent that is clot specific and is produced within the blood vessels. Treatment with tissue plasminogen activator must be accomplished within several hours after the ischemic event. Thus the patient must be rapidly deemed as an appropriate candidate and transferred to a participating institution.

- Surgical Interventions
  1. Carotid endarterectomy may be performed to minimize the risk for stroke in patients with documented stenosis of the carotid arteries.
  2. Patients who would benefit most are those with TIAs and severe stenosis of the carotid vessels. The benefit of performing this procedure on all patients with carotid disease is receiving renewed attention by the medical community.[3]
  3. The performance of extracranial anastomoses to intracranial vessels (EC-IC bypass) has been used when large areas are infarcted from a thrombotic event but remains a controversial procedure. The most common vessels used are the superficial temporal artery to the middle cerebral artery.

HEMORRHAGIC STROKE SYNDROMES

Hemorrhagic events occur less frequently than ischemic ones, accounting for about 15% of strokes. The etiology of the hemorrhage may be a

- hypertensive bleed
- ruptured aneurysm or arteriovenous malformation
- bleeding dyscrasia

The morbidity and mortality associated with hemorrhagic events is greater than that associated with ischemic strokes. The recovery potential of those who survive these episodes is, however, better than with ischemic events because the area of infarction is usually less.

Hypertensive Intracerebral Hemorrhage

Intracerebral hemorrhage (ICH) caused by hypertensive bleeds generally occurs quickly, over the course of minutes to within twenty-four hours. The pathophysiology involved is

- extravasation of blood into the brain parenchyma, which may continue as long as the blood pressure is elevated
- continued bleeding that enlarges the clot site and may displace anatomical structures and cause shifting of intracranial contents
- blood may be displaced into the subarachnoid space or ventricles

The vessels that bleed from continued high blood pressures are the smaller penetrating branches of the major cerebral vessels. The most common sites for hypertensive ICH are

- the putamen and nearby internal capsule
- deep portions of the central white matter
- thalamic area
- cerebellum
- pons

The patient may complain of a headache or unusual sensation in the head and then immediately present with unilateral motor weakness. Vomiting is not uncommon. Speech may be garbled or nonexistent. The level of consciousness may progress from confusion to stupor to coma. Focal seizures may occur during the acute phase. Lumbar puncture will reveal bloody cerebrospinal fluid (CSF), and the hemorrhage will be apparent on CT scan.

Management of ICH

Surgical evacuation of intracerebral hemorrhage is not generally undertaken unless the clot is large enough or located in a site to place the patient at significant risk for herniation. The focus of care is on

- supporting vital systems
- managing increased ICP if present
- maintaining normotensive blood pressures

Blood pressures often need to be maintained in the hypertensive range for patients with acute ICH to maintain cerebral perfusion pressure (CPP). Some of the patients will benefit from intracranial pressure monitoring to facilitate CPP management. The insertion of ventricular drainage may be performed to decrease increased ICP.

Ruptured Cerebral Aneurysms

Cerebral aneurysms are localized, weakened areas of the cerebrovasculature that may result from congenital malformations or traumatic injury to the vessel. The aneurysm most frequently seen is berry shaped or saccular but may also be elongated (fusiform). Septic emboli from pathological processes occurring elsewhere in the body (eg, subacute bacterial endocarditis) may cause development of a mycotic aneurysm. Head trauma may disrupt vessel integrity and create a weakened area such that an aneurysm might later develop.

The size of intracranial aneurysms is usually in the range of 2 to 10 mm, although "giant aneurysms" of up to 3 cm can occur.

Rupture of an aneurysm causes bleeding into the subarachnoid space that then permeates the CSF distribution. Ischemia to the area normally perfused by the involved vessel may lead to infarction. Three major sequelae to subarachnoid hemorrhages from ruptured aneurysms are

- hydrocephalus
- vasospasm
- rebleeding

The patient is at risk for developing communicating hydrocephalus as the blood in the CSF occludes its absorption by the arachnoid villi. The vessels adjacent to the ruptured aneurysm frequently experience vasospasm, further compromising cerebral perfusion. Physiological lysis of the clot approximately seven to ten days post-hemorrhage places the patient at risk for further bleeding.

Patients with subarachnoid hemorrhages from aneurysmal rupture have a high morbidity and mortality rate. The most common site for aneurysms is in the anterior cerebral circulation of the circle of Willis, frequently at points where the vessels bifurcate. The anterior communicating artery is the site of 60% of cerebral aneurysms, while 25% occur at the bifurcation of the internal carotid and middle cerebral arteries.[4]

Clinical Presentation of Subarachnoid Hemorrhages

Most patients do not have any prodromal symptoms of the rupture, although obscure symptoms such as headache or visual disturbances may exist and go unheeded. Rupture most often occurs while the patient is alert and physically active. The person often complains of having a terrible headache, unlike any they have ever had before. Depending upon the severity of the bleeding, the level of consciousness may not change or the patient may lose consciousness.

The presence of blood in the subarachnoid space serves as an irritant focus to the blood vessels, meninges, and spinal nerve roots, creating meningeal signs that may not be clinically apparent until several hours after the bleed. Meningeal signs that one can expect are:

- photophobia
- nuchal rigidity—stiff neck
- Kernig's sign—inability to passively extend the knee with the hip flexed at a 90-degree angle from a supine position. The patient will complain of leg pain and spasm.

- Brudzinski's sign—flexion of the hips and knees when the head and neck are passively flexed onto the chest

Symptomatology reflecting aneurysms of specific cerebral vessels is summarized in Table 9-1.

Classification of Severity

A consistently used classification system for gauging the surgical risk associated with intracranial aneurysms has been described by Hunt and Hess.[5] The higher the grade, the poorer the patient's condition and prognosis (Table 9-2).

Table 9-1 Common Deficits Associated with Cerebral Aneurysms

Middle cerebral artery (MCA):	Motor deficits (hemiplegias); seizures; homonymous visual field defects; speech and sensory disturbances
Anterior cerebral artery (ACA):	Unilateral visual loss; anosmia; personality changes; lower-extremity weakness; akinetic mutism
Anterior communicating artery (ACoA):	Visual loss in lower half of both visual fields; personality changes
Posterior cerebral artery (PCA):	Third cranial nerve disturbances
Basilar artery (BA):	Weakness; extraocular movement (EOM) dysfunction; dementia and headache (hydrocephalus); autonomic disturbances (hypothalamic injury); fifth and seventh cranial nerve disturbances; brain stem signs
Vertebral artery (VA):	Ataxia, bulbar signs, brain stem signs

Table 9-2 Hunt and Hess Classification of Subarachnoid Hemorrhages

Grade	Patient Presentation
I	Minimal headache; no neurological deficits; (minimal hemorrhaging)
II	Alert, with mild-to-moderate headache; slight neurological deficit (cranial nerve palsy); nuchal rigidity; (mild hemorrhaging)
III	Confused, lethargic; nuchal rigidity; focal deficits (hemiparesis); (moderate hemorrhaging)
IV	Severely decreased level of consciousness; nuchal rigidity; may have increased hemiparesis, dysphasia; (moderate to severe hemorrhaging)
V	Stuporous to comatose; pathological reflexes and posturing (decerebration); (severe hemorrhaging)

Source: Adapted from *Journal of Neurosurgery*, Vol. 28, pp. 14–19, American Association of Neurological Surgeons, © 1968.

Management of Ruptured Aneurysms

The focus of treating subarachnoid hemorrhages from ruptured aneurysms centers upon managing rebleeding, vasospasm, and hydrocephalus.

Rebleeding. The clot that forms at the rupture site serves as a barrier to further bleeding by the vessel. Physiological lysis of the fibrin clot seven to ten days posthemorrhage places the patient at risk for rebleeding from the site. The administration of the antifibrinolytic agent aminocaproic acid (Amicar) may be initiated as soon as possible to avert rebleeding from the aneurysm, although its use remains controversial. The usual dose is up to 30 g/day. It can be given via IV administration or in an oral elixir.

An immediate measure instituted to help minimize the risk of rebleeding is to place the patient in as quiet and calm an environment as possible. Most institutions have standard protocols for subarachnoid hemorrhage or aneurysm precautions. The protocol usually includes

- bed rest in a quiet room
- darkened environment to minimize the symptoms of photophobia
- restriction of visitors
- avoidance of activities that may contribute to increased anxiety (catastrophic news events, loud music)
- use of sedation evaluated on an individual basis
- assistance as needed with activities of daily living
- avoidance of Valsalva's maneuver, which causes increased intracranial pressure (ICP)
- initiation of bowel program to prevent constipation and straining, both of which can cause increased ICP

Because these patients may be on bed rest for an extended period of time, attention to providing passive range of motion is necessary to minimize disuse phenomena to joints and muscles. The potential for deep-vein thrombosis is increased, and daily evaluation of the extremities is warranted. The application of external pneumatic compression therapy is becoming more widespread to approximate the lower extremity venous pressures normally present with activity. Antihypertensive agents may be necessary to control hypertension in some individuals, while others may need volume expanders to help ensure adequate cerebral perfusion.

Because of the sensory deprived atmosphere in which these patients are placed, it is not unusual for them to lose track of time. Providing constant orientation whenever in the room can help maintain the patient's perception of temporality.

Vasospasm. While vasospasm occurs physiologically within minutes to hours following a hemorrhage, to decrease blood flow and to minimize the risk of rebleeding, development of the syndrome of clinical cerebral vasospasm presents a multitude of problems for patient management. The exact mechanism that causes this syndrome is not fully understood, but it develops within the first four to ten days after a subarachnoid hemorrhage, peaking in incidence around day 7 to 10 and usually resolving by day 21. Vasospasm may continue to persist after surgical repair of the aneurysm.

Vasospasm is an abnormal narrowing of the cerebral vessels adjacent or distant to the site of aneurysmal rupture. While arteriographic narrowing of cerebral vessels from vasospasm is evident around day 3 or 4 after the hemorrhage, the patient does not always exhibit clinical evidence of ischemia caused by the narrowing. Approximately 30% of the patients who have incurred a major subarachnoid hemorrhage will develop clinical symptomatology related to ischemic changes.[5]

The onset of clinical vasospasm may be heralded by an increasing blood pressure and complaints of a worsening headache. Characteristically the patient will display

- gradual onset of confusion, lethargy
- deteriorating level of consciousness
- focal deficits such as dysphasia and hemiparesis

The syndrome may present as a minor focal deficit and remain so or may progress to cause major deficits, including coma.

The potential impact on adequate cerebral perfusion is severe; vasospasm initially begins with the vessels adjacent to the ruptured one yet can diffuse to involve major cerebral vessels distal to the site of rupture. The arterial narrowing increases cerebrovascular resistance, and in the presence of an altered autoregulatory system, as often occurs following aneurysmal rupture, the CBF becomes dependent upon CPP (see Chapter 4). The resulting ischemia can progress to infarction if the spasm is major.

The cause of vasospasm remains elusive, but its occurrence is related to the presence and amount of blood within the subarachnoid space. The presence of spasmogenic substances (serotonin, prostaglandins, angiotensin, and hemoglobin, among others) within the subarachnoid space may also contribute to cerebral vasospasm. A number of hypotheses currently exist as to the cause of cerebral vasospasm:

- contraction of smooth muscle within cerebral arteries in response to vasoactive substances in the CSF

- vasodilatory dysfunction
- proliferative vasculopathy
- immune response
- inflammatory process
- mechanical phenomena[6]

Because the cause of cerebral vasospasm is as yet undetermined, a variety of therapeutic modalities have been and continue to be investigated in an attempt to identify the most effective method to control vasospasm. Vasospasm management requires aggressive management of blood pressure, fluid volume, and cerebral perfusion. Drug therapy aimed at reducing arterial wall constriction may include

- intravenous nitroprusside (Nipride)
- beta blockers such as isoproterenol (Isuprel), although lidocaine may be a necessary adjunct to treat the dysrhythmias caused by isoproterenol
- calcium channel blockers (nifedipine, nimodopine)
- papaverine hydrochloride
- prostaglandin inhibitors

A regimen of kanamycin and reserpine has been used to decrease serum serotonin levels. While it demonstrated success in preventing postoperative vasospasm, it had little effect in preventing preoperative vasospasm.[7] Hypervolemic hemodilution is being used by some centers to manage vasospasm by maximizing CPP.

Regardless of the current mode of therapy, since it changes frequently, aggressive management of vasospasm is a major priority in treating subarachnoid hemorrhages. Because of the magnitude of the therapies employed, these patients require constant monitoring, which includes pulmonary capillary wedge pressures, intracranial pressures, and arterial pressures.

Hydrocephalus. The presence of blood in the subarachnoid space not only serves as an irritating focus to the meningeal and vascular tissues but also can obstruct the arachnoid villi, through which CSF is absorbed. The communicating hydrocephalus that results can contribute to decreased cerebral perfusion and increased ICP. The placement of a ventriculostomy affords the ability to measure ICP and to drain CSF to decrease ICP.

Surgery. The decision when to operate and to surgically ligate or seal the ruptured aneurysm is yet another area of controversy. Some advocates recommend surgical intervention within the first two to four days postbleed before vasospasm develops, while others recommend waiting until the vasospasm has abated. Early surgical intervention is generally not appropriate in patients with grade IV or V aneurysms.

Surgical intervention may involve ligating the affected vessel, clipping the aneurysm with specially designed aneurysm clips, or coating the aneurysm with an acrylic-based agent to prevent further rupture. Some patients may be candidates for embolization of the aneurysm, which is accomplished by guiding a catheter through a femoral artery puncture up through the cerebrovasculature to the aneurysm site. The aneurysm can be occluded by the insertion of a thrombosing material or deposition of a balloon. This technique is considered in patients who are not good surgical risks or whose aneurysms are difficult to approach surgically.

Arteriovenous Malformations

Arteriovenous malformations (AVMs) may result from a developmental anomaly or from a head injury that subsequently required the development of a shunt around the traumatized area. Further information regarding arteriovenous malformations is listed below.

- The clinical presentation of the patient resembles that of the patient who has incurred a subarachnoid hemorrhage.
- The management of AVMs is similar to that of subarachnoid hemorrhages.
- Surgical intervention is aimed at dissecting the entire malformation from the cerebral vasculature. Large AVMs often necessitate embolization, achieved in several stages, to shrink the AVM sufficiently for surgical resection.
- Proton-beam therapy is an additional avenue of treatment for surgically inaccessible AVMs.

NURSING MANAGEMENT CONCERNS

Goals of nursing care after a cerebrovascular event include

- monitoring neurological status
- maintaining the airway
- providing general body-system support
- minimizing the occurrence of complications

The patient may have concomitant body-system disease that requires additional specialized nursing care and may be exacerbated by the cerebral event.

Frequent Neurological Assessment

Ongoing monitoring of neurological status is necessary to evaluate progression or resolution of deficits. The level of consciousness may wax and wane during the initial acute phase; periods of confusion are not unusual.

Airway Maintenance

Ensuring an unobstructed airway is necessary to prevent aspiration as well as hypoxemia. Decreased level of consciousness and the possible presence of cranial nerve deficits place the patient at increased risk for airway obstruction and aspiration. Patients unable to protect their airway will be electively intubated and mechanically ventilated. This measure also provides the ability to hyperventilate the individual in the event of increased ICP.

Management of Increased ICP

As with other neurological conditions, aggressive management of increased ICP is necessary to maintain cerebral perfusion pressure at optimal levels and to minimize hypoxic and ischemic damage to areas not directly involved in the cerebrovascular event. The details of managing increased ICP are presented in Chapter 4.

Seizure Control

Seizure activity may occur in patients who incur cerebrovascular events. Prompt and aggressive management of any seizure activity will minimize further compromise of the cerebral environment. Seizure precautions should be instituted if indicated.

Fluid and Electrolyte Balance

Fluid intake, urinary excretion, and electrolytes require close monitoring to assess for adequate fluid volume, renal function, and electrolyte balance. Inadequate or overtreatment with fluids may precipitate concomitant problems with ICP as well as with respiratory, renal, and cardiac systems.

Caloric Intake

Achieving adequate nutritional intake may initially be managed through parenteral or enteral feeding programs. The involvement of the lower cranial nerves in the brain stem places the patient at high risk for aspiration and choking while ingesting food and fluids. Consults to speech therapy or a dysphagia team can elucidate the capabilities of the patient in managing fluids and food.

Bowel Function

Administration of a stool softener should begin once nutritional support is instituted. Prevention of constipation will minimize straining that can trigger a Valsalva's maneuver, causing increased ICP.

Bladder Function

Initiation of an appropriate bladder program should be done once the need for an indwelling catheter is passed.

Hazards of Immobility

The paresis or paralysis and sensory alterations that can result from a disruption in the cerebral blood supply place the patient at risk for pressure ulcers and joint dislocations. Compromised nutritional status and bladder and bowel incontinence may be further contributors to tissue breakdown. Foam or water mattresses should be used to promote pressure relief. The use of low air-loss bed therapy may be a treatment consideration in patients with tissue breakdown. Diligent attention to the skin integrity is crucial.

The possibility of deep-vein thromboses (DVT) of the lower extremities and pulmonary emboli requires continual assessment to evaluate their occurrence. Use of sequential compression devices on the legs might be considered to minimize venous stasis of the lower extremities along with frequent assessment of the calves for signs of DVT and the lungs for decreased breath sounds.

Mobilization of the patient into a chair should begin as soon as the patient is through the acute phase. Transfer of patients with paretic or paralyzed upper extremities should be accomplished with the affected extremity supported in a sling or by another person. Shoulder subluxations can easily occur in patients who have suffered a stroke.

Physical and occupational therapy consults should be initiated during the acute phase to provide advice regarding optimal positioning of the patient, depending upon the degree of neuromuscular involvement. These therapists are also invaluable in making recommendations as to the efficacy of prosthetic and orthotic devices (braces, splints, activities of daily living aids) in maximizing patient function.

Psychosocial Alterations

The cognitive, perceptual, and emotional changes that can occur with a stroke depend upon the areas of the brain affected and to what extent. The degree to which many of the possible alterations occur may not be evident until formal neuropsychiatric testing is obtained. Behavioral manifestations most likely to occur during the acute phase include

- emotional lability that was not present in the patient's premorbid behavior. The patient may cry for seemingly unprovoked reasons.
- behavior reflecting lack of social appropriateness. The patient may demonstrate sexual disinhibitions, express vulgar language, or act out inappropriately.
- inability to integrate environmental stimuli, such that the patient is easily agitated by the surroundings. The normal noise and activity levels in an intensive care unit (ICU) can prove to be overwhelming to some patients, and they may demonstrate their confusion and agitation by yelling or continually calling for their nurse.

Families need to be counseled that the behavior they see their loved one demonstrating is a result of the stroke and is not being consciously demonstrated by the patient.

NOTES

1. Mark L. Dyken, Philip A. Wolf, H.J.M. Barnett, John J. Bergan, William K. Hass, William B. Kannel, Lewis Kuller, John F. Kurtzke, and Thoralf M. Sundt. "Risk Factors in Stroke: A Statement for Physicians by the Subcommittee on Risk Factors and Stroke of the Stroke Council." *Stroke* 15(1984):1105–1111.
2. Raymond D. Adams, and Maurice Victor. *Principles of Neurology* (New York: McGraw-Hill, 1977), 518–520.
3. Constance M. Winslow, David H. Solomon, Mark R. Chassin, Jacqueline Kosecoff, Nancy Merrick, and Robert H. Brook. "The Appropriateness of Carotid Endarterectomy." *The New England Journal of Medicine* 318(1988):721–727.

4. Richard W. Leech, and Robert M. Shuman. *Neuropathology: A Summary for Students* (Philadelphia: Harper & Row, 1982), 31–32.
5. William E. Hunt, and Robert M. Hess. "Surgical Risk as Related to Time of Intervention in the Repair of Intracranial Aneurysms." *Journal of Neurosurgery* 28(1968):14–19.
6. Susan K. Mitchell, and Rowena R. Yates. "Cerebral Vasospasm: Theoretical Causes, Medical Management, and Nursing Implications." *Journal of Neuroscience Nursing* 18(1986):315–324.
7. J. Philip Kistler, "Management of Subarachnoid Hemorrhage from Ruptured Saccular Aneurysm." in *Neurological and Neurosurgical Intensive Care*, ed. A. Ropper, S. Kennedy, and N.T. Zervas (Rockville, MD: Aspen Publishers, 1983), 175–187.

SUGGESTED READINGS

Awad, Issam A., L. Philip Carter, Marjorie Medina Spetzler, and Fred W. Williams, Jr. "Clinical Vasospasm After Subarachnoid Hemorrhage: Response to Hypervolemic Hemodilution and Arterial Hypertension." *Stroke* 18(1987):365–372.

Bohachick, Patricia A. "Pulmonary Embolism in Neurological and Neurosurgical Patients." *Journal of Neuroscience Nursing* 19(1987):191–197.

Crowell, Robert M. "Surgical Management of Cerebrovascular Disease." *Nursing Clinics of North America* 21(1986):297–308.

Fode, Nicolee C. "Nonatherosclerotic Carotid Occlusive Disease—A Guide to Patient Education." *Journal of Neurosurgical Nursing* 17(1985):280–287.

Gelmers, Herman J., Kasper Gorter, Cees J. De Weerdt, and Hans J.A. Wiezer. "A Controlled Trial of Nimodipine in Acute Ischemic Stroke." *The New England Journal of Medicine* 318(1988):203–207.

Gorelick, Philip B. "Cerebrovascular Disease: Pathophysiology and Diagnosis." *Nursing Clinics of North America* 21(1986):275–288.

Grotta, James C. "Current Medical and Surgical Therapy for Cerebrovascular Disease." *The New England Journal of Medicine* 317(1987):1505–1516.

Heros, Roberto C., and Yong-Kwang Tu. "Is Surgical Therapy Needed for Unruptured Arteriovenous Malformations?" *Neurology* 37(1987):279–285.

Hopkins, Marybeth, Barbara M. Valberg, and Lynda M. Robinson. "A Report on the EC/IC Bypass Study." *Journal of Neuroscience Nursing* 18(1986):211–213.

Hummel, Susan K. "Cerebral Vasospasm: Current Concepts of Pathogenesis and Treatment." *Journal of Neuroscience Nursing* 21(1989):216–224.

Jackson, Linda O. "Cerebral Vasospasm after Intracranial Aneurysmal Subarachnoid Hemorrhage: A Nursing Perspective." *Heart & Lung* 15(1986):14–21.

Kastrup, Erwin K., ed. *Drug Facts and Comparisons*. Philadelphia: J.B. Lippincott, 1987.

Kasuya, Akiko, and Karyn Holm. "Pharmacologic Approach to Ischemic Stroke Management." *Nursing Clinics of North America* 21(1986):289–296.

Kocan, Mary Jo. "Electrocardiographic Changes Following Subarachnoid Hemorrhage." *Journal of Neuroscience Nursing* 20(1988):362–365.

Lechat, Ph., J.L. Mas, G. Lascault, Ph. Loron, M. Theard, M. Klimczac, G. Drobinski, D. Thomas, and Y. Grosgogeat. "Prevalence of Patent Foramen Ovale in Patients with Stroke." *The New England Journal of Medicine* 18(1988):1148–1152.

Martin, Evangeline M., and Ann B. Hummelgard. "Detachable Balloon Occlusion of Carotid-Cavernous Fistula." *Journal of Neuroscience Nursing* 19(1987):132–140.

Martin, Evangeline M., and Ann B. Hummelgard. "Traumatic Aneurysms." *Journal of Neuroscience Nursing* 18(1986):89–94.

Mitchell, Susan K., and Rowena R. Yates. "Cerebral Vasospasm: Theoretical Causes, Medical Management, and Nursing Implications." *Journal of Neuroscience Nursing* 18(1986):315–324.

O'Brien, Mary T., and Phyllis J. Pallet. *Total Care of the Stroke Patient*. Boston: Little, Brown, 1978.

Oertel, Lynn Bishop. "The Dilemma of Cerebral Vasospasm Treatment." *Journal of Neurosurgical Nursing* 17(1985):7–13.

Rigamonti, Daniele, Mark N. Hadley, Burton P. Drayer, Peter C. Johnson, Karen Hoenig-Rigamonti, J. Thomas Knight, and Robert F. Spetzler. "Cerebral Cavernous Malformations." *The New England Journal of Medicine* 319(1988):343–347.

Rudy, Ellen B. *Advanced Neurological and Neurosurgical Nursing*. St. Louis: Mosby, 1984.

Stewart-Amidei, Chris, and Sue Penckofer "Quality of Life Following Cerebral Bypass Surgery." *Journal of Neuroscience Nursing* 20(1988):50–57.

Vinters, Harry V, Mark J. Lundie, and M.B. Kaufmann. "Long-Term Pathological Follow up of Cerebral Arteriovenous Malformations Treated by Embolization with Bucrylate." *The New England Journal of Medicine* 314(1986):477–483.

Wald, Madeline E. "Cerebral Thrombosis: Assessment and Nursing Management of the Acute Phase." *Journal of Neuroscience Nursing* 18(1986):36–38.

10
Seizures and Status Epilepticus

It is estimated that about 1.4 million people in the United States have a seizure disorder.[1] In some persons the cause is readily identified, while in others it may remain obscure. Critical care nurses care for a patient population at risk for seizures due to any number of predisposing factors or pathological states. This chapter will present the classification of seizure types and the nursing and medical management appropriate for seizure activity in the acute care setting.

DEFINITION OF SEIZURE ACTIVITY

Seizure activity can be defined as the chaotic, paroxysmal discharge of energy from neurons within the brain. The exact mechanism that precipitates the abnormal discharge of electrical activity is not known. It may be caused by hyperexcitability of neurons or inhibition of normal neuronal activity. The amplitude and frequency of discharges can affect nearby neurons, causing them to discharge abnormally with the spread of seizure activity from a localized area of the cortex across to the opposite hemisphere.

The clinical demonstration of seizure activity displayed by the patient may reflect a localized zone of activity (focal seizure) or the involvement of major areas of the brain (generalized seizure). Seizure activity is a symptom of damaged neurons, whether the cause of the damage is known or not. Seizures may be identified as being idiopathic or acquired.

Idiopathic Seizure Activity

Idiopathic seizures are those for which no etiology can be identified. The seizure activity is recurrent yet episodic. Patients with longstanding seizure disorders in whom an identifiable cause has not been found are often referred to as having epilepsy. These patients are usually managed by referral to neurologists for medication management. Idiopathic seizures generally occur before the age of 20 years and seldom after the age of 30 years. The attributable etiology is thought to be due to congenital defects or birth injury.

Acquired Seizure Activity

Acquired seizures are those in which an identifiable cause for the abnormal discharge can be located. The seizure activity may be transient or recurring. Among the conditions that contribute to acquired seizure activity are

- hyperpyrexia
- central nervous system (CNS) trauma—Patients with a prior history of head trauma may develop partial or generalized seizure activity up to two years postinjury.
- CNS disease (cerebrovascular accident [CVA], tumors, infection)—Space-occupying lesions within the cranial cavity may make their presence known through a focal or generalized seizure, and patients who have incurred a CVA are also prone to development of seizures. Infectious processes of the CNS may also present with seizure activity.
- metabolic disturbances—Water intoxication, hyperglycemia, or hyponatremia are additional causes of seizure activity. Alcohol withdrawal and drugs may also contribute to seizure activity developing by lowering the seizure threshold.
- anaphylaxis

Precipitating Factors

Seizure activity can be precipitated or triggered by internal and external stimuli. Examples of such stimuli include

- stress
- electrolyte imbalance
- environmental stimuli (light, noise, odors)
- hyperthermia
- alcohol consumption
- noncompliance with or changes in medications
- menstruation

Seizure activity is usually spontaneous in its occurrence, although patients with longstanding seizure disorders may learn to alter the environmental stimuli to avert seizure activity (such as avoiding strobe lights).

CLASSIFICATION OF SEIZURE ACTIVITY

Seizures may be broadly classified as being in one of three categories: partial, generalized, or unclassified.[2] The onset of seizure activity may be marked by an aura, which is the presence of sensory manifestations such as unusual tastes or orders and visual, auditory, or other stimuli.

Partial Seizures

Partial seizure activity arises from a localized area of the brain, with the frontal, parietal, and temporal lobes being the most common sites. Partial seizures are further subdivided into categories.

Simple Partial Seizures

Simple partial seizures do not involve a loss of consciousness. The symptomatology accompanying this seizure activity will reflect the point of origin on the cerebral cortex. Patients may have

- focal motor, sensory, or somatosensory signs
- autonomic involvement (epigastric distress, pupillary dilation)
- psychic symptoms such as sensations of déjà vu or inappropriate affect

Complex Partial Seizures

Complex partial seizures are also referred to as psychomotor seizures. This partial seizure activity does involve an alteration in consciousness. The manifested behavior may involve any combination of cognitive, sensory, or psychomotor symptomatology. Automatisms, which are repetitive and involuntary motor activities such as lip smacking, grimacing, and fumbling with clothing, are common. These seizures may last two to three minutes and are followed by a period of confusion, fatigue, and amnesia.

Secondarily Generalized Seizures

Secondarily generalized seizures are partial seizures from either the simple or complex category that advance to generalized seizures with tonic-clonic manifestations.

Generalized Seizures

Generalized seizures usually involve a loss of consciousness. These seizures involve both sides of the brain. Several subcategories of generalized seizures are identified.

Tonic-Clonic Seizures

Also known as a grand mal seizure, it may be frequently seen in the intensive care setting. Most tonic-clonic seizures last about three minutes and involve an immediate loss of consciousness; they may or may not be preceded by an aura. The initial tonic phase consists of

- a symmetrical increase in muscle tone with extension of the extremities. If standing, the patient may fall.
- duration of about ten to twenty seconds

The clonic phase follows, marked by rhythmic bilateral contraction and relaxation of the skeletal musculature that lasts for thirty to sixty seconds.

During tonic-clonic seizures, circumoral pallor from apnea is not uncommon, nor is bladder incontinence. Saliva caught in the mouth may be forced out during exhalation and present as frothing. The pupils may dilate and be unreactive to light.

As the seizure activity ceases, the patient will become more responsive. The energy reserves used during the seizure activity may deplete the body stores to the point where it is not unusual for patients in the postictal (after the seizure) phase to sleep deeply for several hours.

Tonic Seizures

Tonic seizures are generalized seizure activity characterized by sustained increase in muscle tone. The seizures start abruptly and produce a generalized stiffening of all extremities.

Clonic Seizures

Clonic seizures are generalized seizure activity characterized by sustained rhythmic contraction and relaxation of skeletal muscle, especially the upper extremities.

Atonic Seizures

Atonic seizure activity involves a spontaneous loss of postural muscle control that lasts just a few seconds and that usually does not involve a loss of consciousness.

Myoclonic Seizures

Myoclonic seizures are characterized by involuntary muscle jerks that usually appear as symmetrical contractions of the extremities.

Absence Seizures

Absence seizure activity is also known as a petit mal seizure, which is more common in children. This seizure activity is characterized by brief and frequent staring episodes. Other associated behavioral changes may not occur. These are frequently seen before the age of five years, and may completely disappear or develop into another type of seizure disorder.

Unclassified Seizures

Seizures placed into the unclassified category include those seizure activities for which there is insufficient data to describe the seizure activity (eg, neonatal seizures).

DIAGNOSIS OF SEIZURE ACTIVITY

Since seizure activity is a symptom of underlying pathology, an adult presenting with a first-time seizure requires a complete medical evaluation to determine its cause. The diagnostic procedures ordered may include

- complete history and physical examination
- neurological evaluation
- computed tomography (CT) scan/magnetic resonance imaging (MRI)
- lumbar puncture
- skull series
- angiography
- electroencephalogram (EEG)
- toxicology evaluation
- positron emission tomography (PET) or single photon emission computed tomography (SPECT) scan, where available

Identification of abnormal electrical activity on an EEG supports diagnosis of seizure disorder; however, it is important to note that the absence of abnormal activity does not preclude the diagnosis. EEG telemetry with video monitoring is frequently used for a day or longer to document seizure activity in those patients for whom a distinct diagnosis is elusive.

TREATMENT OF SEIZURE ACTIVITY

The treatment of seizure activity is predicated upon treatment of the underlying cause. Patients without an identifiable cause (idiopathic seizure disorders) are managed on a long-term basis with one or more anticonvulsant drugs. Advances with diagnostic techniques such as CT, MRI, and PET scans as well as microsurgical techniques have contributed to localization and resection of suspect lesions in brains of patients with intractable seizure disorders.

Identifiable lesions such as tumors or clots can be surgically resected or excised. Long-term anticonvulsant drug therapy is often indicated. Seizures related to alcohol and drug abuse most often require short-term manageament. Seizure activity related to metabolic imbalance or infectious processes usually do not recur once the underlying cause is treated.

Patient teaching regarding medication regimens and drug interactions is a major component in ensuring adequate seizure control. Noncompliance with medications is a major factor in poorly controlled seizure disorders, particularly among younger patients. The duration of anticonvulsant drug therapy is dependent upon the individual patient and the etiology of the seizure activity. Practice obviously varies, but gradual withdrawal of anticonvulsant drugs is often initiated once patients are seizure free for two years or longer.[1]

Anticonvulsant Drug Therapy

There are a variety of drugs available for the treatment of seizures, and many patients require more than one drug to control the seizure activity. The more commonly used drugs are presented in Table 10-1; note that this listing is not inclusive. There are also a number of drugs currently being studied for their efficacy in treating seizure activity. It must be remembered that attainment of seizure control in some patients may require frequent changes in the dosage or type of drug used.

Patients with active seizure disorders, in whom seizure activity has been demonstrated within the past twenty-four hours, should be placed on seizure precautions (Exhibit 10-1). Anticonvulsant drug levels should be monitored to ensure that therapeutic levels are present in the serum.

Table 10-1 Major Anticonvulsant Drugs

Drug	Usual Dose	Side Effects	Toxic Signs
Dilantin (phenytoin)	300–400 mg/day intravenously (IV)/ orally(PO)	Gingival hyperplasia Rash Facial coarsening Fever Dermatitis Leukopenia	Nystagmus Ataxia Tremor Drowsiness Constipation Nausea
Phenobarbital	90 to 180 mg/day IV/intramuscularly (IM)/PO	Rash Dependency	Sedation Psychic changes Nystagmus Ataxia
Mysoline (primidone)	750 mg to 1.5 g/day	Rash Dependency	Same as for phenobarbital Gastrointestinal (GI) tract upset
Tegretol (carbamazepine)	400–1200 mg/day	Bone marrow depression Lens opacities Lethargy	Diplopia Dizziness Nausea Vomiting Ataxia
Depakene (valproic acid)	15–60 mg/day	Thrombocytopenia Transient hair loss Hepatic toxicity Inhibited platelet aggregation	Drowsiness Nausea Vomiting Diarrhea
Zarontin (ethosuximide)	750–1500 mg/day	Headache Leukopenia Erythema multiforme Pancytopenia	Nausea Vomiting Dizziness Anorexia Hiccups
Klonopin (clonazepam)	20 mg/day	Rash Thrombocytopenia	Drowsiness Ataxia Dizziness Hypotonia Slurred speech Hyperactivity

Assessing Seizure Activity

Accurate assessment and description of seizure activity is of paramount importance in patient management. Because of the brief duration most seizures have, it

Exhibit 10-1 Seizure Precautions

- Bedrails should be padded. If the patient is ambulatory, the bed should be kept in its lowest position.
- Oral airways should be at the bedside of patients who are not intubated or have a tracheostomy.
- Padded tongue blades are not recommended because of the danger of biting off and swallowing or aspirating portions of the tongue blade.
- Supervised showers are recommended over tub baths if the patient is ambulatory.
- Axillary or rectal temperatures are recommended rather than oral temperatures.

is often easiest to assess seizure activity in a systematized format. Seizure activity can be classified as having three stages: preictal (just prior to the seizure), ictal (during the seizure), and postictal (following the seizure).

Preictal Stage

Patients may recognize the impending onset of seizure activity through the presence of an aura.

Ictal Stage

While the patient is having a seizure, systematic assessment and monitoring of patient activity provides an accurate summary of patient status. It is helpful to note the time of the seizure onset to accurately describe its duration. Assessment and monitoring of the patient should include the following:

- Point of seizure activity onset—Did the seizure begin in any one portion of the body: hand, arm, foot, leg, face?
- Body parts involved—Was the activity focal or generalized? Describe the body movements: tonic, clonic, tonic-clonic, myoclonic. Protect the patient from the immediate environment but do no attempt to restrain movements, as injury may result.
- Eye movements—Assess for the presence of nystagmus and the response of the pupils to light. Note whether the eyes moved in any one direction predominantly.
- Respiratory status—Assess for the presence of apnea or dyspnea. Note presence of circumoral pallor or cyanosis of the lips and nailbeds. Suctioning an actively seizing patient is not recommended, although it may be necessary; turning the patient to the side will allow saliva or vomitus to drain from the patient's mouth.
- Level of consciousness—Assess the patient's responsiveness to verbal stimuli. Note the duration of unconsciousness.

- Automatisms—The display of automatisms by patients with complex partial seizures should be noted but not interrupted.
- Incontinence—Note whether there was urinary or fecal incontinence during the seizure.

Postictal Stage

As the seizure activity resolves, patients who were unconscious will begin to respond to stimuli. Headache, confusion, and amnesia for the event are not uncommon with generalized seizures. Vital signs and neurological status should be assessed immediately and continued until the patient returns to baseline. The patient should be assessed for potential injury to body parts that may have occurred during the seizure, including radiographic studies if indicated.

It is not uncommon for the patient to be extremely drowsy and to express the desire simply to "sleep" after a seizure. The energy expended during the seizure activity may result in the presence of neurological deficits in the postictal stage that resolve with time. Examples of such neurological deficits include

- visual field defects
- varying degrees of aphasia
- Todd's paralysis (weakness of an extremity following a focal motor or generalized seizure)

STATUS EPILEPTICUS

Status epilepticus is repetitive or prolonged seizure activity such that recovery between events does not occur. It constitutes a medical emergency because the patient is at risk for respiratory arrest. Status epilepticus is frequently due to inadequate serum anticonvulsant levels or the abrupt withdrawal of anticonvulsant medications. It may involve partial or generalized seizure activity.

Immediate Management

Immediate management of status epilepticus involves the following:

- Establish airway; intubation may be indicated.
- Maintain airway free from secretions, vomitus.
- Monitor blood pressure.
- Establish and monitor IV site for drug infusions.
- Anticipate orders for oxygen, blood studies.

Seizure Control

Pharmacologic interventions for status epilepticus involve the following:

- Diazepam (Valium)—0.3 to 10 mg IV push (IVP) at ≤ 2 mg/min; may repeat every ten minutes up to 30 mg maximum. Acts rapidly to suppress seizure activity. Monitor respiratory status. Lorazepam (Ativan) may be the preferred drug in some institutions.
- Phenytoin (Dilantin)—up to 1,000 mg IVP at ≤ 50 mg/min. It may be infused in a saline solution over a twenty-minute period. Please note that phenytoin is unstable even in saline after twenty to thirty minutes. Monitor blood pressure and heart rate. Often used in conjunction with diazepam, they are a very effective regimen in controlling status epilepticus.
- Phenobarbital—60 to 180 mg IVP at ≤ 30 mg/min; may administer higher doses but will need ventilator support. Monitor blood pressure, heart rate, and respiratory status; drug often increases respiratory depression when given in conjunction with diazepam.
- Diazepam drip—concentration of 50 mg in 250 mL dextrose at a rate of 40 mL/hour may be administered if seizures are refractory to above measures.
- General anesthesia—Neuromuscular blockade may become necessary to abolish seizure activity.

NOTES

1. J. Kiffin Penry, ed. *Epilepsy: Diagnosis—Management—Quality of Life* (New York: Raven Press, 1986), 1–36.
2. Ibid., 36.

SUGGESTED READINGS

Brewer, Kathleen, and Michael R. Sperling. "Neurosurgical Treatment of Intractable Epilepsy." *Journal of Neuroscience Nursing* 20(1988):366–372.

Callaghan, Noel, Andrew Garret, and Timothy Goggin. "Withdrawal of Anticonvulsant Drugs in Patients Free of Seizures for Two Years." *The New England Journal of Medicine* 318(1988): 942–946.

Commission on Classification and Terminology of the International League Against Epilepsy. "Proposal for Revised Clinical and Electroencephalographic Classification of Epileptic Seizures." *Epilepsia* 22(1981):489–501.

DeVroom, Hetty L., and Elaine P. Considine. "Advances in the Localization of Epileptic Foci for Surgical Resection." *Journal of Neuroscience Nursing* 19(1987):77–82.

Hartshorn, Jeanette C., and Edward A. Hartshorn. "Nursing Interventions for Anticonvulsant Drugs." *The Journal of Neuroscience Nursing* 18(1986):250–255.

Hickey, Joanne. *The Clinical Practice of Neurological and Neurosurgical Nursing*. Philadelphia: J.B. Lippincott, 1981.

Kastrup, Erwin K., ed. *Drug Facts and Comparisons*. Philadelphia: J.B. Lippincott, 1987.

Ng, Stephen K.C., W. Allen Hauser, John C.M. Brust, and Mervyn Susser. "Alcohol Consumption and Withdrawal in New-Onset Seizures." *The New England Journal of Medicine* 319(1988): 666–673.

Raimond, Jeanne, and Joyce Waterman Taylor. *Neurological Emergencies: Effective Nursing Care*. Rockville, MD: Aspen Publishers, 1986.

Rudy, Ellen B. *Advanced Neurological and Neurosurgical Nursing*. St. Louis: C.V. Mosby, 1984.

Santilli, Nancy, and Teresa L. Sierzant. "Advances in the Treatment of Epilepsy." *The Journal of Neuroscience Nursing* 19(1987):141–157.

Taylor, Joyce Waterman, and Sally Ballenger. *Neurological Dysfunction and Nursing Intervention*. New York: McGraw-Hill, 1980.

11

Infectious Processes

The central nervous system (CNS) can be invaded by a variety of organisms to produce bacterial, viral, fungal, and parasitic infections. To discuss every form of infection that can affect the CNS is beyond the scope of this text. The more common infectious processes will be presented: bacterial and viral meningitis, encephalitis, brain abscess, and the neurological complications of acquired immune deficiency syndrome (AIDS). It is often the case that neurological and associated systemic deterioration requires that patients with CNS infections be admitted to intensive care units (ICUs).

ACCESS ROUTES

Pathogens can gain access to the CNS through a number of mechanisms.

- The most common route is through the circulatory system. Any number of systemic processes can infect the CNS if carried there by the circulating blood.
- Direct access to the CNS is afforded pathogens through anatomical defects (meningomyeloceles), penetrating wounds, neurosurgical procedures, and extension from nearby anatomical sites (sinusitis, mastoiditis, otitis, osteomyelitis of cranial bones).
- Cerebrospinal fluid (CSF) may become infected through a dural tear from trauma or during a lumbar puncture or neurosurgical procedure.
- Extension along the peripheral nerves also serves as an entry route. An example of an infectious process gaining entrance through this route is rabies.

The presence of certain factors may make an individual more susceptible to CNS invasion by pathogens. Some of the more common predisposing factors include
1. immunosuppression
2. leukemias, lymphomas, and sickle cell disease

3. debilitated conditions
4. splenectomies
5. immunoglobulin deficiency
6. radiation therapy

MENINGITIS

Meningitis may be bacterial or viral in origin, causing inflammation of the arachnoid and pia layers of the meninges. It is more common in children and the elderly. Bacterial meningitis in its severest form can cause death from septic shock, respiratory failure, or adrenal hemorrhage. Viral or aseptic meningitis is a less catastrophic event.

Bacterial Meningitis

Bacterial meningitis is the most common form of meningitis. In many instances it can often be prevented by prompt treatment of systemic infections and local infections of the head and neck area. It is caused by such organisms as

- *Haemophilus influenzae*
- *Neisseria meningitidis*
- *Streptococcus pneumoniae*—seen in youngsters and the elderly; persons with sickle cell disease and splenectomies are at high risk
- group B streptococcus
- *Escherichia coli*
- *Staphylococcus aureus*[1]

Clinical Presentation

The classical symptoms of meningitis are

- fever—101°F (38.3°C) to 104°F (39.9°C) or higher if bacterial
- headache
- altered consciousness (confusion, lethargy, stupor)
- behavioral changes ranging from mild to combative
- signs of meningeal irritation
  1. nuchal rigidity
  2. photophobia

3. Kernig's sign—inability to extend the lower leg after the knee is flexed to a 90-degree angle with the hip
4. Brudzinski's sign—flexion of the knees toward the abdomen after flexing the head and neck into the chest
- generalized seizure activity
- petechial rash (meningococcus)

Increased intracranial pressure (ICP) may develop as the infection fulminates. Early diagnosis and treatment allows resolution of the presenting symptoms, although adhesions may form in the arachnoid, contributing to the development of hydrocephalus at a future date.

Diagnosis

The diagnosis of bacterial meningitis is predicated upon the patient history, physical examination, and evaluation of CSF. A computed tomography (CT) scan to evaluate for edema and ventricular compression may be done prior to performance of the lumbar puncture (LP). CSF in bacterial meningitis characteristically reveals

- elevated pressure (greater than 180 mm H_2O)
- white blood cell (WBC) count greater than 1000 μL, mostly polymorphonuclear cells
- elevated CSF protein (greater than 50 mg/L)
- decreased glucose (less than 40% of serum)
- cloudy or turbid color
- Gram's stain identification of causative organism
- positive culture of causative organism

Evaluation of serum electrolytes and blood urea nitrogen may be abnormal due to dehydration or inappropriate antidiuretic hormone (ADH) secretion (see Chapter 6).

Management Concerns

Usually a ten- to fourteen-day course of an antibiotic to which the causative organism is sensitive results in resolution of the infection. Patients with severe infections who display signs and symptoms of increased ICP will require interventions directed at managing this complication (see Chapter 4).

Nursing concerns with meningitis center upon

- continuous neurological assessment
- management of increased ICP
- management of pyrexia
- seizure management and prophylaxis
- maintenance of fluid and electrolyte balance
- provision of quiet environment
- infection control management (need for isolation determined by causative organism)

Aseptic or Viral Meningitis

Viral meningitis tends to be seasonal in its occurrence, with most cases seen in the summer and early autumn. It occurs most often in children but can affect all age groups. Causes of viral meningitis include

- Enterovirus (coxsackievirus, echovirus)
- herpes simplex virus
- paramyxovirus (mumps)
- arboviruses (from mosquitos and ticks)

Clinical Presentation

Viral meningitis may present initially with a flulike syndrome and progress to present as bacterial meningitis with

- fever
- headache
- nausea and vomiting
- complaints of general malaise, aches, chills
- confusion, drowsiness, lethargy
- evidence of meningeal irritation

Diagnosis

Diagnosis of viral meningitis is on the same basis as its bacterial counterpart. However, CSF evaluation does not reveal the same characteristics as for bacterial organisms but rather

- normal CSF pressure
- elevated WBC count, mostly lymphocytes
- elevated protein level
- normal glucose level
- turbid color
- isolation of causative organism not usually possible

Management Concerns

An effective pharmacological agent has not yet been developed to treat viral meningitis; therefore treatment is supportive and symptomatic. Aseptic meningitis generally is self-limited, with the patient recovering within two weeks of its onset. The nursing concerns addressed with bacterial meningitis are applicable.

Fungal Meningitis

Fungal meningitis is most common in patients who have systemic disease such as leukemia or lymphoma. It may develop into encephalitis and brain abscess. Recent evidence is revealing an association between AIDS and fungal meningitis. Causative organisms include

- *Coccidioides immitis*
- *Cryptococcus neoformans*
- *Candida*
- *Nocardia*[2]

Once the causative organism is identified, the patient is started on an appropriate antifungal agent (amphotericin B, flucytosine). The duration of therapy may extend over several weeks to months.

ENCEPHALITIS

Encephalitis is the widespread inflammation and degeneration of brain tissue caused by the invasion of some viral agent. The offending organism can be any one of a number of viruses that can affect the neuronal cells. Symptomatology of viral encephalitis varies according to the causative agent, as do treatment modalities. In its early stages it may be difficult to differentiate encephalitis from aseptic meningitis. Causes of encephalitis include

- arboviruses (equine encephalitis)
- enteroviruses
- herpes simplex and herpes zoster viruses
- rabies
- cytomegalovirus (CMV)

Clinical Presentation

Encephalitis may present initially as a meningitis with

- fever
- headache
- signs of meningeal irritation
- altered consciousness
- seizures

The patient with encephalitis may also present with any number of the following neurological deficits, based upon the anatomical infiltration of the virus

- hemiparesis with positive Babinski's response
- aphasia or mutism
- involuntary movements, ataxia
- myoclonus
- nystagmus, ocular palsies
- facial weakness

Diagnosis

As with meningitis, diagnosis is predicated upon patient history and physical examination as well as CSF analysis. CSF findings are usually similar to what is found with viral meningitis.

Management Concerns

Specific pharmacological agents for treating the majority of viruses causing encephalitis do not exist. Herpes simplex encephalitis has shown a positive response to administration of cytosine arabinoside (ARA-C) and acycloguanosine (acyclovir), and duck embryo vaccine is effective in producing active immunity against rabies.

Nursing goals are as for meningitis. It should be noted that some forms of encephalitis can render the patient comatose and dependent upon life-support systems very quickly and for extended periods of time. Because of the destruction that occurs to neural tissues with encephalitis, patients who recover may be left with residual neurological deficits.

BRAIN ABSCESS

Invasion of the brain tissue by infectious organisms from nearby head and neck sites or from distant systemic infections can result in a brain abscess. They can occur in conjunction with meningitis or encephalitis. Common causative agents are

- *Klebsiella*
- *Proteus*
- streptococci

After an initial inflammatory response by the brain tissue, the infected area becomes enveloped within a wall of granulation tissue within several weeks. Satellite abscesses may occur.

Clinical Presentation

During initial development of the abscess, the patient may be asymptomatic or may present with symptoms similar to a flulike syndrome. As the patient receives treatment for the primary infection, symptoms of neurological involvement often subside. Several weeks later, however, symptomatology returns as the enlarging abscess acts as a space-occupying lesion. Extension of the abscess into the ventricles can result in seeding of multiple abscesses throughout the CNS as well as devastating hemorrhage.

Demonstrated symptomatology by the patient is predicated upon the location of the abscess. Depending upon its location, the abscess may extend into the ventricular system and cause hemorrhage.

Diagnosis

Patient history of a recent localized or systemic infection affords the signal that a brain abscess should be part of the differential diagnosis. Focal deficits caused by the abscess will facilitate its location. CT scan and perhaps magnetic resonance imaging (MRI) will identify the abscess as a mass lesion. In some instances a brain abscess may not be a consideration for various reasons, and the lesion may be assumed to be that of a brain tumor.

CSF analysis will likely reveal

- increased pressure
- increased protein
- increased WBC
- normal glucose
- positive cultures for the causative organism

In the event of considerable mass effect by the abscess, an LP for CSF analysis may be contraindicated.

Management Concerns

Identification of the causative organism will direct appropriate antibiotic therapy. Antibiotic coverage will need to be continued for an extended period of time, either systemically or intrathecally through a reservoir system. In the event that culture of a presumed abscess is not possible, administration of a broad-spectrum antibiotic is indicated. Surgical drainage or excision of the abscess will decrease the mass effect. The administration of dexamethasone or prednisolone is frequently initiated to decrease localized edema.

The nursing care is the same as that for meningitis and the patient with a space-occupying lesion (see Chapter 9). The major complicating factor is increased ICP, which requires aggressive management (see Chapter 4), as herniation is a potential outcome.

NEUROLOGICAL COMPLICATIONS OF AIDS

Opportunistic infections of the CNS in patients who have AIDS are increasing in frequency as the number of people with this disease increases. The virus associated with AIDS is currently termed human immunodeficiency virus (HIV). It remains within the body, selectively infecting and destroying T4 lymphocytes, eventually producing an incompetent immune system. The depressed immune system among this patient population facilitates infiltration of the CNS by pathogenic organisms.

Due to the relative "newness" of AIDS, the information available to postulate curative therapies is scant; it is known that these patients have complex medical and nursing needs. The CNS symptomatology manifested by persons with AIDS is the same as in persons not infected with HIV. Among the diagnoses being made are the following:

- Acute atypical meningitis
  1. Aseptic meningitis may occur when the patient seroconverts to HIV positive; it does not occur with all cases.[3]
  2. Occurrence may reflect response of CNS to HIV invasion.
  3. Patient presents with signs and symptoms of meningitis.
  4. HIV may be isolated from the CSF, and there may be associated cranial nerve neuropathies.
- Herpes and cytomegalovirus infections
  1. Herpes simplex and herpes zoster encephalitides produce the same symptomatology as in non-AIDS patients.
  2. These viruses are treated with intravenous (IV) acyclovir.
  3. Herpes zoster may produce inflammatory radiculitis (shingles), which is extremely painful and extends along the involved dermatomes. Invasion of the spinal cord itself may produce generalized motor weakness.
  4. CMV encephalitis is diagnosed by biopsy, as it is difficult to isolate from the CSF.
  5. Clinical drug trials are in progress to identify the most appropriate agent for treating CMV.[3]
- CMV retinitis
  1. Common ocular infection in the AIDS population
  2. Produces hemorrhagic retinitis
  3. Current therapy includes use of investigational antiviral agent to suppress the infection
- Progressive multifocal leukoencephalopathy (PML)
  1. Progressive, demyelinating disorder that presents with focal signs (aphasia, ataxia, hemiparesis) and progresses within weeks to death
  2. Caused by activation of dormant papovavirus in the immunocompromised patient
  3. Biopsy may be performed to rule out other causes of neurological dysfunction
  4. No known treatment
- Toxoplasmosis
  1. Caused by the organism *Toxoplasma gondii*, which is reactivated in the immunocompromised patient
  2. Produces scattered inflammatory abscesses throughout the brain that may appear as brain abscesses or neoplastic growths
  3. Patient presents with altered mental status and fever; focal neurological signs also occur, depending upon the location of the organisms in the brain.
  4. Treatment is combined administration of pyrimethamine (Daraprim) and sulfadoxine.

- Cryptococcosis
  1. Caused by commonly found yeast (*C. neoformans*) that can invade the CNS in immunocompromised individuals
  2. Clinical presentation similar to acute meningitis
  3. Yeast spores can be isolated from CSF via a lumbar puncture.
  4. Treatment consists of amphotericin B and/or 5-fluorocytosine.
- Primary CNS lymphoma
  1. Although not a CNS infection but rather an uncommon CNS neoplasm, it is included here because it is being seen more often in the AIDS rather than the general population.
  2. It may be clinically silent and discovered only incidentally or at autopsy.
  3. Presenting symptomatology may vary, but mental status is altered.
  4. Biopsy is necessary to confirm the diagnosis.
  5. Current treatment modality is radiation therapy. Investigational studies are examining the efficacy of various pharmacological agents.[3]

NOTES

1. Virginia Prendergast, "Bacterial Meningitis Update." *Journal of Neuroscience Nursing* 19(1987): 95–99.
2. Raymond D. Adams, and Victor Maurice, *Principles of Neurology* (New York: McGraw-Hill, 1977), 646–648.
3. Justin C. McArthur, "Neurologic Manifestation of AIDS." *Medicine* 66(1987):407–432.

SUGGESTED READINGS

Beckman, Mari M., and Ellen B. Rudy. "Acquired Immunodeficiency Syndrome: Impact and Implication for the Neurological System." *Journal of Neuroscience Nursing* 18(1986):5–10.

Gryfinski, Juanita. "Intramedullary Spinal Cord Abscesses." *Journal of Neuroscience Nursing* 20(1988):34–38.

Hickey, Joanne. *The Clinical Practice of Neurological and Neurosurgical Nursing*. Philadelphia: J.B. Lippincott, 1981.

Kastrup, Erwin K., ed. *Drug Facts and Comparisons*. Philadelphia: J.B. Lippincott, 1987.

McArthur, Julie H., and Justin C. McArthur. "Neurological Manifestations of Acquired Immunodeficiency Syndrome." *Journal of Neuroscience Nursing* 18(1986):242–249.

Minnick, Ann. "Cysticercosis: Etiology and Nursing Care." *Journal of Neuroscience Nursing* 18(1986):135–139.

Perlstein, Lori M., and Jean-Marie Ake. "AIDS: An Overview for the Neuroscience Nurse." *Journal of Neuroscience Nursing* 19(1987):296–299.

Taylor, Joyce Waterman, and Sally Ballenger. *Neurological Dysfunctions and Nursing Intervention*. New York: McGraw-Hill, 1980.

12

Acute Neurological Conditions

In addition to the pathological processes presented thus far, a number of neurological conditions exist that, if in an acute phase, can render the patient ill enough to require intensive care nursing and medical expertise. This chapter will present an overview of three such neurological diagnoses: myasthenia gravis, amyotrophic lateral sclerosis, and Guillain-Barré syndrome.

MYASTHENIA GRAVIS

Myasthenia gravis is a disease believed to be of autoimmune origin that causes a defect at the neuromuscular junction. It is characterized by voluntary muscle weakness and fatigability with activity. Other characteristics are as follows:

- The weakness and fatigue are attributed to a decrease in the number of receptor sites at the myoneural junction for the neurotransmitter acetylcholine (Ach) and to the presence of antiacetylcholine antibodies that block remaining receptor sites.
- Muscle fatigue and weakness recover with rest and administration of anticholinesterase drugs, which inhibit the hydrolysis of Ach.

Clinical Presentation

Clinical presentation of myasthenia gravis is as follows:

- It affects both sexes; more common in early adulthood and old age. Women tend to be affected more than men during early adulthood, with the distribution being about even in older age.
- Older males with thymomas have a higher incidence.

- Infants born to myasthenic mothers may exhibit transient symptoms of the disease during the first few days of life.

The involvement of voluntary muscles tends to occur in a progressive fashion.

- Muscles controlling ocular movement are usually affected first. The patient may present with palsies of eye movement, ptosis, and double vision. Because the nuclei of the oculomotor nerve are not affected, pupillary responses are normal.
- The next groups affected are the muscles of the face, neck, mastication, and articulation; this is also referred to as bulbar involvement.
- As the disease progresses, extremity and truncal musculature are affected.

Diagnosis

Diagnosis is predicated upon patient history, electromyelographic (EMG) studies, antibody titers for acetylcholine receptor antibodies and an edrophonium chloride (Tensilon) test. Tensilon is an acutely short-acting anticholinesterase drug up to which 10 mg is administered intravenously (IV). Within a minute of infusion a patient with myasthenia will show dramatic improvement in muscle strength. Tensilon may also be used to differentiate between myasthenic and cholinergic crisis.

Classification

Myasthenia gravis can be classified according to the progressive involvement of muscle groups.

- In ocular myasthenia, ptosis and diplopia result from weakness of the ocular musculature. It is the mildest form of myasthenia but the most resistant to medication, and it may progress within two years to a more generalized form.
- Mild, generalized myasthenia occurs gradually and affects the ocular, bulbar, and extremity musculature. Proximal muscle groups are often more seriously affected than distal ones.
- Severe, generalized myasthenia has an abrupt onset with involvement of the respiratory muscles in addition to the groups listed above. The more severe, generalized form will greatly limit activity.
- Myasthenic crisis is the abrupt onset of generalized weakness to the point where paralysis of respiratory muscles occurs. This crisis frequently results

from insufficient medication, while the cholinergic crisis seen with myasthenic patients is the result of too much medication.

The course of the disease is often unpredictable. The disease may progress in some patients and not in others. Periods of remissions may occur but are temporary. While some patients may have a relatively stable disease course, others may go on to develop severe progression of the disease with recurrent episodes of respiratory failure. It is these patients whom critical care nurses are most likely to encounter, in addition to patients in myasthenic or cholinergic crisis.

Management Concerns

There is no known cure for myasthenia gravis. Treatment is symptomatic, and treatment options continue to evolve. Initial treatment involves the administration of anticholinesterase drugs that inhibit or inactivate acetylcholine. Patients who respond poorly to the conservative drug therapy may undergo adjunctive therapies. Most patients learn to manage their medications and to adjust their activity schedules to maximize independence. Reinforcement of information relative to specific drug therapy facilitates compliance.

Anticholinesterase Drugs

The following information about anticholinesterase drugs is relevant to their use in patients with myasthenia gravis:

- The medications used are
  1. neostigmine bromide (Prostigmin Bromide)
  2. ambenonium chloride (Mytelase)
  3. pyridostigmine bromide (Mestinon)
- These drugs are poorly absorbed orally and must be given in large doses to maintain therapeutic serum levels.
- The duration of action is such that doses to maintain muscle action must be repeated every two to four hours for neostigmine and every three to five hours for the other two drugs. Many myasthenic patients become compulsive about taking and receiving their anticholinesterase drug at the exact time due. Medications received later than they are due may make the difference between independence and dependence in activities of daily living.
- Pyridostigmine is available in a timed-release capsule and is the drug most frequently given at bedtime.

Patients learn to organize their activities around the peak action times of their drugs and to adjust to the side effects posed by the anticholinesterase drugs. The side effects include

- miosis
- increased secretions
- flatulence
- cramping and diarrhea
- diaphoresis
- muscle cramps

Symptoms of overdose include exacerbation of the side effects and

- bradycardia
- hypotension
- fatigability and generalized muscle weakness
- scattered fasciculations
- central nervous system (CNS) depression

Immunosuppression

Immunosuppressive therapy is aimed at decreasing production of circulating acetylcholine-receptor antibodies.

- Prednisone is frequently given as an adjunct to anticholinesterase therapy. Patients may require high doses of steroids and are at risk for the complications of long-term steroid therapy.
- Azathioprine (Imuran) and cyclophosphamide (Cytoxan) may also be used to provide further immunosuppression. The cytotoxic implications of these drugs must be weighed against possible benefits for the patient.

Thymectomy

When conservative drug therapy does not improve the patient's status, thymectomy is often recommended. It is thought that the thymus gland enhances development of acetylcholine receptor antibodies. Increased muscle strength often occurs immediately after surgery, or it may be months. Acetylcholinesterase drugs are withheld following surgery, and ventilatory support of the patient may be necessary.

Therapeutic Plasma Exchange (Plasmapheresis)

Plasmapheresis has gained recent success in treating myasthenia because of evidence that the acetylcholine receptor antibodies are protein-bound. These circulating antibodies are washed from the patient's plasma during the pheresis.

The protocol at this institution calls for 7 to 10 exchanges, performed three times a week. The exchanges are performed through a central venous access device to avoid needle punctures to the patient with each treatment. Three liters of plasma are drawn off and replaced with 3 liters of 5 percent albumin. Coagulation studies are monitored daily, as are calcium levels. Hypocalcemia may be problematic during the procedure, as indicated by numbness of the circumoral area or the fingers, and can be treated with intravenous infusion of calcium gluconate.

Myasthenic Crisis or Cholinergic Crisis

Two life-threatening situations that a myasthenic patient can encounter are myasthenic or cholinergic crisis. While many of the presenting symptoms are similar, each type of crisis has its characteristics (Exhibit 12-1). Patient history can be of great value in the differential diagnosis; myasthenic crisis is caused by insufficient medication, while cholinergic crisis is caused by overmedication. The probability of elective intubation is high, regardless of the cause. Common criteria for intubation include

---

Exhibit 12-1 Myasthenic or Cholinergic Crisis

Symptoms common to both
- Anxiety and restlessness
- Generalized muscle weakness; dysphagia; dysarthria; difficulty breathing
- Increased secretions: bronchial, lacrimal, salivary, and diaphoresis

Symptoms common to myasthenic crisis
- Cyanosis, increased pulse and blood pressure due to hypoxia
- Decreased or absent cough and gag reflexes
- Bowel and bladder incontinence
- Decreased urine output
- Positive Tensilon test response

Symptoms common to cholinergic crisis
- Scattered fasciculations
- Severe abdominal cramps with diarrhea
- Diplopia
- Nausea and vomiting
- Negative Tensilon test response

- vital capacity measurements less than a liter
- dyspnea
- use of accessory muscles for respiration
- arterial blood gas indications of hypoxia

Tensilon (edrophonium chloride) is used in differentiating between the two. The patient is given 10 mg IV push. If patient improves it is considered a positive reaction and diagnostic for myasthenic crisis. It will cause the patient's symptoms to worsen if the crisis is cholinergic in origin. Emergency equipment needs to be close by. The effects of cholinergic crisis can be reversed with atropine.

AMYOTROPHIC LATERAL SCLEROSIS

Amyotrophic lateral sclerosis (ALS) is a motor neuron disease of unknown etiology characterized by the loss of motor neurons throughout the CNS. Theories as to its cause include

- genetic defects
- toxic agents such as heavy metals
- vitamin and mineral deficiencies
- metabolic disturbances
- immune deficiencies

The sensory system is not affected, nor is cognition. It is a progressively fatal disease within five to ten years of onset. Males are affected more often than females.

Clinical Presentation

Initial symptoms are insidious in onset, beginning as signs of an upper motor neuron (UMN) lesion. The onset may be more apparent in one extremity than another and may occur with either the upper or lower extremities. Other signs and symptoms are as follows:

- cramping or clumsiness of the legs with eventual spastic paraparesis
- difficulty coordinating fine motor functions of the hands
- dysphagia

As the disease progresses, signs of lower motor neuron (LMN) lesions predominate.

- Atrophy of the shoulder and arm muscles becomes apparent and extends to the truncal and lower-extremity musculature.
- The patient becomes areflexic and hypotonic.
- Involvement of the bulbar region produces dysarthria, dysphagia, tongue atrophy, fasciculations of the facial area, and hypophonia.
- Drooling of secretions is common and poses as a never-ending discomfort to some patients. Anticholinergic drugs such as trihexyphenidyl hydrochloride (Artane) can help to decrease secretions.

Death is usually near once the bulbar and respiratory musculature become involved. Critical care nurses may encounter patients at this stage or after elective intubation or tracheostomy.

Diagnosis

History and physical examination are prime factors in contributing to the diagnosis of ALS. Other diagnostic findings are

- Creatinine phosphokinase (CPK) is elevated, possibly reflecting muscle cell atrophy.
- EMG and nerve conduction studies reveal changes consistent with motor neuron disease.
- Myelography will exclude any treatable spinal condition.
- Muscle biopsy will reveal denervation and degenerative changes.

The diagnosis is often based on the exclusion of other disease processes combined with the history and physical examination.

Management Concerns

The management of the patient with ALS is strictly supportive until, and if, a definitive therapy is found. The usual complications of immobility are present and require standard interventions. Major goals of the supportive care are to

- maintain nutritional status
- establish bowel and bladder programs

- maintain personal hygiene
- maintain tissue integrity
- provide emotional support and promote psychological well-being

Physical therapy is of benefit in delaying muscle atrophy and in minimizing contractures. Occupational therapy can facilitate maximal participation in activities of daily living. Speech therapy assists with the patient's ability to manage secretions and to articulate.

Respiratory insufficiency becomes a major issue in the terminal stages and is the usual cause of death. Denervation of respiratory musculature results in hypoventilation; dysphagia and depressed cough and gag reflexes lead to aspiration with resultant pneumonia. Routine chest physical therapy and postural drainage techniques will promote pulmonary hygiene, as will oral and blind endotracheal suctioning. Ultimately, however, the patient must decide whether intubation or tracheostomy and mechanical ventilation are options to be implemented.

Because sensation and cognition are intact, interventions often are focused on the sensory perceptions and psychological status of the patient. Emotional lability is not uncommon in these patients and may be helped by antidepressant therapy. Bulbar and respiratory involvement obviate that the patient and family make decisions regarding life-support mechanisms.

GUILLAIN-BARRÉ SYNDROME

This syndrome may be referred to by a number of other terms: Landry-Guillain-Barré syndrome, acute idiopathic polyneuritis, or inflammatory polyradiculoneuropathy. Guillain-Barré syndrome (GBS) produces an acute inflammatory response in the axons and nerve roots of the peripheral nervous system, causing demyelination and axonal destruction. The etiological basis for the disease is unknown, but theories for causation include

- hypersensitivity response to viral or bacterial infection
- autoimmune process

The onset of the disease is often within a few weeks of a mild viral infection, surgical procedure, or vaccination. The disease is self-limiting, with full recovery the norm within several months to a year following onset. Both sexes are affected, as are all age groups.

The major characteristic of the disease is weakness that can progress to total paralysis. Patients with extensive motor weakness are at risk for respiratory compromise and are frequently admitted to intensive care unit (ICU) settings.

Clinical Presentation

Clinical presentation of GBS is as follows:

- Motor weakness tends to occur in a fairly rapid, progressive, and ascending pattern over the course of several days, beginning with the lower extremities.
- The extent of axonal demyelination and destruction can be gauged by the severity of clinical symptomatology.
- Variants of the syndrome do exist.

Evaluation of the patient generally demonstrates the following:

- evidence of lower motor neuron (LMN) lesions—Areflexia and hypotonia are usual; muscle atrophy may occur and is generally very slight.
- muscle tenderness upon deep pressure and paresthesias
- loss of proprioception
- autonomic nervous system involvement—fluctuating blood pressure (hypotension more commonly), cardiac dysrhythmias, and anhydrosis (loss of sweating)
- respiratory compromise due to involvement of the muscles of respiration and the vagus nerve
- cranial nerve palsies—inability to close the eyelids, facial paresis, dysphagia, difficulty speaking

Diagnosis

Diagnostic data include a patient history that generally reveals the presence of some form of illness within the preceding month, the rapid onset of the symptoms, and the pattern of muscle weakness. Other confirmatory data are elicited from the following:

- Lumbar puncture at onset of the disease reveals normal protein and cell counts, but protein levels tend to rise without a corresponding significant increase in cell count within a few days. The protein level generally peaks within a month and probably reflects nerve-root inflammation.
- Presence of slight leukocytosis early in the disease, which returns to normal.
- Slowing of nerve conduction velocities soon after development of paralysis. Fibrillations may occur later as the muscle is denervated.

Management Concerns

Management of the patient with GBS is supportive and highly dependent upon nursing assessment and interventions, as the neurological status may change abruptly. Major goals during the acute phase (which may last days or weeks) are to

- monitor neuromuscular function
- monitor respiratory status—Respiratory compromise may occur precipitously; vital capacity measurements below a liter, dyspnea, or arterial blood gas indications of hypoxia may signal imminent need for elective intubation or tracheostomy and mechanical ventilatory support.
- support cardiovascular system—Hypotension may require vasopressor drugs; cardiac dysrhythmias may require drug therapy.
- maintain nutritional status—Dysphagia often necessitates nasogastric or gastric tube placement; paralytic ileus may mandate parenteral nutrition.
- establish bowel and bladder programs—Urinary retention may occur initially; constipation occurs due to decreased gastric motility.
- maintain personal hygiene
- maintain tissue integrity—The paretic or paralyzed state of these patients leaves them prone to pressure sore development; corneal abrasions are a potential if cranial nerve VII is involved.
- maintain comfort—Myalgias and paresthesias may be extremely uncomfortable sensations for the patient and may be alleviated by such drugs as acetaminophen or codeine.
- provide emotional support and promote psychological well-being—Since the patient is alert and cognitively intact, anxiety and apprehension over the loss of motor function and associated symptoms may be frequent behavioral manifestations.

Administration of corticosteroids may be instituted in the acute phase to decrease the inflammatory process, although this is an area of controversy. Plasmapheresis therapy may be an alternative preferred by some physicians.

Passive range of motion should be instituted in the acute phase, with any rigorous physical therapy postponed until the disease process has stabilized. The rehabilitation phase of this syndrome may incorporate months of therapy at a rehabilitation facility. GBS is a one-time occurrence for most individuals. Once the disease process stabilizes, recovery generally occurs in a progressive, descending fashion, with eventual full recovery in most patients. However, plateau states and relapses can occur.

SUGGESTED READINGS

Adams, Raymond D., and Maurice Victor. *Principles of Neurology*. New York: McGraw-Hill, 1977.

Evoli, Amelia, A.P. Batocchi, C. Provenzano, E. Ricci, and P. Tonali. "Thymectomy in the Treatment of Myasthenia Gravis: Report of 247 Patients." *Journal of Neurology* 235(1988): 272–276.

George, Maureen Redmond. "Neuromuscular Respiratory Failure: What the Nurse Knows May Make the Difference." *Journal of Neuroscience Nursing* 20(1988):110–117.

Hickey, Joanne. *The Clinical Practice of Neurological and Neurosurgical Nursing*. Philadelphia: J.B. Lippincott, 1981.

Kastrup, Erwin K., ed. *Drug Facts and Comparisons*. Philadelphia: J.B. Lippincott, 1987.

McCullough, J., and M. Chopek. "Therapeutic Plasma Exchange." *Laboratory Medicine* 12(1981): 745–753.

Noroian, Elizabeth L. "Myasthenia Gravis: A Nursing Perspective." *Journal of Neuroscience Nursing* 18(1986):74–80.

Osterman, P.O., C.A. Vedeler, B. Ryberg, J. Fagius, and H. Nyland. "Serum Antibodies to Peripheral Nerve Tissue in Acute Guillian-Barré Syndrome in Relation to Outcome of Plasma Exchange." *Journal of Neurology* 235(1988):285–289.

Raimond, Jeanne, and Joyce Waterman Taylor. *Neurological Emergencies: Effective Nursing Care*. Rockville, MD: Aspen Publishers, 1986.

Ricci, Marilyn, ed. *Core Curriculum for Neuroscience Nursing Volume II*. Park Ridge, IL: American Association of Neuroscience Nurses, 1984.

Stone, Nancy. "Amyotrophic Lateral Sclerosis: A Challenge for Constant Adaptation." *Journal of Neuroscience Nursing* 19(1987):166–173.

Taylor, Joyce W., and Sally Ballenger. *Neurological Dysfunctions and Nursing Interventions*. New York: McGraw-Hill, 1980.

Index

A

Absence seizures, 198
Abstract reasoning, 38
Acetylcholine, 10, 36
Acetylcholinesterase, 10
Acoustic neuroma, 164–165
Acquired seizures, 195
Acute subdural hematoma, 120
Adie's pupil, 56
Agnosia, 40
Agraphia, 39
AIDS, 209, 212–214
Airway maintenance, 132, 189
Alexia, 40
Amnesia, retrograde, 122, 123
Amyotrophic lateral sclerosis, 120–122
Analgesics, 168–169
Aneurysms, cerebral, 182–188
Anisocoria, 56
Antacids, 95
Anterior cerebral artery syndrome, 176
Anterior cerebral circulation disruption, 175–177
Anterior cord syndrome, 143, 145
Anterior fontanel, 2
Anterior fossa, 4
Anterolateral fontanel, 3
Anterolateral system, 26
Anticholinesterase drugs, 217–218
Anticoagulation, 180
Anticonvulsant drug therapy, 94–95, 168, 199–200
Antidiuretic hormone, 128–130
Anulus fibrosus, 6
Aphasia, 39–40
Apnea, 105
Apraxia, 40–41
Apresoline (hydralazine), 154
Arachnoid membrane, 8, 9
Argyll Robertson pupil, 56
Arterial blood gas monitoring, 93
Arteriovenous malformations, 188
Aseptic meningitis, 208–209
Astrocytomas, 162
Astroglia, 9
Atlas, 6
Atonic seizures, 197
Atrophy, 42
Atropine, 54
Attention assessment, 38
Auditory agnosia, 40
Autonomic dysreflexia, 152–154

Autonomic nervous system, 32, 34–36
Autoregulation, cerebral, 82
Axis, 6
Axons, 10, 11

B

Babinski's response, 44
Bacterial meningitis, 206–208
Barbiturate coma, 96
Barbiturates, 132
Basal ganglia, 10–12, 14, 15
Basilar artery syndrome, 178–179
Basilar skull fracture, 115–117
Bethanechol chloride (Urecholine), 152
Biopsy, 169
Bitemporal hemianopsia, 57
Bladder function, 150–152, 190
Blindness, 57
Blood-brain barrier, 80
Body temperature control, 92, 97, 113, 154
Bond, Michael R., 134
Bowel alterations, 95, 133, 152, 190
Brachytherapy, 170
Brain abscess, 211–212
Brain compliance, 81
Brain death
    application of criteria of, 104–106
    declaration of, 106
    definition of, 103–104
    organ donation issues and, 107–109
Brain injury, 117
    diffuse, 122–125
    focal, 117–122
Brain lacerations, 118
Brain stem, 18
Brain swelling, 84, 125
Brain tumors. *See* Central nervous system tumors
Brain-stem auditory–evoked responses (BAERs), 78, 105
Brain–stem reflexes, 105
Brown–Séquard syndrome, 146
Bullet wounds, 111, 112

C

Calcium channel blockers, 180
Caloric intake, 133, 190
Carbamazepine (Tegretol), 200
Cardiovascular alterations, 91–92, 150–151
Carotid arteries, 26
Carotid artery studies, noninvasive, 73–74
Carotid–cavernous fistula, 127
Caudate nucleus, 12
Cavernous sinus, 29
Central cord syndrome, 145
Central herniation, 86, 87
Central nervous system (CNS), 1
    structures, 11–19
Central nervous system (CNS) tumors
    classification of, 157–158
    clinical presentation of, 158–160
    intracranial, 161–166
    management of, 167–170
    risk factors of, 160–161
    spinal canal, 166–167
Cerebellar function, 37, 46
Cerebellar peduncles, 18
Cerebellum, 19
Cerebral aneurysms, 182–188
Cerebral angiography, 106
Cerebral arteries, 26–28
    anterior, 175–176
    posterior, 178
Cerebral arteriography, 70–71
Cerebral blood flow, 82
    studies, 72–73, 106
Cerebral edema, 83–84, 173
Cerebral function, 37–41
Cerebral hemispheres, 12, 13
Cerebral perfusion pressure, 83
Cerebral vascular resistance, 82
Cerebral vasculature, 26–30
Cerebrospinal fluid (CSF), 8, 9
    drainage of, 97–98, 117
    function and characteristics of, 30–32
Cerebrovascular accidents (CVA)
    classification of, 173–174

diagnosis of, 174
hemorrhagic stroke syndromes, 181–188
ischemic stroke syndromes, 175–179
management of, 179–181, 188–191
risk factors for, 172
Cerebrum, 11, 13
Cervical fracture, 138
Cervical tongs, 148
Cervical vertebrae, 6, 7
Chaplain, 106
Chemoreceptors, 25
Chemotherapy, 16–170
Cholinergic crisis, 219–220
Chronic subdural hematoma, 121
Cimetidine (Tagamet), 95
Cingulate herniation, 85, 86
Circle of Willis, 26–28
Cisternogram, 68–69
Claustrum, 12
Clonazepam (Klonopin), 200
Clonic seizures, 197
Closed head injury, 112
CMV retinitis, 213
CNS structures, 11–19
Coccygeal fracture, 140–141
Coccygeal ligament, 8
Cognitive function, 39–41
Coma, 52
 barbiturate, 96
 caused by head injury, 134
Comminuted fracture
 of skull, 114, 115
 of vertebrae, 138
Communicating hydrocephalus, 126
Complex partial seizures, 196
Complex spinal cord compression, 142–143
Compliance, 81
Compound skull fracture, 115
Compression fracture, 138, 139
Computed tomography (CT), 61–62
Concussion, 122–124
Confusion, 51
Consciousness level, 48, 51–52, 90
Constipation, 95, 133. *See also* Bowel alterations
Constructional apraxia, 41

Contrecoup injury, 113
Contusions, 118
Conus medullaris, 19
Coordination, 44
Coronal suture, 2
Corpus callosum, 12, 14
Corpus quadrigemina, 18
Corticobulbar tract, 25
Corticorubrospinal tract, 25
Corticospinal tract, 25
Corticosteroid therapy, 93, 168
Coup injury, 113
Cranial nerve function, 37, 46–48, 160
Cranial nerves, 30, 32–34
Cranial sutures, 1–2
Cranial vault, 1–4
Craniopharyngiomas, 166
Craniosacral division, 34
Cryptococcosis, 214
CSF. *See* Cerebrospinal fluid
Cytomegalovirus infections, 213
Cytotoxic edema, 83, 84

D

Decadron (dexamethasone), 94
Decerebrate rigidity, 54
Decorticate rigidity, 54
Deep-tendon reflexes (DTRs), 44, 45
Delirium, 51
Dendrites, 10, 11
Depakene (valproic acid), 200
Depressed skull fracture, 114, 115
Dexamethasone (Decadron), 94
Diabetes insipidus, 129–130
Diaphragma sellae, 8
Diazepam (Valium), 95, 132, 203
Diencephalon, 15–18
Diffuse axonal injury, 124–125
Diffuse brain injuries, 122
 concussions, 122–124
 types of, 124–125
Digital subtraction angiography, 71–72
Dilantin (phenytoin), 95, 200, 203
Dipyridamole (Persantine), 179
Dislocations, 141

Diuretics
  loop, 94
  to maintain kidneys for transplant, 109
  osmotic, 94
Doll's eye phenomenon, 57–59
Dopamine (Intropin), 10, 109
Dorsal columns, 26
Dressing apraxia, 41
Drug interactions, 10
Dura mater, 8–9
Dural nerve-root sleeves, 8
Dural sinuses, 28, 29
Dysphasia, 39

E

Edema
  cerebral, 83–84, 173
  spinal cord, 149
Elastance, 81
Electroencephalogram (EEG), 75, 76
  isoelectric, 105
Electrolyte balance, 133, 149, 189
Electromyography, 77
Embolus, 173–174
Encephalitis, 209–211
Encephalopathy, punch–drunk, 124
EOM. *See* Eye assessment
Ependyma, 9
Ependymomas, 163
Epidural hematomas, 8, 118–120
Epidural space, 8
Epilepsy, 194. *See also* Seizures
Epithalamus, 15
Ethosuximide (Zarontin), 200
Evoked responses, 78–79
Exteroceptors, 25
Extradural hematomas, 118
Extradural space, 8
Extradural spinal tumors, 166–167
Eye assessment
  for eye movement, 56–59
  for pupillary responses, 54–56
  signs indicating increased intracranial pressure, 90, 91
Eye donation, 109

F

Falx cerebelli, 8
Falx cerebri, 8
Family, 106, 134
Fasciculus cuneatus, 26
Fascic,ulus gracilis, 26
Fertility, 156
Fibrocartilaginous disc, 6
Filum terminale, 8, 19
Flaccidity, 54
Fluent aphasia, 39–40
Fluid balance, 133, 149, 189
Focal brain injuries
  contusions, 118
  epidural hematomas, 118–120
  explanation of, 117
  intracerebral hematomas, 121–122
  lacerations, 118
  subdural hematomas, 119–121
Fontanels, 2–3
Foramen magnum, 18
Fossae, 3–4
Fractures, vertebral, 138–141
Frontal lobe, 12, 13
Full consciousness, 51
Fungal meningitis, 209
Furosemide (Lasix), 94

G

Gait, 41–42
  ataxic propulsive, 42
  spastic, 41, 43
  steppage, 41
  waddling, 42
Gamma–aminobutyric acid (GABA), 10
Ganglia, 10
Ganglionic blocking agents, 154
Gastric acid secretion, 131
Gastrointestinal motility, 149
Generalized seizures, 197–198
Glasgow Coma Scale, 48–49, 51, 89–90, 147
Glasgow Outcome Scale, 134–135
Glial cell tumors, 161–163

Glial cells, 9
Global aphasia, 40
Globus pallidus, 12
Glycine, 10
Grasp reflex, 44
Gray matter, 10, 21
Guillain-Barré syndrome, 222–224
Gunshot wounds, 111, 112

H

Hangman's fracture, 140
Head trama
　brain injury, 117–125
　head injury, 111–114
　management of, 131–135
　scalp lacerations, 117
　secondary problems following, 125–131
　skull fractures, 114–117
Head wounds, 132
Headache, 92
Hematomas
　epidural, 118–120
　intracerebral, 119, 121–122
　subdural, 119–121
Hemodilution, 180
Hemorrhage, 125–126
Hemorrhagic strokes, 174, 181
　hypertensive intracerebral, 181–182
　ruptured cerebral aneurysms, 182–188
Herniation syndromes, 85–89
Herpes infections, 213
Hess, Robert, 184
Hippus, 56
Histamine receptor antagonists, 95
Homonymous hemianopsia, 57
Hormones, pituitary, 17
Horner's syndrome, 146
Hunt, William E., 184
Hydralazine (Apresoline), 154
Hydrocephalus, 126, 187
Hygromas, subdural, 127
Hyperglycemia, 130
Hypernatremia, 129

Hypertensive intracerebral hemorrhage, 181–182
Hypertrophy, 42
Hypophyseal stalk, 17
Hypothalamus, 17

I

ICP pressure waves, 99–101. *See also* Intracranial pressure
Ideational apraxia, 41
Idiopathic seizures, 194–195
Immediate recall, 38
Immobility hazards, 133, 190–191
Immobilization
　of head trauma patients, 132
　of spinal cord injury patients, 148–149
Immunodeficiency virus (HIV), 212, 213
Immunosuppressive therapy, 218
Incomplete spinal cord compression, 143, 145–146
Increased intracranial pressure (ICP)
　blood–brain barrier and, 80
　brain swellings and, 84
　cerebral blood flow and perfusion and, 82–83
　cerebral edema and, 83–84
　conditions contributing to, 85
　herniation syndromes and, 85–89
　management of patients with, 92–98, 132, 189
　monitoring, 98–101
　Munro-Kellie hypothesis and, 80
　signs and symptoms of, 89–92
　volume–pressure relationships, 81–82
Inferior colliculi, 18
Infratentorial herniation, 86, 88, 89
Infratentorial tumors, 159–160
Internal capsules, 15
Internal carotid artery syndrome, 176
Internal jugular vein, 28, 29
Interoceptors, 25
Interstitial brachytherapy, 170
Interstitial edema, 83, 84
Intervertebral discs, 6

Intracerebral hematomas, 119, 121–122
Intracerebral hemorrhage, 181–182
Intracranial pressure monitoring, 98–101. *See also*, Increased intracranial pressure
Intracranial tumors, 161–166
Intradural spinal tumors, 167
Intraparenchymal intracranial pressure monitoring, 98
Intraventricular hemorrhage, 125–126
Intropin (dopamine), 10, 109
Involuntary movements, 44
Ischemic strokes, 173, 175
    anterior circulation disruption in, 175–177
    management of, 179–181
    posterior circulation disruption, 177–179
Isoelectric EEG, 105
Isoproterenol (Isuprel), 109
Isuprel (isoproterenol), 109

J

Jefferson fracture, 138, 139
Jennett, Bryan, 49, 134
Judgment, 39

K

Kidney transplants, 108–109
Klonopin (clonazepam), 200

L

Lacerations, brain, 118
Lacunar infarcts, 176–177
Lambdoidal suture, 2
Lasix (furosemide), 94
Lateral medullary syndrome, 178
Laxatives, 95
Lethargy, 51
Levarterenol bitartrate (Levophed), 109
Levophed (levarterenol bitartrate), 109
Ligaments, spinal, 6
Light, 90
Lightening, 52
Limbic system, 15

Linear skull fracture, 114–116
Lumbar cistern, 9
Lumbar puncture, 67
Lumbar vertebrae, 6, 7

M

Magnetic resonance imaging (MRI), 62–63
Mannitol (Osmitrol), 94
Medication. *See individual drugs*
Medulla oblongata, 18
Medulloblastoma, 165
Memory assessment, 38
Meningeal system, 8–9, 19
Meningiomas, 163–164
Meningitis, 206–209, 213
Mestinon, 10
Metabolic disruption, 128–130
Methylprednisolone (Solu–Medrol), 94
Microglia, 9
Midbrain, 18
Middle cerebral artery syndrome, 175–176
Miotics, 54
Motor function, 37
    alterations indicating increased intracranial pressure, 91
    assessment of, 52–54
    components of, 41–45, 147
Motor neuron lesions, 142
Motor neurons, 21, 24
Munro-Kellie hypothesis, 80
Musculoskeletal alterations, 155
Muscle, 42–43
Myasthenia gravis, 10, 215–220
Myasthenic crisis, 219–220
Mydriatics, 54
Myelogram, 69–70
Myoclonic seizures, 198
Myoneural junction, 11
Mysoline (primidone), 200

N

Nembutal Sodium (pentobarbital sodium), 96

Nerve-conduction velocity studies, 77–78
Neurodiagnostic procedures
  cerebral arteriography, 70–71
  cerebral blood-flow studies, 72–73
  cisternogram, 68–69
  computed tomography, 61–62
  digital subtraction angiography, 71–72
  electroencephalogram, 75–76
  evoked responses, 78–79
  lumbar puncture, 67
  magnetic resonance imaging, 62–63
  myelogram, 69–70
  nerve-conduction velocity studies, 77–78
  noninvasive carotid artery studies, 73–74
  single-photon emission-computed tomography, 63–64
  skull radiographs, 65
  spine radiography, 66
  transcranial Doppler sonography, 75
Neurogenic bladders, 151
Neurological assessment
  factors evaluated for, 48, 51–60
  flow chart for, 49, 50
  in head trauma patients, 132
  purposes of, 48
  in stroke patients, 189
  use of Glasgow Coma Scale for, 48, 49, 51
Neurological examination components
  cerebellar function, 46
  cerebral function, 37–41
  cranial nerves, 46–48
  motor function, 41–45
  sensation, 45
Neurological status, 93
Neurons, 9–11, 21, 24
Neurotransmitters, 10
Nitrogen balance, 130
Noncommunicating hydrocephalus, 126
Nonfluent aphasia, 39
Noninvasive carotid artery studies, 73–74

Nonpenetrating head injury, 112
Norcuron (vecuronium bromide), 132
Norepinephrine, 10
Normal pressure hydrocephalus, 126
Nucleus, 10, 11

O

Obstructive hydrocephalus, 126
Occipital lobe, 12, 13
Occupational therapy, 155
Oculocephalic reflexes, 57–59
Oculovestibular reflexes, 57, 58
Odontoid, 6
Odontoid fracture, 140, 141
Oligodendroglia, 9
Oligodendrogliomas, 162
Open head injury, 111, 112
Organ donation, 107–109
Orientation, 38
Osmitrol (mannitol), 94
Osmotic diuretics, 94
Otorrhea, 117

P

Pancuronium bromide (Pavulon), 132
Paraphasias, 40
Parasellar tumors, 165–166
Parasympathetic nervous system, 34, 36
Parietal lobe, 12, 13
Peripheral nervous system, 30, 32,–36
Parkinson's disease, 42
Partial seizures, 196
Pavulon (pancuronium bromide), 132
Penetrating head injury, 111, 112, 132
Pentobarbital sodium (Nembutal Sodium), 96
Persantine (dipyridamole), 179
Phenobarbital, 95, 200, 203
Phenytoin (Dilantin), 95, 200, 203
Pia mater, 8, 9
Pilocarpine, 54
Pineal body, 15
Pineal tumors, 164
Pituitary gland, 17

Pituitary tumors, 165–166
Plasmapheresis, 219
Platelet antiaggregants, 179–180
Pons, 18
Positioning, 96–97
Positron emission tomography (PET), 63
Postconcussion syndrome, 123–124
Posterior cerebral arteries, 178
Posterior cerebral artery syndrome, 179
Posterior circulation disruption, 177–179
Posterior columns, 26
Posterior fontanel, 2
Posterior fossa, 4
Posterolateral fontanel, 3
Postganglionic neurons, 32
Posture, 41, 42
Preganglionic neurons, 32
Pressure sores, 154–155
Primary CNS lymphoma, 214
Primidone (mysoline), 200
Pro-Banthine (propantheline bromide), 152
Progressive multifocal leukoencephalopathy, 213
Propantheline bromide (Pro–Banthine), 152
Proprioception, 45
Proprioceptors, 25
Prosopagnosia, 40
Psychosocial alterations, 191
Punch-drunk encephalopathy, 124
Pupillary responses, 54–56, 90
Putamen, 12

Q

Quadrantopsia, 57

R

Radiation necrosis, 169
Radiation therapy, 169
Ranitidine (Zantac), 95
Rebleeding, 185
Reflexes, 44–45
Respiratory function alterations, 91, 150

Respiratory management, 93, 147–148
Respiratory patterns, 59, 60
Reticular activating system (RAS), 18–19
Reticulospinal tracts, 25
Retrograde amnesia, 122, 123
Rhinorrhea, 117
Rotational injury, 113–114
Ruptured cerebral aneurysms, 182–188

S

Sacral fracture, 140–141
Sacrum, 6
Sagittal suture, 2
Scalp lacerations, 117, 132
Secondary generalized seizures, 196
Sedation, 132
Seizures
    classification of, 196–198
    control of, 133, 189
    definition of, 194–196
    diagnosis of, 198–199
    post-traumatic, 126–127
    status epilepticus, 202–203
    treatment of, 199–202
Sella tumors, 165–166
Sella turcica, 17
Semicoma, 52
Sensation, 45
Sensory function, 37, 52, 91, 147
Serotonin, 10
Sexuality, 155–156
Shearing forces, 113–114, 122
Simple fracture, 138
Single-photon emission-computed tomography, 63–64
Skin care, 154–155
Skull
    lacerations to, 117
    management of fractures to, 116–117
    radiographs of, 65
    types of fractures to, 114–116
Social worker, 106
Solu-Medrol (methylprednisolone), 94
Somatosensory-evoked responses, 78

Spinal canal tumors, 116–117
Spinal column, 4–7
Spinal cord, 6, 19–26
Spinal cord compression
  complete, 142–143
  incomplete, 143, 145–146
Spinal cord edema, 149
Spinal cord injuries, 6
  functional loss from, 144–145
  management of, 146–150
  mechanisms of, 137
  secondary problems resulting from, 150–156
  types of, 141–146
  vertebral fractures, 138–141
Spinal ligaments, 6
Spinal nerves, 19–21, 30
Spinal shock, 143, 152
Spinal vasculature, 30
Spine radiography, 66
Spinocerebellar tracts, 26
Squamosal suture, 2
Stab wounds, 111
Status epilepticus, 202–203
Strength assessment, 43
Strokes. *See* Cerebrovascular accidents
Stupor, 51
Subacute subdural hematoma, 120–121
Subarachnoid hemorrhage, 125–126, 183–184
Subarachnoid space, 8
Subdural hematomas, 119–121
Subdural hygromas, 127
Subdural space, 8
Substantia nigra, 15
Subthalamus, 17
Superficial reflexes, 44, 45
Superior colliculi, 18
Superior sagittal sinus, 29
Supratentorial herniation, 85, 86
Supratentorial tumors, 158–159
Sympathetic nervous system, 32, 34
Synapse, 10
Syndrome of inappropriate antidiuretic hormone secretion (SIADH), 128–129

T

Tactile agnosia, 40
Tagamet (cimetidine), 95
Teasdale, Graham, 49, 134
Tectospinal tract, 25
Tegretol (carbamazepine), 200
Temporal lobe, 12, 13
Tentorium cerebelli, 8
Thalamus, 15
Thoracic vertebrae, 6
Thoracolumbar system. *See* Sympathetic nervous system
Thrombolytic therapy, 180
Thrombosis, 173
Thymectomy, 218
Tonic seizures, 197
Tonic-clonic seizures, 197
Toxoplasmosis, 213
Traction care, 150
Transcranial Doppler sonography, 75
Transection, 142–143
Transplants. *See* Organ donation
Transtentorial herniation, 87
Transverse sinus, 29
Tumors. *See* Central nervous system tumors

U

Uncal herniation, 86–88
Uniform Anatomical Gift Act, 107
Urecholine (bethanechol chloride), 152

V

Valium (diazepam), 95, 132, 203
Valproic acid (Depaken), 200
Vascular injury, 127
Vasogenic edema, 83–84
Vasopressor drugs, 109, 151
Vasospasm, 186–187
Vecuronium bromide (Norcuron), 132
Venous system, 28, 29

Vertebral arteries, 26, 177
Vertebral column, 4–7
Vertebral fractures, 138–141
Vertebro-basilar system, 26, 28
Vestibulospinal tracts, 25
Viral meningitis, 208–209
Visual agnosia, 40
Visual-evoked responses, 78
Visuospatial agnosia, 40
Vital signs, 59–60
Volume-pressure relationships in brain, 81–82
Volume-pressure response (VPR) test, 81
Vomiting, 92

W

Watershed infarcts, 176, 177
White matter, 10, 12, 21

Z

Zantec (ranitidine), 95
Zarontin (ethosuximide), 200